Primitive Art

A VOLUME IN *THE ARTS OF MAN* SERIES

Pri

A CHANTICLEER PRESS EDITION

mitive Art

Douglas Fraser

Assistant Professor of Art History and
Archaeology, Columbia University

DOUBLEDAY & COMPANY INC.

Garden City, New York

Published in 1962 by
Doubleday & Company, Inc.,
Garden City, New York

Planned and produced by
Chanticleer Press, New York

TO MY PARENTS

Library of Congress Catalog Card No. 62-13342

CONTENTS

Preface

To describe and analyze the arts of primitive man in a single volume is no easy task. For not only are these arts extraordinarily diverse in form and character but also they are scattered throughout the world. Moreover, since only a few of the great art-producing tribes are still active today, access to the ideas held by primitive peoples must be gained through the literature on them. This literature, ranging from missionary records to anthropological reports and specialized studies of primitive art, is vast and very diffuse.

But perhaps the greatest problem confronting the prospective writer on primitive art is the almost complete lack of information concerning the origins and development of styles. Unlike western art, which passed through various phases such as Romanesque, Gothic, Renaissance, and Baroque, each standing in a clear relationship to the other, primitive art has no historical frame of reference. All of its styles appear to be equally ancient, all of its achievements equally unique. Thus to place primitive art forms in relation to one another or to other things is inherently difficult.

Fortunately, there are some redeeming circumstances. During the past hundred years or so, scholars have collected a great deal of information on primitive life and culture. Thus, if the writer wishes, he can discuss primitive art forms in terms of their context, their magico-religious functions and their social roles. This has been done with considerable skill in a number of instances. But there is a danger in this approach: by concentrating on local conditions, the author may blind himself to relationships of a larger sort, that is, between his immediate subject and others somewhat distant from it. Only by stepping back slightly from his material can he discern its true position in the broad development of world art and thought. I have tried in this book to incorporate the best features of both the closeup and the broad approaches.

My viewpoint throughout has been essentially that of the art historian rather than of the anthropologist; but I have of course dealt with anthropological factors wherever they seemed important. To present a systematic survey of primitive art I have sifted and studied the available records of each local style; at the same time I have not hesitated to introduce new and broader observations where these seemed useful and valid. My aim has been to see each style in relation to its local setting and, wherever possible, in relation to other styles both near by and far away. I have suggested no relationships for which I do not have ample corroboration, though it was often impossible in a general book to present all the evidence. How such relationships between the various areas came about, it is generally impossible to say. But it need hardly be added that the discovery of such a relationship can cast much light not only on the origins of a style but also on the forces that molded it.

For reasons of space, I have had, in a few instances, to curtail or omit altogether the discussion of certain styles; for this I apologize. Conversely, certain little-known styles have received special attention because their importance seemed to warrant it. In sum, then, the book is intended as a comprehensive, though by no means exhaustive, consideration of primitive art.

Finally, I wish to express my gratitude to countless anthropologists, art historians, government officers, native informants, missionaries, museum curators, and theoreticians without whose detailed observations and helpful analyses this book would have been impossible. Unhappily I can acknowledge here only my most obvious debts. Raymond Firth's remarkable chapter on the social framework of primitive art has greatly influenced my notion of what the primitive carver can and cannot do. The seminal articles of Robert Heine-Geldern have proved more valuable to me in reconstructing Asian prehistory than any other source. Felix Speiser, Julius Glück, Carl Hentze, Gordon Ekholm, and Joseph Greenberg have through their various writings shed much light on the material covered by this book.

Equally important have been discussions with colleagues, including: B. A. L. Cranstone, Philip Dark, William Fagg, A. A. Gerbrands, John Haskins, Paul Hinderling, Simon Kooijman, A. C. van der Leeden, Charles Mountford, Douglas Newton, Edith Porada, Carl Schmitz, and Frank Willett. L. Langewis of the Royal Tropical Museum, Amsterdam, called my attention to the discoveries made by Ling Shun-Sheng and also by Alfred Salmony, whose book *Antler and Tongue* has been of enormous value. For special kindnesses, my thanks go also to Robert Goldwater and Allan Chapman of the Museum of Primitive Art, Harry Shapiro and Philip Gifford of the American Museum of Natural History, Frederick Dockstader of the Museum of the American Indian, Bernard Karpel of the Museum of Modern Art, and Jane Rosenthal of the Brooklyn Museum. To my teachers, Meyer Schapiro, Rudolf Wittkower, and especially Paul Wingert, who have provided constant stimulus and encouragement, my gratitude is warm. I wish to thank Milton Rugoff and Wallace Brockway for their careful editing of the manuscript. Jean Tennant devoted many hours to the difficult task of organizing the illustrations, and Ulrich Ruchti by his care in designing succeeded admirably in the very complex problem of fitting the illustrations and text together.

Werner Bruggmann, Elwin J. Daniel, Eliot Elisofon, Friedrich Hewicker, Malcolm Knapp, Peter Moeschlin, Frank Newens, Gesa Sarkany, Jr., Edwin Smith, Charles Uht, I. Zaffrir, and others have my thanks for their splendid photographs. Without the work of these and many more, this book could not have been brought forth.

My greatest debt is to my wife who participated enthusiastically in every phase of the work.

Douglas Fraser
New York City   January, 1962

Introduction

The revolutionary development of modern painting and sculpture in the opening decades of this century created a vast new audience for primitive art. Just when most native peoples were beginning to lose their old artistic traditions, twentieth-century taste rescued their art from the obscurity of the curio shop and the ethnographical museum. Westerners who would once have shuddered at the primitive artist's unclassical use of proportion found they could enjoy and admire the work of an African sculptor. Today objects originally destined for grisly rituals rest upon museum velvet or upon patrician coffee tables. And the more one looks at such objects, the more one finds in them the qualities—beauty, relevance, meaning—which earlier generations could detect only in Western art.

The pace of this discovery has been breathtaking. Forty years ago collectors sometimes assigned primitive art objects to the wrong continent, twenty years ago to the wrong area, ten years ago to the wrong tribe. Today primitive art is so firmly implanted in twentieth-century sensibility and the study of it so advanced that only the most difficult pieces still defy classifi-

cation. That a subject once despised and neglected should have progressed so rapidly is proof—if any were needed—that primitive art has had its life span extended indefinitely.

Earlier Attitudes

The increased breadth of our modern approach becomes dramatically evident when we compare it with earlier views of primitive art. Until the middle of the eighteenth century, Westerners virtually ignored all ideas not embraced in the narrow, Renaissance point of view. Then, with the breakdown of classical values and discoveries overseas of alien cultures by such great voyagers as Captain Cook, there came a sharp increase of interest in the "noble savage" and his supposedly untrammeled life. At first, primitive art seemed to the West as exotic and outlandish as its makers. Objects brought back by sea captains and sailors in the late eighteenth century were regarded as curiosities; they attracted little more than passing attention. But after 1800, missionaries, who took a very different view, began to arrive in the South Seas. For them, primitive carvings were idols made by degraded savages and worthy only of destruction. The objects that they burned or encouraged the natives to destroy would probably have filled a score of museums.

There was, however, a bright side to this picture. Unlike some of the early conquerors, Christian missionaries did not seek to overwhelm the native peoples or enslave them; they hoped only to save their souls. Once the native had been converted and his idols taken away, a missionary could look upon primitive carvings as symbols of his own victory over evil. Quite a number of pieces survived for just such a reason. These trophies, collected during the first half of the nineteenth century, together with sailors' souvenirs, are some of our finest and oldest examples of primitive art (Plates 74, 75 and 115).

In the second half of the century a new approach—the scientific study of primitive man—was developed. In this era, which began with Darwin and Huxley, much stress was laid on the origins and evolution of primitive

1   Beaded mask. Cameroons. H. 26¹/₄" (Denver Art Museum).

man. His artifacts and forms of ornament, it was believed, might provide insights into man's later social and technical development. To house the increasingly vast collections of objects, museums were founded; these served to stimulate and organize further research. Before the end of the century, anthropology had emerged as a distinct field of learning with a solid claim to importance.

No sooner had interest been aroused and objects become available than speculation arose as to the nature and purpose of primitive art. The first really systematic view was that of the evolutionists. They regarded primitive art as an early stage in the development of a realistic view of the world and considered its changes simply a natural process determined by circumstances. But their theory failed not only to provide any explanation of underlying causes, it also did not consider the artist's intentions. Both of these aspects, however, found a place in the second great theory of primitive art—that propounded at the turn of the century by Franz Boas, father of American anthropology. Deriving his ideas mainly from the technologist Gottfried Semper, Boas stressed the importance of materials, manufacturing techniques, and intended purpose. These, he concluded, gave rise to form, to patterns of ornament, and even pleasurable aesthetic response. For Boas and the technological school, representational art was merely a copy of nature as modified by the artist's personal experience. Because it minimizes social, historical, and psychological factors, this approach today seems overly automatic and materialistic.

At about the same time, many Western artists were becoming interested in primitive art. Prior to the twentieth century, theirs had been largely the rather lackadaisical interest one artisan takes in the work of another. Even Gauguin, who lived in the South Seas, seems to have had only a fleeting concern for primitive art. But with the rise of modern art, it was possible for Vlaminck, Picasso, Matisse, and others to "discover" African sculpture. Then a more passionate reaction toward this style developed. Modern artists consciously imitated primitive art and hailed its outspoken "visual freedom." This in turn led to a broader examination of primitive art than was possible on a purely technological basis.

Thus, in the 1920's, interest veered from the formal qualities of primitive art to its content. A series of books appeared, mainly in Germany, purporting to give the final psychoanalytical interpretation of the subject. During the following decade, partly as a corrective, scholars and artists began to join forces, comparing the visual evidence on the one hand with anthropological data on the other to discern the artist's intentions. The 1930's also saw the earliest careful stylistic classifications of art areas and the first exhibition based on aesthetic standards. In recent years numerous illustrated publications and detailed studies have at last given the public easy access to the full range of primitive man's finest works of art.

The Scope of Primitive Art

Primitive art may be defined most succinctly as the high art of low cultures. This is of course a working definition and hardly covers all examples. It is helpful mainly in order to distinguish our subject from (1) the lesser arts, usually called crafts; (2) the subordinate art of high cultures, called folk art; and (3) the products of advanced civilizations such as our own.

Closer examination of the arts of primitive people will make clear their unique nature. An object may be extremely handsome and interesting in its own right, yet still not be worthy of the name of art. Such objects we call crafts. It is true, of course, that primitive man, not having a word for art as such, would not trouble himself over what is and is not "Art." But in his daily life he almost always differentiates between objects produced by a slow, repetitive process, such as weaving or pottery (crafts), and other objects of paramount significance for his culture. He relegates craft work to inferiors (i.e., women); only men, as a rule, practiced carving and painting. Primitive man also discriminates mentally between those objects whose use is practical and secular—thus easily replaced—and those of high spiritual value, which he cannot afford to lose. He may part with a valued work of art, but only after it has been properly despiritualized. Connected with every important art object is an essential spirit that it would be a sacrilege to offend and a catastrophe to ignore.

Several other types of art are often confused with the primitive kind. One is folk or popular art. This is usually a provincial style that stems from minority or peasant groups of strongly conservative outlook rather than from true primitives. Although sometimes ascribed to a primitive stage in society, folk art usually draws heavily on older high art; this in turn makes it appear to be aesthetically and psychologically timid. In comparison with primitive art, which exists, so to speak, at the *top* of its culture, popular art betrays a consciousness of lower social and artistic status that amounts to an inferiority complex.

Another art very different in character from that of primitive peoples is the so-called high art of advanced civilizations. The styles of these societies focus on specific visual problems, on complex political institutions such as the state, or on religious ideas alien to primitive thought. These civilizations use rare metals, massive stone masonry, and imported materials which no primitive society can ordinarily command. The artists of such advanced societies have learned through centuries of experiment to achieve, by means of perspective, the realistic representation of the visible world on a two-dimensional surface. The lack of perspective in the primitive artist's work does not of course discredit the value of his work. It merely repeats the relatively simple organization typical of primitive life in general.

Although his close-knit society limits the native artist's expression, the fact does not necessarily follow that primitive art as a whole is simple and easily understood. A glance at the books on styles of certain areas will quickly dispel any such misconception. Behind the primitive's style lie ideas and relationships we have yet to begin to apprehend. We are so accustomed to accepting easy, almost simple-minded explanations of primitive style that we fail to perceive just how vast and varied the material really is. But before we try to recognize new qualities in primitive art, we must compare the points of view which formerly governed so much thinking on the subject.

Basically there seem to be two main views of the scope and significance of primitive art. The first is that of the professional anthropologist who takes an interest in native art objects mainly in connection with his chief concern—the society as a whole. Among his first preoccupations are how an object was made, who paid for it, who used it and for what purposes. When he "enjoys" primitive art, it is as something in a cultural setting. At the opposite extreme is the attitude of the art lover. He sees each piece as the unique product of a human mind; cherishing its artistic qualities for their own sake, he ignores the environment out of which the object came. Instead the object provides an aesthetic stimulation which, for him, is its true and ultimate meaning.

Both points of view have their validity but both need amplification. The anthropologist justifiably points out that once an art object is uprooted from its native environment, almost any statement about it, no matter how absurd, may pass as truth. A good example of this was the Cubist painters' enthusiasm over the "purity and freedom" of African art. As the anthropologist sees it, the meaning of forms evolves only in a context of belief and opinion shared by a social group.

It should be noted, however, that a sensitive person who is visually attracted to primitive art may find in it important ideas, even though he misunderstands the purpose or function of a work. Lack of knowledge did not prevent the Cubists from discovering in African sculpture qualities and formal concepts which have since revolutionized Western art. Similarly, archaeologists, often limited to examining only a few artifacts, gain enormously valuable insights into the life of lost civilizations simply by looking carefully at the surviving objects and classifying the results of their observations. In our effort to understand primitive art, therefore, we will try to combine all the advantages of the strictly anthropological or functional method with those of close visual analysis.

The Character of Primitive Art

Having broadly indicated the scope of the subject, we turn to the character of primitive art as it is understood today. One of the first things we must realize is that this art is not intended to serve aesthetic ends. The artist merely responds to the needs of his society; he produces precisely the number of objects—no more and no less that his patrons require. Moreover, all the works he makes have an ulterior function: either they assist in ritual or they perform a social role. Any time or energy left over to the artist will be spent in other activities—not in the further production of art. Thus the Western idea of art for art's sake would mean little to the primitive artist. He does not dream that the sole purpose of an object could be to give himself and others that joy in artistic performance we call aesthetic pleasure.

Equally meaningless to the primitive artist is the Western artist's stress on exact imitation of nature as developed in the Renaissance. Bound to a long, strict tradition, the primitive artist repeats again and again only that version of reality accepted in his society. His symbols are perpetuated because they have the weight of the past behind them. Neither a spontaneous, emotional outpouring nor a mystical, intuitive creation, primitive art is an endless incantation given visual form.

The aims of the primitive artist are essentially those of his group. He may be asked to help placate supernatural powers, to glorify the living, or to commemorate deceased members of the community. Ancestors and supernatural powers, it is believed, could influence or alter the physical and economic well-being of the living. When he has produced prestige objects and other emblems of rank, the artist has helped to give order to human affairs. Thus, far from being passive in the face of reality, primitive peoples have tried constantly to manipulate the forces which surround them. Because this effort has been unabating, the artist has enjoyed a steady demand for his work.

Before turning to specifically aesthetic matters, then, we must consider some of the external influences which help mold the character of primitive art.

The Effect of Environment

Although the primitive artist does not imitate forms as they appear in life, nature herself imposes various conditions on his art. Weather and physical environment determine the materials available to him. If he chooses to work in wood, the columnar shape of a tree may inspire him to organize his design accordingly. Or he may be guided by the form inherent in his subject matter, as when he makes the human figure tall and postlike or gives a mask a lateral curvature. The extent of the influence of materials on ideas, therefore, remains highly uncertain in primitive as

16

in other arts. A medium may challenge or inhibit the primitive craftsman; it can hardly fix the precise character of his work. Moreover, if the artist substitutes one material for another, as often happens, the forms and the style usually remain unchanged. In Tibet, for example, all sculpture has a common visual pattern, though it may be produced in wood, metal, or yak butter. Basically, it is the artist's mental conception, not the material he uses, that determines the character of his art.

On the other hand, there may be a general relation between the appearance of nature and the art produced in a particular area. The world of the Micronesian artist of the Pacific atolls is, so to speak, thin-drawn and linear—atoll art often has such characteristics. In Melanesia, with its plunging defiles, sluggish rivers, and craggy mountains, art seems to parallel in its violence and contrast the harsh shapes of the landscape. Some vistas such as the mesa country of the American Southwest and the escarpments of the West African Sudan may perhaps overwhelm the viewer with their massive grandeur. The constrained, geometric styles of these areas may reflect the impact of the natural setting upon the local artist. Even more speculative is the possibility that the endless open spaces of prairie, tundra, and desert may have influenced man in a negative way, turning him in-

2 and 3   Healing figures. Used as charms against spirits causing ailments such as swollen legs (far left) and backache (left). Borneo. H. 15¹⁄₂" and 14¹⁄₂" (Pitt Rivers Museum, Oxford University).

17

4 (Left) Aztec death
God, Xolotl, twin of
Quetzalcoatl. Mexico.
Jade. H. 9"
(Württembergisches
Landesmuseum, Stuttgart).

5 Mask worn at secret
military society rites.
Bushongo, Central Congo.
Wood with beads and
shells. H. 9" (von der
Heydt Collection, Reitberg
Museum, Zurich).

ward toward self-contemplation. In any event, physical surroundings are but the broadest of many factors influencing the primitive artist.

The Influence of Tools and Technique

The traditional tools of the primitive artist were made of stone, bone, horn, teeth, shell, and, in some areas, metal. He used his adze, chisel, or knife with such ease that even after European tools became available he often modified these into the preferred native forms. Obviously, the old tools were effective enough for his purpose. They were perhaps a little less efficient than modern devices but, since the artist had as much time as he required, this made little difference.

Tools and the way they are used sometimes contribute directly to the artist's final achievement. The adze, for example, requires steady rhythmic strokes delivered at the same angle and in one direction. Carvers in the Northwest Coast area of North America leave the adze marks on the surfaces, creating pleasing textural patterns and a direct sense of the artist's handiwork. In Polynesia, where the carver has a different attitude toward surface and finish, the marks of the carving process are carefully obliterated. The artist's technique sometimes leads him to innovation. The use of wood shavings in the decoration of East Siberian carvings is an instance of the impact of pure technique on design. But on the whole, technical factors are of minor importance as compared to those yet to be discussed.

Social Forces

The importance of the society in which a primitive artist works in shaping his ideas can hardly be overstated. Living in a community closely knit by ties of kinship and marriage, the artist needs the full sanction and approval of his group even to begin his work. Quite naturally he absorbs its viewpoint and attitudes, and, whatever his particular status, he functions as an integral part of the group. The idea that the artist is rebellious, temperamental, and generally antagonistic toward his society is a Western notion that dates no earlier than the Renaissance. The primitive conception of the artist's role is altogether different.

The Primitive Artist

What then distinguishes the primitive artist from his fellow men? Here we have reached a point where generalities can be expected to yield to specific instances. If there is one thing that can be said about the native artist, it is that in the eyes of his group he does not seem very different from anyone else. In societies such as those of the Australian aborigines and the New Hebrides, all men engage in some form of art production. Even when the artist enjoys special status, he still can scarcely be called a professional or a specialist, for he continues to fish, herd cattle, or raise crops. In other words, no matter how important the primitive artist is to us, in his own society his primary identity is more the result of his social and economic position than his work as an artist. Unlike the Western artist, the primitive carver gains little from skilled performance alone.

Nevertheless, in primitive life artists are selected for their tasks. Different groups do this in different ways. In Africa, one clan often dominates a particular trade. Children are therefore more or less obliged to pursue their parent's craft. This helps to concentrate economic power in the family unit and in turn increases political stability. Another approach is that of the Mundugumor of New Guinea. They select as artists those who have proved their magic powers in infancy—for example, children who are born with the umbilical cord wrapped around their necks and thus believed immune to danger. A third method of selection occurs among the Ibo of Nigeria. Here the artist works not for prestige or financial reward but because he enjoys carving and feels his products are useful.

The training given the primitive artist has varied just as widely as the process of selecting him. Often a mature artist has taken his young son or nephew as an apprentice, thus keeping craft secrets within the family. There seem to have been no special requirements for the role other than a liking for ritual. For besides participating in tribal ceremonies, the artist has had to perform his own private rites to appease the spirits connected with carving. As we might expect in such a situation, the mediocre sometimes find a place along with the gifted. But where artistic standards have been high, as among the Tchambuli of New Guinea, the would-be artist has had to achieve a high level of performance.

The artist's training commenced usually about the time of puberty and continued till maturity. In rare instances, mainly in Africa, an artist might begin carving only in his middle years or later life. In general, then, maturation as an artist has closely paralleled the general development of the individual. Learning to carve or paint, like acquiring fishing or hunting skills, came largely through participation in the work itself. As in medieval Europe, the apprentice begins by making his own tools and discovering the potentialities and limitations of his medium. His immediate goal is to master his teacher's repertoire, since the aim of all his training is to ensure accurate reproduction of the forms approved by tradition. Far from being objectionable—as it would be in our society—exact imitation is felt by primitive man to be the essence of creativity. The right to make and use a specific design is, therefore, a form of property which belongs sometimes to the artist, but more often to the patron. This "copyright" privilege can in certain circumstances be traded, sold, or even given away. We know of at least a few instances of outright and, from a Western point of view, outrageous plagiarism. Good examples of this are copies of Bella Coola and Ibibio masks made by the neighbors of these tribes. But, in general, stealing designs from one's fellow artists was, in the primitive craftsman's mind, worse than ordinary thefts of property because it meant tampering with the supernatural. Not infrequently the punishment for plagiarism was death.

So much for the training and development of the artist. Having learned something about his background and outlook, we are in a position to decide whether the primitive artist really resembles certain present-day types with whom he is often compared. One is the mentally disturbed person who produces an incomprehensible art. We might note that this is exactly the opposite of the primitive artist's intentions and results. What distinguishes the disturbed individual is the fact that his outlook differs from the one that is generally accepted. Not only does the primitive artist strive to be understood, but also every step of his selection and training forces him in a traditional direction. It is true that primitive man sometimes sought to induce trances and visions. But this was considered "normal" in primitive life and had little impact on art. Many native artists declare that motifs or designs came to them "in a dream." This is probably as good an explanation of the creative process as one could find; yet the objects these artists produce

6   *Mask used in initiation rites. New Hebrides. Painted vegetable fiber and boar's tusks. H. 12$\frac{1}{2}$" (Suva Museum, Fiji).*

conform very closely to prevailing types. That the native artists of a single group agree so closely with one another suggests that primitive art is fundamentally a rational form of communication and expression.

A second art form often compared with primitive art is that of children. In view of his lengthy apprenticeship and demonstrated skill, the native artist would have a right to resent such a comparison. For children's art with its fantasy and technical inadequacy belongs to the child's mysterious and very private world. Not having the experience of adults, the child uses only his immediate resources to solve visual problems. The tendency to complete and to enclose forms may assist him; but each achievement seems to be a unique one, dependent upon the mental state and development of the child at the moment of creation. Moreover, studies of Australian aboriginal children show that the child acquires the conventional symbols of his society during the second decade of his life. It is as though the need for standardization and perpetuation has replaced the childhood desire for growth and self-expression. Other than a vague similarity such as we see in stick figures, there is little to connect the art of children with that of primitive man.

The Question of Realism

An interesting question related to the problem of children's art is the ability of the artist faithfully to reproduce nature—something no child can ever do. We have already suggested that the primitive artist lacks interest in realism per se. But some writers have insisted that primitive carvers could have carved naturalistic portraits "if they had wanted to." This is like arguing that elephants can really fly—but just do not want to. To say a people can accomplish something they did not attempt invites misunderstanding. Many primitives carved likenesses of the human face; but few achieved more than an approximation of the real forms. Apparent examples of naturalistic portraiture in primitive art, such as seated figures from the Congo, illusionistic heads from the Northwest Coast, and Maori house figures from New Zealand are often cited as evidence of the primitive artists' skill in realism. All of these probably involve Western influence. What is more, the closer we look at these examples, the more they seem to be generalized rather than specific likenesses.

A glance at the history of portrait-making reveals why the primitive artist paid so little attention to this seemingly important art. Before the ancient Greeks achieved individual likeness in their art, they had first to interest themselves in man as a general type worthy of accurate representation. The Greeks began by depicting the gods as men, first in an abstract, intellectual way, later in an increasingly specific way, and finally, in Hellenistic times, in true portraits. Never having admired mankind in the abstract, the primitive artist saw little significance in the facial details that distinguish each individual. Instead, he sought to represent certain standard entities—the ancestors, the spirits, or the gods—which for him existed independently and without reference to specific human beings.

Nature Versus Western Judgment

In spite of ritual requirements and cultural inertia, the primitive artist did have some freedom to invent new forms and to modify old ones. This varied, of course, from culture to culture. Where changes occurred, they usually took the form of a gradual shift of emphasis or a novel combination of existing elements. Drastic alterations of style such as we see in modern art, simply would not have been understood or appreciated. But given a traditional style that they recognize, members of a primitive society can identify the work of individual artists among a large group of objects. To recognize distinct "hands" they may even use the same kinds of visual criteria we use, but this is uncertain. All that can be said is that their reasons for identifying the artist's work differ sharply from our own. As in medieval art, religious significance and other nonaesthetic factors entered into visual judgment. Either a carving fulfilled expectations and it was good; or it was eccentric and therefore worthless. The poorly painted design failed not only because it seemed clumsy and aesthetically inadequate, but also because it was thought incapable of performing its social or religious function. The artist's part in producing the object was, in the eyes of his society, more or less a passive one. Forms emerged through him almost as through a medium in a seance.

It is very difficult for us to accept this attitude toward art. Westerners tend usually to see art in terms of the artist's personality. We think of Picasso's work in relation to his entire life. Even when an anthropologist visits a communal society to study its art, he always sits down to watch the artist at work, asking him questions, recording each gesture, and noting down every grunt. But, unlike Westerners, when primitives talk about art, they speak of the objects themselves. And though they lack special aesthetic terms and a critical apparatus for discussing their work, they are by no means indifferent to the products of their art.

Which viewpoint is correct? Is it possible that we have been deceived by our own idea of what an artist really is, and that, as far as primitive art is concerned, the native artist is not of the utmost importance in native art? The answer is apparently yes. For if we ask the artist why he does something, he will answer: "It has always been done so," or "This is what the gods decreed," or simply, "I don't know." In each instance he reveals an attitude toward himself and his art identical with that expressed by his society. He regards his work neither as an extension of himself nor as an expression of his personality.

That is why comparisons between Western judgments of primitive art and those of the natives who produce it have proved so inconclusive. Thus it is said that the views of the Dan-Guere peoples of the Ivory Coast accord with our own, whereas those of Nigerians do not. The mistake is in trying to compare their judgment with ours. The attitude of Westerners alters constantly as new ideas and fashions circulate among them; that of the native group remains essentially unchanged. An appreciation of primitive art is enhanced by an understanding of both viewpoints.

Patronage

Primitive society expresses its view of the artist through its demands for his work more than through any conscious concern for him personally. The artist's commissions almost always have come from social institutions—the chief, the secret society, the priesthood, or head of the family—rather than from individuals in their private capacities. Consequently, primitive art serves institutional rather than personal ends. Although religion provides a

7   *Clay figure, Remojadas style. Veracruz, Mexico. H. 22″ (Stavenhagen Collection, Mexico City).*

pretext for artistic effort, social attitudes usually determine just what form art objects will take. As the anthropologist Raymond Firth observes, such themes as landscape, still life, and the self-portrait, which are comparatively devoid of broad social meaning, have little place in primitive art. Favored above all other subjects are the human face and figure or a reasonable facsimile thereof. When animals or plants appear, they almost inevitably in one way or another have reference to social position. Thus through its patronage each primitive community shapes the artist's works to fit the goals of the society.

Being controlled by social aims, primitive art tends to reflect public institutional attitudes. The insignia, shapes, and symbols that to us seem so weird or distorted form in fact a sort of official language usually understood throughout the group. In Melanesia, for instance, women and children often know exactly what certain masks and figures mean, although theoretically their society insists they should be ignorant of the hidden content and should continue to be mystified year after year. This is to distinguish fixed roles for certain segments of the community, thereby contributing to social order. So, because of its close ties with local native institutions, primitive art becomes an excellent vehicle for communicating attitudes and proclaiming values within the group. It also tends to be forthright and easily understood. What is more, it is undeniably optimistic.

Such a statement calls for more than a little justification. It has always been customary to look upon our subject—primitive art—as an art of fear, hatred, or dread. Now, thanks largely to Raymond Firth, we can see the errors of that viewpoint. To be sure, primitive man has his problems. His world is a difficult one, with food shortages, disease, and sudden death often confronting him. To be able to face these unpleasant situations he has developed a series of magical responses which, while inadequate from our point of view, serves him very well. The more we look at his art, the more we see that each object, in satisfying the society's demand, reinforces the status quo. No one, we agree, is likely to question solutions when they are backed by the authority of generations and the sanction of all of one's ancestors.

8   Rice shed door with ancestor figure. Sumatra. H. 34¹/₄" (Royal Tropical Museum, Amsterdam).

Far from denying the power of institutions to cope with the world, primitive art affirms their superiority and value.

If we assume, then, the positive character of primitive art, it is easy to understand why there is no art of social protest among primitive peoples. The art supports authority just as did all Western art prior to the sixteenth century. True, there were caricatures of chiefs, foreigners, and neighboring peoples in Hawaiian, Eskimo, and Northwest Coast carvings. But lampooning rivals and ridiculing strangers actually helped the great leaders of the local group to maintain their power.

This brings us to another issue—that of racial contribution to primitive art. It is an interesting problem, but one that is beclouded by emotion. What information we have indicates that as far as primitive art is concerned, the artist's racial origin is completely incidental. The three main races of the world, black, yellow, and white, have all contributed major styles and innovations, and yet some of their representatives, such as the Caucasoid Australian aborigines, have hardly progressed beyond the Old Stone Age level. Ideas have passed back and forth among races to such a bewildering extent that no one group can claim to have invented this or that motif. A truly valid classification of primitive art either along racial or social lines must await the clarification of local and historical differences.

The Importance of Historical Relations

Primitive man has always been extraordinarily conservative. Every facet of his religious and social life encourages stability and permanence. Consequently, the art forms produced today probably resemble very closely those made by his forefathers centuries ago. The more isolated a style is from the mainstreams of world art, the greater will be its tendency to remain unchanged. The most primitive of peoples always have the most ancient of art styles—unless historical accident has introduced new visual ideas. Then the modification of the style will reveal the sources of influence, while the traditional elements remaining will be a good indication of how the ancient

9   *Mother and child roof pinnacle figure. Pende, Central Congo. H. 45³⁄₄″ (Musée Royal de l'Afrique Centrale, Brussels).*

style appeared before the change took place. The art of Mexico just after the Spanish conquest is a good example of this. The new elements brought in by the Spanish are easily distinguished from those which belonged to pre-Columbian art. Yet the blending of the two produced—for a time at least—a new style that was, strictly speaking, neither Indian nor Spanish. Without European contact or other upheaval, the Aztecs would have gone on reproducing their traditional style indefinitely.

There are two ways of looking at culture: one, paying great attention to history, the other, ignoring it. In the historical view, an art object is part of a long artistic tradition; no matter when or where it was made, it has a definite relation to its forerunners and is dependent on them. The opposing functional view considers relationships simultaneously without reference to time. If, for example, an art object is used in a dance, it interacts with the spectators and with their milieu. Its function is what counts, not its history.

Both of these approaches are helpful in understanding primitive art. Partly because we do not know what primitive art looked like in ages past, the functional approach has usurped more than its proper share of the field. But all conceptions about an art style must to some degree be based on a view of its history even when the past is obscured. To assume that a style has no past and is entirely a local phenomenon is in itself a historical view—and an untenable one—which condemns art objects to solitary confinement in an artistic limbo. We will try to correct this distortion.

The evidence of the history of primitive art available to us is of several kinds. Unfortunately the legends of their own origins given by primitive peoples are usually garbled beyond the point of usefulness. Frequently "edited" for one reason or another and full of borrowings, their myths are almost impossible to verify; and in many instances they can be shown to be downright false. As for the archaeology of primitive cultures, this is still in its infancy, except for that of the Indians of the United States and perhaps that of Nigeria. And unfortunately most truly primitive objects used in the past were of wood, fiber, or skin and therefore perished long before the archaeologist lifted his spade. In short, to see the real history of these artifacts we must turn to the art forms themselves.

The first question that arises in any historical study of objects is: what is a valid historical connection? On our answer the whole idea of primitive art depends. For if we approach the subject with rigid anti-historical conceptions, we will find few new relationships. On the other hand, we may

10 *Rubbing of ancestor plaque. Taiwan. H. 36¹/₄″ (T'aitung Prefecture Library, Taiwan).*

admit that when art objects have much in common, they must be histori-cally connected. In the latter case we may even discover new relationships between widely separated areas. Madagascar is nearly half way around the world from Polynesia; yet linguistic evidence completely supports the ob-vious relationship between the two areas as discerned in their arts. Our idea of what makes a valid link will become clearer when we consider specific examples in subsequent chapters.

But there are dangers in the historical approach to primitive art. One danger is that a historian's overriding idea of primitive history may lead him completely astray. Thus students of Polynesian culture have long searched in Indonesia, India, and China for the origins of that civilization, never realizing that the concept of Polynesian unity was false to begin with. Another still more absurd example of self-deception in viewing the past appears in the case of the several masks from the Nile that for nearly thirty years were exhibited in the United States as Bella Coola Indian carvings. The owner, an expert in his field, knew that this Northwest Coast tribe came originally from a much simpler culture, and he died firmly convinced that the Nile masks were specimens of the "ancient" Bella Coola art style.

The historical connections that are easiest to demonstrate are those of objects close to one another in time and in space. But such links, being obvious, are comparatively uninteresting. Nor do they alter drastically our present thinking. Much more exciting is a relationship such as that—which we shall discuss later—between New Zealand and Taiwan, over 6000 miles apart (Plate 10). The most interesting connections of all, of course, are those that are far away in time as well as in space. An excellent example of this is a Bushman painting from South Africa which seems to illustrate a com-plex sexual relationship between large animals and fish. Exactly the same theme appears on Greek pottery of the eighth century B.C. There are four possible explanations of this: first, independent convergence; second, Greek influence on the Bushmen; third, Bushman influence on the Greeks; fourth, an earlier common prototype. The first seems unlikely in view of the com-plexity of the theme; the second and third are improbable because of the lack of other connections. The fourth explanation is in fact correct. A com-mon prototype dating from the Old Stone Age has been discovered by a European scholar, Carl Hentze.

Now we must remember that Bushman art, like Bushman culture, rep-resents essentially the Old Stone Age level of development. Thus, though probably made within the last few centuries, the Bushman painting is actually closer to the original source than the Greek version. The Bushman conception is a living fossil whereas the Greek is truly a later interpretation of an Old Stone Age theme. In other words, as far as style is concerned, their chronology should be reversed. If we had no Stone Age prototype to examine, we would still have to say that the eighth-century B.C. treatment was derived from a lost earlier model of which the modern Bushman example is a fairly accurate reflection. With techniques such as this, we are able to delve into the dim past of primitive art with at least some hope of success.

Psychological Factors

Very little is yet known about the psychology of primitive art. One theory, popularized by the late Ralph Linton, American anthropologist, held that the primitive artist visualizes the final form of his work in his mind's eye before beginning to work. Attractive as this idea is, there is no evidence to support it. Moreover, we lack any means of proving such a theory. The only other observations that emerge from earlier discussions concern the temperament of the artist himself: in some instances, he is described as an excitable type; in others, he is characterized as a plodder. Ability to work with others and to accept criticism seem to have been fairly widespread prerequisites. Apart from these generalities, defining the psychological components of primitive art remains a problem for future study.

We have seen how natural, social, historical, and psychological factors help to shape primitive art. In subsequent chapters we shall examine areas where the aesthetic qualities of the various styles become clear. Each of us may decide for himself what significance or force the artist's particular ideas have. But it is important that thoughtful people the world over take note of the concepts primitives are rapidly discarding. As primitive man emerges from his world into the modern one, he trails in his wake attitudes, perceptions, and sensibilities which so-called civilized man can ill afford to ignore. Unless we continue to extend our patterns of imagination to include the exotic, we shall remain as limited in our aesthetic responses as were the old-fashioned missionaries when they saw in primitive art only the "idols of the heathens."

A F R I C A

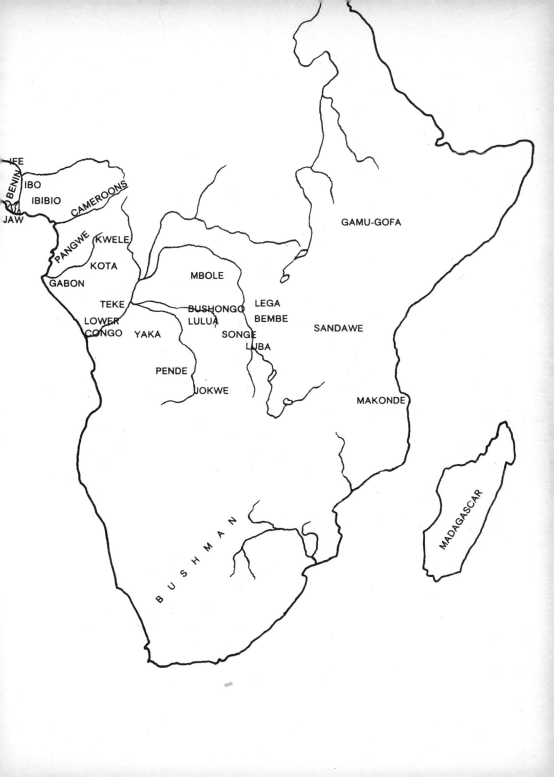

IFE

BENIN

IBO

IBIBIO

JAW

CAMEROONS

PANGWE

KWELE

KOTA

GABON

MBOLE

TEKE

BUSHONGO

LEGA

LOWER
CONGO

LULUA

BEMBE

GAMU-GOFA

YAKA

SONGE

SANDAWE

LUBA

PENDE

JOKWE

MAKONDE

B U S H M A N

MADAGASCAR

I

The People

Up to the latter half of the nineteenth century, Africa was the Dark Continent—an unknown land to Westerners. They conceived of this blank space on the map as representing a vast jungle inhabited by wild animals and uncivilized tribes. Gradually the continent yielded its secrets to explorers and colonizers. Now, with breathtaking suddenness, events have made Africa and its peoples a focus of world attention. Even the remotest areas have become familiar to newspaper readers, and one misconception after another has been dissipated. We now know, for example, that this land is only one-fifth forest, the rest being savannah and desert.

On a higher level, we now also realize that it was not an inherent inferiority that kept African tribes from organizing great political states. Indeed, it seems obvious that the rapid formation of power blocs both inside and outside their own countries would not have been possible without extensive schooling in political affairs from time immemorial. Compared with the native of New Guinea, for example, the African was politically sophisticated long before the beginning of European exploitation.

The traditional African system of political control is based on a family unit. Each individual owes allegiance to certain family elders whom he honors and obeys. These in turn defer to a hereditary headman or local chief. The latter pays homage to a paramount tribal chieftain or in some areas to a king. Thus Africans align themselves in an essentially feudal way. Advancement to power in these societies is as clearly laid down beforehand as is the succession of a European monarch. When a leader dies, his successor is automatically determined by the inheritance system.

Another misconception about Africans is the belief that they all belong to the same race or ethnic group. Actually, there are in Africa several distinct races varying widely in language and culture. Racial types, however, do tend to fall into certain groups; and these groupings are useful for the light they cast on the historical development of African life.

Racial Types

The earliest Africans who still survive are the Bushmen of South Africa and the Pygmies of the Congo Basin. Neither group is really Negro. The Bushmen have yellowish skin, tightly curled "peppercorn" hair, and long slender limbs. Standing apart from all other Africans, they belong to an ancient race that may have Asiatic origins. The languages the Bushmen and their relatives the Hottentots speak form a distinct group, notable for frequent use of clicking tongue sounds. Although confined today to such marginal areas as the Kalahari Desert, the Bushman must at one time have dominated most of southern and eastern Africa. For their living they have always depended on hunting and food gathering, the most primitive and insecure form of livelihood known to man.

The other early people, the Pygmies, also lead a somewhat precarious life in the forest lands of the Congo. Short and dark, the Pygmies are of Negroid origin but differ from the true Negro in significant respects. Pygmies are not dwarfs; they are a small, well-proportioned people of considerable intelligence who happen to average about four and a half feet in height. Originally they probably ranged over the entire Congo basin. Yet today they cannot even call their small hunting territory their own. For they live as satellites of the more sophisticated Negro groups of the Congo who give them iron and other valuables in exchange for forest products. Perhaps

because of this subordinate role, the Pygmies have lost the independent languages they once must have spoken.

Both the Pygmies and the Bushmen represent the hunting and food-gathering stage of cultural development. Basically, this means that their way of life was nomadic. Lacking the ability to accumulate great quantities of food, they could never settle in one place long enough to develop agriculture, pottery, weaving, or any of the amenities of life. But like all peoples, they had time for magic because it was just as essential as food. Their ritual life, while not of great variety, did give rise to some forms of art.

A third racial type in Africa is the Negro. His history and relations with other groups are still rather unclear. The Negro may have originally come from southern Asia, since other Negroid peoples are found in Oceania. On the other hand, he may have originated in western Africa, where his type is known in its purest form. Negro intermarriage with peoples of Caucasian blood in northern and eastern Africa has further confused the matter.

The Negro's way of life represents an important advance over those of earlier peoples. Long ago, probably in the western Sudan, he learned to grow crops, in particular pearl millet and sorghum, a maizelike cereal grain. He also acquired cattle from western Asia. He thus achieved a freedom from want and an ability to concentrate wealth that

11   Mother and child dance staff. Yoruba, Nigeria. H. 12¹/₂" (Dubiner Collection, Tel Aviv).

12 *Figures holding bowl.
Cameroons. H. 17¹/₂" (Lindenmuseum, Stuttgart).*

earlier peoples would have thought unbelievable. Moreover, these advances
enabled him to turn to political organization and elaborate forms of art.

The Art

Viewed historically, African art follows the pattern of the culture that produces it. The Pygmies have virtually no art. The Bushmen, on the other
hand, created wonderful rock engravings and rock paintings, some of which
date back centuries. The Negroes of northern and eastern Africa produced
almost no visual art. But the peoples of western Africa carved the magnificent masks and figures so envied by modern artists today. There is obviously some significance in this distribution. Careful study of each area may

help us discern what the pattern of historic development in African art really is.

The Bushman

The gentle, half-starved Bushman of today no longer produces the paintings that have made him world famous. In older times, before the Negro and the white man pushed into Bushman territory, he ranged over the land in small groups, living on the game he killed. He also painted and engraved animal and human designs on rocks. In these works the animals were often shown singly; and human figures usually appeared with weapons or in pursuit of animals. The colors were applied in flat even tones without any attempt to express light and shade. In the human body, movement—an important concern of the artist—was achieved through slanting lines and a somewhat arbitrary shaping of the body. Animals were seldom depicted in motion (Plate 13). Bushman artists used neither ground line nor perspective.

As for style, Bushman painting, particularly that of human figures, has a vivacity and directness of expression that wins our immediate admiration. Simple and unsophisticated though his work may have been, the artist conveyed his message in purely aesthetic terms. Forms take on a human appearance not only because they include such lifelike details as the sway-back and prominent buttocks of the Bushmen but also because the forms themselves have the vitality we associate with human beings. The treatment of animals is different. They are depicted with great fidelity to nature, yet show little feeling. Whatever the artist's attitude toward the real animals may have been, or the emotions he felt in painting them, he did not project these feelings into his painting; there is no counterpart here to the Delacroix who made every animal snort or rear.

This brings us to the question of origins. The isolation of the Bushmen makes it seem unlikely that they have been influenced to any degree by the developed civilizations of Asia and Africa. The theme of animals and hunters immediately suggests a relationship to the Old Stone Age cave paintings of the so-called Franco-Cantabrian tradition in southern France and northern Spain. In support of this theory, scholars have piled up considerable evidence. Their case rests mainly on a similarity in the designs themselves; and, in fact, there are strong connections between the animal styles of the

Bushmen and of the Lascaux and other Paleolithic artists. The Bushman figure style, however, is not paralleled in the art of the cave painters.

If we turn to a somewhat less well known Stone Age art, that of the East Spanish tradition, which is somewhat later than the famous cave paintings, we find active silhouette figures closely resembling Bushman designs. Running, hunting, and gesturing, the East Spanish human figures have all the impetuous movement of the historic Bushman styles. The two even share artistic conventions, such as the raising of one arm and the lowering of the other at a different angle, used in both areas to express motion. It appears, then, that the Bushman tradition is a mixture of stylistic in-

13 Bushman rock painting. Zamenkomst, Maclear District, Cape Province. H. 3' 6"
(South African Museum, Capetown).

fluences that find an early expression in the paintings of the Franco-Cantabrian region and of eastern Spain.

How, then, did ideas originating roughly ten to fifteen thousand years ago get to southern Africa? No one seriously believes that the Bushmen migrated from Spain. On the other hand, since the Bushmen have remained at the Paleolithic level, the Stone Age styles may have spread southward among hunting peoples for thousands of years, by way of northern and eastern Africa. Then, as more advanced people replaced the hunters, the older styles were probably forgotten except in such a very isolated area as southern Africa. Evidence of this movement should appear, then, in eastern Africa, especially among the more primitive inhabitants. And that is in fact the case. Rock paintings from this region, especially from the Sandawe people of Tanganyika, show a Paleolithic-Bushmanlike style. Significantly, the Sandawe are probably relatives of the Bushman to begin with, as their language contains the peculiar click sounds. Still further north are the recently discovered prehistoric rock paintings of Tassili and other sites in the central Sahara. These too have a distinct Bushman character.

We must not make the mistake, however, of insisting on linguistic or cultural support for artistic connections. Art changes faster and travels further than culture, language, or race because it offers every group the blessings of its "big magic." Easily understood and quickly reproduced, it may be adopted more readily than a new technique or a new language. The people of Arnhem Land in Australia, completely unlike the Bushmen in language and race and comparable to them only in having a food-gathering and hunting culture, nevertheless produce strikingly similar rock paintings. Both styles must have drawn their inspiration from the common well of Late Paleolithic style (Plate 59).

The Negro

Negroes occupy a vast strip of Africa extending from the Senegal on the Atlantic coast to the Limpopo River in the east. Except for the southern tip

14 Mask with heart-shaped face. Kwele, Gabon. H. 11" (Margaret Plass Collection, Philadelphia).

of Africa, this area includes virtually all of Africa south of the Sahara Desert. Although hundreds of languages are spoken in this area, the American linguist Joseph Greenberg has recently shown that all these tongues belong in three great families—the Afro-Asiatic, Sudanic, and Niger-Congo groups. The first includes the languages of the Lake Chad region and the Cushitic tongues of eastern Africa. Among their close kin are Egyptian, Berber, Arabic, and Hebrew. The Sudanic group includes such languages as Masai, Shilluk, and many tongues of the Shari-Nile region. But for our purposes, these areas are less important, for they produce very little visual art.

The most interesting language group, from our point of view, is the third—the Niger-Congo family. Almost all the people embraced by a line drawn from the Senegal around the Niger River and past the Congo drainage speak related Niger-Congo languages. As if this were not enough, Greenberg has also shown that the languages of the Congo and those further to the south and east, collectively called Bantu, are actually but a single, relatively recent child of the great Niger-Congo parent stock. The entire spread of Negroid culture south and east of Nigeria is apparently due therefore to a series of migrations by Bantu-speaking peoples whose ancestral roots lie in eastern Nigeria. In view of the fact that their languages are so closely related, these people must have pushed eastward within relatively recent times—say, the last fifteen hundred years. Some got as far as southern Africa though at best they were still late comers. The Bantu Zulu, for example, were still moving southward through Bushman territory and had not yet reached the Cape of Good Hope when the Dutch arrived there in the seventeenth century. Other Bantu peoples penetrated into East Africa where one Bantu dialect—Swahili—became popular as a *lingua franca* or trader's tongue. In other words, the Bantu simply spread out over large sections, whereas other equally important language groups in the Niger-Congo family stayed at home. The area that all the Niger-Congo languages once occupied—western Africa—remains therefore the ultimate homeland of the Negro.

African Negro Art

What a surprise it is, then, to find that Negro sculpture is confined almost exactly to the Niger-Congo region. The art of this vast area, moreover, is so homogeneous that it is obviously the product of a single cultural tradition.

If we look closely at African Negro sculpture, we discern at least one complex visual idea that runs throughout. This pervading motif is the heart-shaped face. Appearing with greatest clarity in Kwele masks from the Gabon region (Plate 4), its characteristics are as follows: the face is shown as a smooth depression or concave surface which extends from the underside of the eyebrows to the vicinity of the mouth. Within this heart-shaped plane, the nose appears in relief as a downward extension of the forehead and the eyes as raised oval shapes. The whole conception is so arbitrary that it can hardly have been invented independently all over the Niger-Congo area.

The heart-shaped face appears in the extreme western region among the Baga and Mende, on the Ivory Coast, in parts of the Cameroons, and throughout the Congo Basin, and even among the Zulu of South Africa and the Makonde of Tanganyika. Curiously, the one area where the heart-shaped face is rare is in the middle of sculpture-producing Negro Africa—that is, in Nigeria. Even here there is an inconsistency. The art of the aristocratic centers of Ife and Benin and of the Yoruba and grasslands Cameroons peoples shows a different style; while that of the Ibo, Ibibio, and Ijaw, the more primitive groups living in this territory, often employs the heart-shaped face. Apparently, this motif belongs to the oldest and most widespread traditions of the Niger-Congo area. Since it accompanied the Bantu in their expansion, it must be at the very least fifteen hundred years old. What is more, the superceding of the heart-shaped face by the aristocratic styles of Nigeria means that this motif must predate the development of high culture. If that is true, the heart-shaped motif must be very old indeed.

Attempts to place African sculpture in a historical context usually give Egypt credit as the initial cultural stimulus. It is pointed out that just as Negro Africa is famous for wood sculpture, so the Egyptians excelled first in this medium and only later in stone. But, aside from this, African art has hardly any stronger connection with the sculpture of Egypt than with that, say, of the Ancient Near East. The heart-shaped face, for example, is not readily apparent in either area of the ancient world. In other words, if the African motif has any connection with the outside world, it must be with a style older, in terms of history, than the styles found in Dynastic Egypt and the Ancient Near East.

It so happens that the heart-shaped motif is seen in several art styles of

very great age. It appears, for instance, in five-thousand-year-old ivory figurines recently excavated from Neolithic sheepherding villages in Palestine, near Beersheba. This distinctive facial type occurs also in wooden images preserved in bogs in Scandinavia and in the Urals of Russia, the latter dating from the third millenium B.C., and of Neolithic origin. Thus archaeology confirms what the African distribution of the heart-shaped face suggests: namely, that this motif, antedating the rise of high cultures, stems from Neolithic times, that is, from the phase when man had begun to produce his own food but before he had developed metallurgy.

The heart-shaped face seems particularly persistent in an aspect of Neolithic culture which we may call the Megalithic tradition. The term Megalithic, meaning "big stone," refers to the most conspicuous custom of these peoples, their habit of erecting great slablike stone monuments. But early Megalithic peoples also used wooden statues, mainly images of ancestors, it seems. Judging by the art of tribes in southern and southeastern Asia that perpetuate the Megalithic tradition (discussed in Chapter II), these images had heart-shaped faces.

Megalithic carving tends to be associated with funeral rites. This is also true in Africa, though perhaps to a lesser degree. The

15 and 16   Memorial figures placed on graves. Gamu Gofa, Southwest Ethiopia. H. 16¹/₂" (above) and 18¹/₂" (right). (Sammlung für Völkerkunde, Universität Zürich).

people of southern Ethiopia, long recognized as Megalithic, carved grave effigies (with heart-shaped faces) of their dead warriors (Plate 15). These they surrounded with images representing the people and animals the warrior had killed. The same custom prevails among the Naga of the Assam highlands between Burma and India. Aristotle reports the use of wooden grave posts among the primitive early inhabitants of Spain, where megaliths abound; and in ancient Greece, crude wooden images known as *Hermae* used to flank the doorways of tombs. Admittedly, these examples cover a vast area, but the fact is that the spread of Megalithic culture was vast.

To reduce the problem of African origins to reasonable scope, we must focus on limited areas where single objects may be studied in detail. Because their style has been comparatively isolated in the southern Congo, we shall start with a tribe of that region, the Pende.

The Pende

Of the very numerous masks and figures used by the Pende, the simplest consist merely of two huge round hollow disks attached to a woven headpiece and decorated with raffia or feathers. Some of these, known as *minganji* were worn by the men who policed the initiation ground. There the young boys were secluded and instructed in tribal lore; after circumcision and the other painful ordeals, they were made members of the group. The masks helped frighten away all the uninitiated and the women and young children. The type

itself seems to be older and more sacred than the *mbuya*, a mask used in festivals celebrating the return of the initiated youths to the village. More realistic and more sculptural than the guardian masks, the *mbuya* represent human and animal characters as well as spirit beings. These masks often show the heart-shaped treatment of the features.

Masks of the *minganji* type were also used at dances held during the building of the chief's ceremonial hut, where cult objects were stored. This house is of the utmost importance because of what it tells us of Pende origins. It consists of a moundlike roof covered with thatch. The door is framed by two carved wooden posts and a lintel; crocodiles, lizards, snakes, Maltese crosses, human heads, figures, and pairs of hornlike outward spirals decorate the entrance. An ax is incised between the spirals over the door and a carved figure on top of the roof frequently holds a cup in one hand and an ax in the other. All of these motifs are found all over western Asia and Europe. Wooden postlike figures representing spirits are also sometimes found in front of Pende ceremonial houses. Their faces are all of the heart-shaped type.

Animal masks are rather rare among the Pende. One type seen in the eastern Pende area has horns above an ordinary face (Plate 17). Another belongs to a tradition that is widespread in Africa: it consists of a muzzle flaring downward from a rounded helmetlike head covering, and horns or ears that extend upward in the opposite direction. Worn horizontally on top of the head, this three-part animal mask represents, in this case, a buffalo. In other areas masks may depict a hippopotamus, an elephant, an antelope, a bird, or a human head. The three-part mask, however, always has horns or tusks, suggesting a Megalithic origin. Probably very old, this type of carved mask is found throughout most of the Niger-Congo area.

The Jokwe

If the style of the Pende tends to seem rather reticent and discreet, such terms cannot be used to describe the art of their neighbors to the south, the Jokwe. Basically nomadic hunters, the Jokwe have only partially adopted agriculture. Hunters play a privileged social role in this culture, and many of the magical rites stress the importance of the chase. In the seventeenth century the Jokwe were conquered by the Lunda, but within the last cen-

17 *Animal mask. Pende, Central Congo. Wood with raffia. H. 15" (American Museum of Natural History, New York).*

tury their relationship has been virtually reversed. Today the Jokwe are famous for their toughness, intelligence, and aggressiveness.

Jokwe art has a remarkably dynamic appearance. Whereas most African styles are fundamentally static and seem to indicate an acceptance of the status quo, the Jokwe forms appear to pulsate with energy. Rippling surfaces emphasize dramatic tensions and contrasting shapes. In figures belonging to this powerful tradition, the most expressive elements, the heads, hands, and feet, are greatly enlarged. Jokwe carvings often adorn some utilitarian object such as a chair or a stool, which may also have been a symbol of authority; from their form it seems evident that these chairs were introduced by Portuguese traders during the sixteenth century.

Jokwe masks also express strength and animation (Plate 18). Some of those used in secular pantomimes mimic the foolish ways of men and women. Those worn by women represent the men and are effeminate in form, whereas the female impersonators' masks often have stylized beards. The tight-fitting netted costume worn with both types has a marked resemblance to costumes worn by Ibo dancers in Nigeria, far to the north. In view of the many Bantu ties with that area, such a connection seems quite understandable. But the expressionistic treatment of the forms is unique to the Jokwe.

The Yaka

To the west of the Jokwe live the Yaka, a group whose principal interests have also been hunting and raiding. The art of the Yaka consists mainly of masks and figures. The masks play an important part in festive dances celebrating the end of the boys' year-long initiation period. All sorts of gay combinations of colors and forms appear in these objects. Using themes taken from mythology, the best artists compete to see who can produce the most arresting interpretation. Animal designs predominate; beneath are white spirit faces, more uniform, and probably sacred (Plate 19).

In comparison with that of other areas, Yaka style seems to be vigorous, localized, and primitive. The Yaka emphasis on animals, and the gro-

18   Dance mask. Jokwe, Central Congo. H. 11" (Museum für Völkerkunde, Hamburg).

tesque noses resembling Cyrano's, are unparalleled in Africa. They suggest continuing totemism and phallic worship, forms of religion that in neighboring areas have given way to more sophisticated kinds of worship. Yaka figurines or fetishes known as *nkisi* are also very primitive; each is thought to contain a spirit that a man may dominate and control for his own ends, often to bring success in the hunt. The Yaka use them at initiation time in particular; the statues are recarved or restored for such occasions. A special hut is built where the initiates are taught the meaning of the figures and how to take proper care of them. Then, after sacrifices have been made, the initiates are instructed in certain sexual taboos, the observation of which guarantees that the medicinal and protective powers of the *nkisi* will not be lost to the clan.

Yaka masks are of several sorts. One type, worn with a raffia costume, is shaped somewhat like a mirror and is held in front of the face. A second type is a giant face mask, which is worn by the old man or woman who supervises the initiation rites. Sometimes these *kakungu* are hung up in the circumcision hut where they are supposed to cure the sick, expel evil, and restore fertility. A third Yaka mask form, the helmet type, is composed of a hollow wood cylinder that completely covers the wearer's head and shoulders. This type has its closest parallel among the nearby Suku people. Of rough surface, these Yaka masks are usually characterized by a very menacing expression.

The Lower Congo Tribes

To the west of the Yaka, at the mouth of the Congo, live people of a very different type. In the late fifteenth century, when the Portuguese first landed in the area, they discovered an advanced society—the kingdom of the Kongo people—already established there. The Portuguese helped the Kongo in their struggle against the warlike Yaka of the hinterland, and converted their leaders to Christianity. But as Portuguese influence waned, the Africans reverted to pagan practices, and in the nineteenth century when Euro-

19   Masked youth dancing at the public climax of initiation rites. Yaka, Western Congo. Photographed in 1951.

54

peans encountered them again they showed little evidence of their earlier Catholicism.

The recent art of the people of the Lower Congo area includes many examples of a small wooden figure depicting a mother nursing her child (Plate 20). These naturalistic figures, set up in shrines to honor ancestors, have provoked violent controversy among scholars. One group regards them as independent inventions of the Congolese sculptors; the other believes the mother and child figures to be derived from Madonna and Child images of the Portuguese.

In an attempt to resolve this disagreement, those who believe in the African origin of the type make the following points: suckling is of course a common sight in Africa and may be an expression of the ever powerful concept of fertility; secondly, mother and child images are also found in northern Nigeria, in the Ivory Coast, and in other parts of the Congo (Plate 9), so the type is widespread. But, as we have seen time and again, natural forms are not a basic source of primitive art, nor is there any particular reason why suckling, an altogether natural and commonplace event, should have ceremonial meaning; moreover, while mother and child images are not uncommon in Africa, they occur almost always in areas strongly tinged with European influences.

Examining the maternal figures themselves, we may be able to learn more about their origin. Perhaps the most striking aspect of these sculptures is the intimate, personal character, and the tender naturalism: a warm psychological relationship exists between mother and child. Equally unprecedented in African art is the mother's cross-legged sitting position and the asymmetrical placement of her hands, one under the child's head, supporting it, the other resting over the little body as if to protect it.

The truth is that this maternal image had been developed in western Europe long before and was carried to the Congo by Portuguese missionaries. Around the middle of the fourteenth century, the Italian artist Simone Martini devised a new kind of religious image, the Madonna of Humility. Based partly on classical models, Simone's new type of image depicts Mary seated on a cushion and giving her breast to the Child. This very human and domestic concept of Mary symbolized her dual role as the Mother of God and the maternal protectress of mankind. Images of the Madonna of Humility reached the Iberian peninsula before 1375; by the time Portuguese caravels arrived at the mouth of the Congo, the figure had become firmly established as a provincial favorite. As the Portuguese priests began their campaign to convert the Congolese leaders, the humble Madonna image apparently was particularly useful, its self-evident symbolism appealing to the child-loving people of Africa. In any event, the gesture of one hand over the Child and one hand under is faithfully preserved in the African version, and the plinth on which the mother sits corresponds exactly to Mary's cushion. Intimacy in the relationship between mother and child also carries through the African version.

The realization that Lower Congo mother and child figures develop from European forerunners is of major importance in understanding African art, and suggests that naturalism may be a rather recent and somewhat alien achievement of the African artist. At the same time, the realization enables us to gauge more accurately his unique indigenous accomplishments. The Teke people, not far from the Congo mouth, produce stiff and angular fetish figures which are entirely African in concept. However, were we to find highly naturalistic figures (in particular, mother and child images) among the Teke or neighboring tribes (Plate 21), we might suspect indirect European inspiration. Such maternal figures as do appear have the same intimate relationship, the seated posture, the one-hand-over, one-hand-under placement as the Lower Congo images. The Madonna of Humility, introduced by Christians and adopted for a different pagan purpose, is the inspiration of these naturalistic forms.

The importance of Madonna symbolism in the Lower Congo suggests that other local art forms may have had a European origin which is now partly obscured. Grave markers carved of soapstone, either in the round or in relief, owe a debt to Christian tomb sculpture. Those having a figure supporting the head with one hand stem from the European tradition of mourning. But the most striking instance of Christian influence is perhaps the wooden fetish figure known as a *konde* (Plate 23). Used variously in magic rites, these figures often bristle with nails driven into them by the sorcerer priests. It was believed sometimes that the nail would hurt a particular enemy who, if he wished relief, must pay to have the nail—and thus his pain—removed. In other instances a man might get rid of a bad habit by persuading another person to drive a nail into the figure. But these *konde* power images were ultimately based on an idea quite alien to the origin of the usual African fetish figure. The Africans must have known of some powerful spirit, mutilated with nails yet capable of performing super-

20 *Mother and child figure based on Madonna of Humility. Lower Congo. H. 10$^1/_2$" (Brooklyn Museum).*

natural feats—and the answer is, of course, the figure of Christ introduced by the Portuguese. The pagan sculptors of the Congo, not understanding the Christian concept of God, transformed the crucifixion to accord with their own traditional use of fetishes. Thus certain *konde* brandishing spears aggressively in their right hands are probably based on the figure of the risen Christ carrying the slender staff and banner of the Resurrection which symbolize His victory over Death. By a slight change in setting, even the meaning of small details has been totally altered and sometimes even reversed. An example such as the *konde* enables us to understand the process of change taking place in primitive as in other arts.

The Bushongo

Establishing the link between Lower Congo mother and child figures and the Madonna of Humility helps also to clarify the art of a related group called the Bushongo. The Bushongo is comprised of tribes sharing many traits and acknowledging a common king. The memory of these kings is kept alive both in oral genealogy and by means of carved wooden portrait statues depicting the monarch seated tailor-fashion on a plinth. Fortunately, an eclipse of the sun mentioned in the royal chronicles enables us to date with considerable accuracy the various reigns. Prominent above all others was that of the great Shamba Bolongongo, who became king about A.D. 1600. Before ascending the throne, Shamba is said to have made a trip far to the west. Upon his return he introduced the custom of carving royal portraits (Plate 22) and the use of new techniques for making and ornamenting cloth, a new and less dangerous sword to replace the old deadly throwing knife, as well as a new board game, *mankala*, to offset a tendency towards excessive gambling.

It is generally agreed that the portrait type of statue introduced by Shamba stems from the Lower Congo area, where he doubtless spent some time. More important, this should prove that the statue type existed at the Congo mouth as early as A.D. 1600, a fact we would otherwise be unable to verify.

Like the Lower Congo figures, the Bushongo royal portraits commemorate and glorify the deceased as a superior sort of being. Now if Shamba's ideas of kingship derive solely from the Congo area, he can only have

learned such things in the Kongo kingdom near the river's mouth. On the other hand, the sword introduced by Shamba, many of the decorative patterns he brought in, and the new courtly ceremony and ritual are all strikingly reminiscent of the Benin kingdom of Nigeria. Since Portuguese voyagers and missionaries were in touch with both the Benin and Kongo kingdoms from the end of the fifteenth century on, it is conceivable that Shamba may have brought his ideas all the way from Nigeria. In any event, to his ambition and energy alone we owe the establishment of an advanced kingdom in the Congo jungles.

Much of Bushongo art is crystalized around the king's person: cloth-making, for example, is a royal monopoly. Even his sculptors were so highly respected they were allowed a seat on the advisory council and wore the brass rings of the nobility.

In nearby areas less dominated by the court there are a great variety of masks (Plate 25), many of them used in the *babendi*, a series of initiation rites. One type, known as *mashamboy* and associated with the Ngongo and Mbala sub-tribes, is of raffia cloth covered with gaily-colored beads and cowrie

21 *(Far left) Fetish figure. Teke, Western Congo. Wood with textile. H. $9^1/_4''$ (Náprstek Museum, Prague).*

22 *Portrait statue of King Shamba Bolongongo, who reigned ca. 1600 to ca. 1620. Bushongo, Central Congo. H. $21^1/_4''$ (British Museum).*

23 *Nail fetish. Ngangi Village, Lower Congo. H. $33^1/_2''$ (Pitt Rivers Museum, Oxford University).*

24 (Left) Commemorative
ancestor figure. Dengese,
Central Congo. H. 31"
(American Museum of
Natural History, New York).

25 (Right) Secret society
initiation mask. Bushongo,
Central Congo. H. $17\frac{1}{2}$"
(U.S. National Museum,
Washington, D.C.).

shells. Another, though it is carved in wood, has similar decorations. In most Bushongo masks the surface design, consisting of minute multi-colored triangles, conflicts violently with the bold, sweeping sculptural planes.

The Lulua

Attention to minute surface detail reaches its African climax in the art of the Lulua tribe, whose lands lie southeast of the Bushongo. The Lulua are a belligerent people famous for their love of conquest and strife. Yet their art is comparatively serene. Although decoration dominates the surfaces, Lulua forms always retain their crisp, clear silhouettes (Plate 26). Unfortunately, the function of Lulua figures is not well documented. Some seem to be ancestor images, but others may be fetishes or protective charms. One variant represents a mother holding her child with the now familiar over-and-under position of the hands. Almost all these appear to be the work of a single gifted carver; the Lulua Master of the Madonnas, as we may call him, must have had contact with Lower Congo images.

Lulua masks are comparatively rare. Some examples are heavily dependent on Bushongo masks; others, large and round-eyed, suggest Jokwe or Lunda origins. A third type, meant to be held in the hand, may even link up with Yaka masks. All seem to have been used in the festive, dramatic post-initiation dances so popular in the central Congo.

The Songe

Like the Lulua, the Songe are an aggressive people who have borrowed many ideas from other tribes around them. Unlike Lulua carving, however, Songe art is comparatively rough and unrefined.

Songe figures function mainly as fetishes, a role well suited to their hostile, primitive appearance (Plate 27). The small images are used by individuals to protect their property or bring disaster on an enemy; large figures are considered village fetishes, and priests use their potency for the benefit of the entire group. To increase the magical power of the figures, certain substances are applied to it. These include horn, beads, snakeskin, metal, shells, and animal and human secretions. Beneath the applied material, sculptural forms are revealed, often developed in summary fashion with arbitrary changes of direction and little uniformity of shape. Occasionally, this gives Songe figures a directness and an immediacy as unrelenting in expression as it is ruthless in execution.

Many Songe figures appear to be wearing masks of a type peculiar to various parts of the Songe country (Plate 28). Known as *kifwebe*, these masks seem originally to have had a religious function. The earliest accounts say that a slave was cut in two and the mask placed between the halves of his body; then it was thrown into a fire, where it was believed to become a powerful spirit. Copies of the *kifwebe* were worn during moments of crisis—at the death of the king, in time of plague, or just before the outbreak of war. In later times the mask came to be more secular, of aid in welcoming visitors to the tribe. However, according to recent reports a secret antisocial organization has again taken up use of the *kifwebe*.

The *kifwebe* is superbly suited to its original role in the fearful religious ceremony which the Songe conduct. It has an insistence and an arbitrary treatment of features awesome even to an impartial observer. Said to represent the lion, this mask has much of the majesty and imperious authority of that beast. All in all, the Songe *kifwebe* is probably the most arresting and most openly aggressive of all African masks.

26   *Carved head. Lulula, Central Congo. H. 5″ (Elisofon Collection, New York).*

65

The Luba

The tribes of the southeastern Congo, though far from being homogeneous racially, share a common linguistic and artistic tradition. This cultural uniformity is the result of an early but purely African imperialism. In the sixteenth century the Luba united many diverse peoples under their leadership, and have maintained considerable hegemony over them ever since. The Luba's organizing of a large-scale kingdom probably had some inspiration from areas to the east and southeast. There, around the great lakes and at Zimbabwe and other sites of the Monomotapa kingdom of southern Rhodesia, in the fourteenth and fifteenth centuries great empires were formed. Whether or not artistic influences spread to the Luba from this source we are not sure. But the art of Luba is unquestionably more aristocratic in form than any other style in the eastern Congo (Plate 29).

An emphasis on subtle formal qualities pervades every aspect of the Luba artist's work. Acutely attuned to plastic values, he tends to avoid all use of color in favor of pure sculptural shapes. Even the masks of the Luba are as a rule monochromatic. Those taken over from the Songe *kifwebe* have a black and white coloring, but this is cushioned by a rounding and a softening of forms that is typically Luba. In one famous monochromatic Luba mask two gracefully carved wooden horns swing down along either cheek, echoing the shape of the face. Somewhat different is a very rare type with a long pointed chin believed to be from the southern Luba. Of its function nothing is known. Yet stylistically it has the same calm and sureness of shape seen in all Luba sculptures.

Among the most impressive Luba carvings are figures and stools. A dozen or so have been shown to be the work of a single great anonymous carver who lived in the village of Buli. The figures made by the Buli Master, as he is now called, are serene and beautifully balanced. But in spite of this they are full of distortions for aesthetic purposes. The heads are deliberately enlarged and facial features expanded beyond ordinary proportions. Half-

27 *Village fetish figure with small images attached. Songe, Eastern Congo. Wood with beads, metal, horn, snakeskin and hide. H. 35¹/₂" (Ethnographical Museum, Antwerp).*

closed eyes, sharply raised eyebrows and fleshy noses add a sensuous quality
to the faces. In this way, the artist introduces an emotional quality into his
figures rarely equalled in primitive art (Plate 30).

The figures that the Buli Master carved on stools call attention to his
remarkable sense of tactile values. Not only do the forms themselves seem
to have been caressed and molded into shape, but the artist exaggerates the
size of the hands with almost expressionistic fervor. This tactility, adapted
to the kneeling pose, gives the figures an appearance admirably suited to
the purpose of exalting the sovereignty of the chiefs for whom the stools
are made.

Among the Buli carver's other masterpieces are *kabila* or sorrowful men-
dicant figures holding begging bowls. These were often used by sorcerers to

28 *(Left Mask used in terroristic rites. Songe, Eastern Congo. H. $11^1/_2''$ (Dubiner Collection, Tel Aviv).*

29 *Neck rest. Luba, Eastern Congo. H. $7^1/_4''$ (Kjersmeier Collection, Copenhagen).*

contain their medicines; others, it seems, were set out in front of the huts where women in childbirth were secluded. Passersby placed offerings of food or objects of value in the bowls to ensure an easy delivery and a quick recovery.

It is possible, as Frans Olbrechts, the Belgian ethnologist, believed, that the Buli Master's style influenced that of his contemporaries. On the other hand, because of his extraordinary visual expression, the Buli carver must himself have been influenced by some outside source, perhaps ultimately European in origin. As a matter of fact, far from contributing to Luba art, his style seems to move away from local tradition. Whatever the truth of this, the Luba style and the Buli Master's work stand side by side in the forefront of Congo sculpture.

The Bembe

So much for the well-documented traditions of the Congo. The lesser-known arts of the northern Congo, while closely linked to those of the south, also reveal many connections with the local tribes as well as with those of the so-called Middle Congo and Gabon regions. Moreover, the styles in this area, being comparatively isolated, contrast vividly with the less primitive traditions we have already discussed. Consider, for example, the art of the Bembe tribe located near Lake Tanganyika. A typical Bembe wooden figure looks like a travesty on the great Buli Master's work, with some elements of Songe style mixed in. The eyes are placed high on the head and slant downward on either side, giving the figures a weak-minded look. The surface detail of the Bembe ancestor figure has probably been borrowed from Luba images but the facial forms underneath are clearly heart-shaped. The same is true of the Bembe mask, a much more striking object that does not seem to have drawn on the rather weak Luba mask tradition. They share their "coffee-bean" eyes and other details with the Teke masks of the Lower Congo and those of the Kwele far away in Gabon (Plate 31).

The Mbole

Another major link between the northern Congo and the coastal region a thousand miles away appears in figures from the Mbole people (Plate 32). Often attributed to Gabon tribes, these rare figures are carved by members of the Mbole secret society, the Lilwa, and are carried around by them in their dances. According to reports, the figures represent sorcerers or evil-doers who have been put to death for disclosing cult secrets. Supposedly the power they once possessed remains in the effigies to watch over the community. In function these images differ from the typical commemorative Congo ancestor figures, operating more in the manner of a fetish or protective spirit. Their heart-shaped faces closely resemble those seen near the coast in Gabon.

30 Chief's stool. Luba (Buli), Eastern Congo. H. 20¹/₂" (Musée Royal de l'Afrique Centrale, Brussels).

The Kwele

The masks of the Kwele of the Middle Congo-Gabon region are among the purest expressions of the heart-shaped face we find in Africa (Plate 33). Here we see the perfect swoop of the concave face interrupted in the center by the nose. Against this depression the "coffee-bean" eyes, as in many Congo masks, stand out sharply. Within the strict and very stylized format, however, considerable variation occurs. Some masks have two long horns that curve around the face and admirably echo its shape. Others employ isolated eye shapes in repetition, as seen also among the Bembe. Still a third type has the muzzle and vertical horns of the three-part mask. In all types the shapes are played off against one another with a crispness and elegance that are a marvel to behold. Unhappily, Kwele masks are very rare and their functions as yet virtually unknown.

The Kota

A number of tribes occupy the forest region south and west of the Kwele area. Known as the Kota, these tribes have attracted attention because of the flat, metal-covered figures which now delight so many lovers of modern art (Plate 34). (Though usually associated with the Kota, this type of figure is also produced by other neighboring tribes.) In the Kota country skulls of important persons, kept in baskets, are thought to give guidance when properly contacted. The metal-covered images are set on top of the baskets, apparently to protect the skulls and also to warn off any unwary person. Known as *mbulu ngulu*, these are decorated with strips of brass and copper, the back being left plain, presumably because the baskets are placed against a wall. A few—known as *mbulu viti*—have two aspects, set back to back in Janus fashion—one side male and the other female. A third type, often referred to as *osyeba* but more properly called *naja*, is even more stylized and simplified in appearance. Structurally this type differs from the

31 Boy's initiation mask. Teke, Eastern Congo. Wood painted white and dark brown. H. 12" (Dubiner Collection, Tel Aviv).

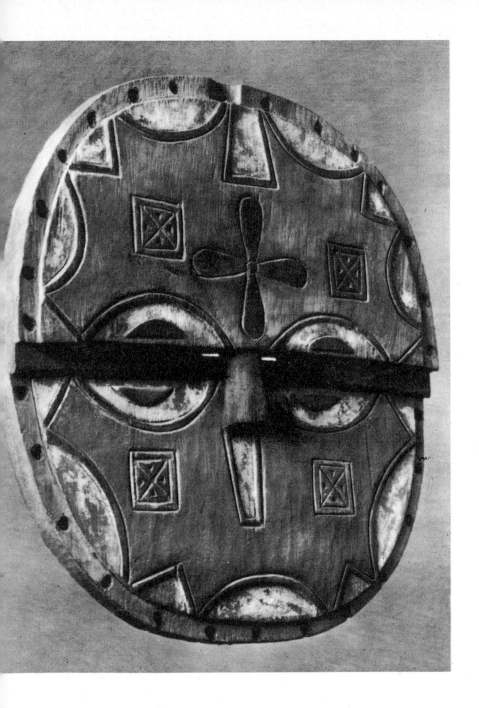

mbulu ngulu only in the base, which opens up forward and backward instead of to either side. The curious diamond-shaped trunk of the Kota figures does not represent the body of the image but is simply an exaggerated version of the arms-akimbo position. Several rare full-length figures from this area confirm this interpretation.

No matter how highly stylized the forms of the Kota guardian image may seem to be, its details often stem from life. The headdress, for example, derives from hair decorations and pendants similar to those depicted more realistically in Pangwe sculpture. The heart-shaped face also is seen in a majority of examples. In the view of Efraim Andersson, the leading authority on the Kota, the *mbulu ngulu* symbolize the spirit of the dead. Despite their realism, the images do not seem to symbolize the ancestors themselves so much as the *essence* of their spirit power—suggesting the role of Lilwa figures in the Mbole tribe. As Andersson also notes, the use of the figures as images of the spirit of the dead is a widespread custom associated with the Neolithic.

The Ogowe River Tribes

The Kota and other Ogowe River tribes also carve masks of singular beauty which have often been attributed to the Lumbo or Pangwe groups (Plate 35). At first glance, the style of these masks appears to break sharply with Kota tradition, for the faces are as realistic in detail as they are human in conception. The artist stresses the elaborate surface divisions and handsomely contrasts these with the elegant sweeping planes of the face. Coiffures and scarification vary slightly from specimen to specimen. The basic elements — white faces, full lips, and black-brown hair—remain unchanged. The Ogowe River mask, in style, reverses the concavity of the Kota spirit figurine and fills out the forms with lifelike flesh. But the "coffee-bean" eyes and heart-shaped contour of the face relate very closely in style to the Gabon-Congo mask forms.

32 Representation of Lilwa society member executed as traitor. Mbole, Northern Congo. Wood with raffia skirt. H. 30" (American Museum of Natural History, New York).

Worn by men in funeral dances, Ogowe River masks represent deceased female ancestors. Sometimes too they are evidently used in stilt dances and in ancestor cult worship, and are then placed in baskets of skulls. Although some writers have linked them with secret societies, Andersson found no evidence among the Kota of such a function.

The Pangwe Tribes

Masks of far less sophistication but nevertheless of related style are carved by the Pangwe peoples (often known as the Fang) to the north of the Ogowe River. Until recently these tribes led a wandering life, shifting from one agricultural area to another. They had no cohesive political organization, and each village engaged in constant skirmishes with its neighbors.

The southern Pangwe produce unusual white-faced masks. Some have long noses and high bulbous foreheads, and look almost like comic-strip characters; others seem so witty and yet so ingenuous they might pass as the work of Paul Klee. All have a certain stylized treatment that distinguishes them from the Ogowe River carvings.

There is a sharp disparity in style between Pangwe masks and figures. Both are extremely vigorous, but the masks tend to be rather simplified, and aloof, whereas the fig-

33 Dance mask. Kwele, Gabon. H. 24″ (Dubiner Collection, Tel Aviv).

ures are aggressive and statuesque. The former appear somewhat constrained, the latter
bursting with physical energy. Perhaps differences in function account for this astonishing contrast in technique. Many Pangwe masks
are used when evildoers and sorcerers must
be disciplined. The abstract and awesome
quality of the heart-shaped face is stressed, its
length or crisp outline exaggerated. The figures, on the other hand, like those of the Kota,
serve as guardians for boxes of ancestral skulls.
Their purpose is to repel evil and protect the
unwitting from contact with the dangerous
skull spirit. Dancers sometimes clutch the figures in their arms as they perform ritual
steps. This suggests a connection ultimately
with the Lilwa carvings of the Mbole in the
northern Congo—which were also carried
around by dancers. The Pangwe are believed
to have migrated from the northern Congo
within the last few hundred years, arriving
in their present locality about 1870.

The origins of Pangwe style must lie in
the heart-shaped face tradition. Indeed, the
carved post figures used in the meeting houses
of this tribe still have the old motif, although
in the features of the guardian images it is
seldom very obvious. What is more, Pangwe
and Kota figures, ostensibly so different from
each other in appearance, are similar in function; both originated within the Neolithic
heart-shaped face tradition. But the round-
ness of Pangwe statues indicates that there are

34 Skull guardian figure. Kota, Gabon. H. 21³/₄"
(Charles Ratton Collection, Paris).

still other influences in the style. The dark, oily wood used for Pangwe figures is like that of the Congo, but the exaggeration of body muscles is very similar to that of Cameroons carvings.

Cameroons Highlands

From the southern Cameroons northward, the heart-shaped face begins to give way more and more to the rounded face. This tradition continues west throughout Nigeria and into Dahomey. There are, however, a few tribes in the northern Cameroons and in southern Nigeria that have been unaffected by the new ideas and have continued in the old tradition. The Mambila and Kata tribes of the Cameroons mountains have made small ancestral figures with heart-shaped face, round eyes, and three-part totemic masks. These are clearly survivals of the ancient Niger-Congo style.

The Ibo

The Ibo, although numbering some four million, also reflect a tendency to conserve the old Niger-Congo traditions. They live in the fertile lowlands of the Niger valley and cultivate all sorts of edible roots and cereal crops. With the Ibibio, a Bantu-speaking people who live nearby, the Ibo have developed several distinctive regional styles and stylistic variations (Plate 36). Prominent among their many art objects are masks worn by members of a religious confraternity called the Mmwo, a group which devotes much effort to the administration and the performances of the ancestor cult. The men, usually in family groups, put on dances representing maidens and their mothers at festivals and funerals. The dances, which are public, are characterized by vigorous, rapid foot movements. The Mmwo mask, by far the best-known Ibo type, has a stark white face, an elaborate hairdo, and a shallow, heart-shaped facial depression. In style Mmwo masks are finicky and effeminate; they link up with female masks of the Ogowe River tradi-

35 *Spirit mask. Collected in 1875. Ogowe River, Gabon. H. 9″ (Pitt Rivers Museum, Oxford University).*

tion. The costume with which they are worn and the delicacy of female representation are also highly reminiscent of the far-off Jokwe and Makonde styles.

Other Ibo festival masks belong to a different tradition. They run the gamut from large, grotesque monster masks to small, delicately modeled face coverings. The mixture of styles and traditions is bewildering and is probably due to the enormous eclecticism of the Ibo, who borrow plays and designs from one another and from their Ibibio neighbors. Many masks are worn during thanksgiving festivals held at harvest time. In subject matter there are chimpanzees, goats, and the massive Elephant Spirit which is often paired with the Maiden Spirit to form a "Beauty and the Beast" theme. This combination of extreme opposites delights the Ibo people.

Ibo figures are also of several types. A seated figure, known as an *ikenga*, often holds an enemy's head and a knife, or other symbolic objects (Plate 37). Its purpose is to protect a young child and imbue him with power, and this is symbolized by the phallic horns of the ram on the figure's head. The pieces are not commissioned individually but are made in the artist's spare time and are

36   (Left) Festival mask. Ibibio, Nigeria. Wood with raffia. H. 19³/₄" (Museum für Völkerkunde, Basel).

37   Protective "power" figure. Ibo, Nigeria. Wood painted yellow, blue and white. H. 21" (Museum of Archaeology and Ethnology, Cambridge University).

38 (Left) Ancestor screen. Ijaw, Nigeria. H. 36" (Pitt Rivers Museum, Oxford University).

39 (Right) Helmet mask. Bobo-Fing, Western Sudan. H. 13" (Elisofon Collection, New York).

sold in the Ibo market place. Despite their repetitiveness of style, the *ikenga* have a naturalism and an alert pose that are most ingraciating. They are, as a group, evidently outside the heart-shaped tradition, probably having been introduced relatively recently into the Ibo area. The unimportance of their role in Ibo society reinforces this theory.

The Ijaw

Turning south from the Ibo country to the swamps of the Niger Delta, we find a primitive fishing group known as the Ijaw. As compared with Ibo art, Ijaw masks and figures belong to a backwater existence. As a rule the masks are crude, blackened rectangular versions of the three-part mask. They represent water spirits who are propitiated in cycles of dances or plays. Like most three-part types, the Ijaw masks are worn horizontally on top of the head. Those of a more human cast belong very decidedly to the heart-shaped tradition. Unaffected and plain as they are, the Ijaw face carvings are notable for their strength and for a primitive condensation of form.

The Sudan Area

This completes our survey of the older traditions of Nigeria. Skipping for the moment over the more recent Nigerian styles, we may begin on the southern fringe of the western Sudan. Here the dense rain forest and savannah give way to semiarid scrub and grassland. Perhaps because the sparse cover produced a scarcity of game, the Sudanese long ago domesticated and developed certain crops such as pearl millet and sorghum, which later spread over much of Negro Africa.

The Sudanese have profited greatly from outside influences which have enriched their culture more than that of the Congo-Gabon region. One of the principal trans-Saharan trade routes running down from northern Africa ends in the western Sudan. Along this route for perhaps three thousand years, and certainly since Phoenician times, men have made their living by exchanging salt, cattle, and other goods for gold and slaves. The profits and tribute exacted by Sudanese leaders enabled them to form great kingdoms, and these attracted the Arab trader with his supercargo of Islamic

culture and religion. Timbuktu in the heart of the Sudan had mosques and a flourishing university where the Greek classics were cherished and studied.

The effect of Islamic culture on the primitive pagan population was relatively minor but that of the Moslem law against making images was not. Many of the indigenous peoples gave up making representational art; others, whose art is of great importance today, took refuge in the open plains and the high escarpments of the Niger bend. The Bobo, Dogon, Bambara, and Baga are still producing arresting images that predate, historically speaking, the Islamic tide that overwhelmed figure sculpture in other parts of the western Sudan.

The Bobo

Perhaps the most primitive of the Sudanese people are the Bobo-oule or Red Bobo of the Upper Volta area. Predominantly cultivators, they seem to have preserved in the masks they use in agriculture rites some of the oldest styles of the region. Representing the village guardian *Do*, these masks, formed of a flat disk with circular eyes, are held in front of the face by means of a handle. Above the face is a vertical slab elaborately decorated with geometric shapes; and a shaggy full-length costume completes the ensemble. To some

40   Ancestor figure. Dogon, Western Sudan. H. 13¹⁄₂″ (Margaret Plass Collection, Philadelphia).

85

extent these Bobo masks resemble masks used in the south by the Baoule in their *goli* dance. In both areas the masks represent village tutelary spirits who appear at funerals and harvest rites to help drive away evil and misfortune. The upper part of the Bobo *Do* mask represents stylized animal and human forms, possibly of totemic significance. In style Red Bobo masks are comparatively slapdash, doubtless due to the fact that after being used they are simply allowed to decay.

Somewhat more permanent are the helmet masks of the Black Bobo or Bobo-Fing (Plate 39). These, as Paul Wingert, the American art historian, points out, strongly remind us of the *banda* mask used by the Baga of the western Guinea coast. The similarity is clear in the flat facial plane in which eyes, nose, and mouth are set almost arbitrarily.

The Dogon

Like the Bobo, the Dogon style represents one of the older traditions of the Sudan. Politically anarchic, the Dogon concentrate power in male and female confraternities which are entrusted with the conduct of sacred rites and secular pageants. These groups make their own equipment—masks, costumes, and so on—for their dances, though their figure sculpture is done by professional carvers. As a result Dogon masks often tend to be rather crude and, by European standards, unattractive. Like most art objects from the Sudan, these masks are conceived as vertical forms broken at intervals by horizontal planes. They have a stately elongation punctuated by abrupt momentary tensions. As the over-all feeling is one of stiffness and formality, Dogon style has often been called austerely abstract.

Thanks to the work of French ethnologists, especially Marcel Griaule, the nature of Dogon dramatic performances and beliefs is quite well known. The most important Dogon ceremonies commemorate the death of the First Ancestor—the Sigi; funeral rites in memory of recent as well as ancient ancestors vie in impressiveness with the *Dama*, during which the souls of the dead are sent to the world beyond and the mourning taboos lifted. Each of these cults requires a series of masks of different degrees of sanctity and of varying appearance. The finer ones show carefully shaped stylized forms organized on architectonic lines. Openings or voids help define the shapes. Simplicity rather than severity seems to be the artist's intention. Partly because so much is known of the Dogon masks, writers have tended to stress their religious as opposed to their visual interpretation. Actually in these masks we still discern the typical Sudanic treatment of the heart-shaped face.

Dogon figures represent ancestors, usually engaged in ritual acts (Plate 40). They are shown with raised hands or arms extended above the head, imploring the gods to unleash the rains; other figures show royal ancestors on their thrones. The design of such figures almost always stresses their verticality. This trait gives the figures a lean, ascetic look and this is often attributed to Islamic influence. But the Dogon have had relatively little contact with Moslems until recent times. And in truth verticalism pervades all Dogon art forms, including even architecture. We must look elsewhere than to Islam for the impetus in the peculiar elongation of Dogon design.

It seems likely that one particular Dogon architectural form, the granary, may be of great significance. These Dogon granaries stand like lofty conical anthills of mud huddled in the shadow of cliffs. They contrast markedly with domestic buildings in the valley below, which are either flat-roofed mud structures built up in stories or cylindrically walled mud huts with conical grass roofs. No buildings quite like the Dogon granaries exist elsewhere in Negro Africa.

Unique as the Dogon storage buildings are, they are strikingly similar to the towers of Berber towns in northern Africa. These towers are fortresses and lookout posts, but they also serve as granaries. The houses around these strongholds are rectangular and have flat terraced roofs. The Berbers are the indigenous people of northern Africa. Basically Neolithic and Megalithic, their culture has been enriched by the invasion of Arabs since the seventh century A.D. Although outwardly converted to Islam, some Berbers still retain much of their pre-Islamic culture. They perhaps started the trans-Saharan trade and they still partially control it. Today there are Berber-speaking people living within a few miles of the Dogon. It seems quite possible, then, that the Dogon acquired many of their alien culture traits from the pre-Islamic Berbers rather than from their later Moslem heritage.

The Bambara

West of the Dogon, on both sides of the Niger, are the Bambara, a people famous for their rich art and thriving culture. The largest and most im-

41 *Antelope headdress. Bambara, Western Sudan. H. 15" (Pierre Verité Private Collection, Paris).*

portant group in the western Sudan, the Bambara are among the descendants of Negroes who long ago domesticated certain food plants in this region which later became staples throughout Africa. In this area the first great African empires—Ghana and Mali—flourished briefly, then vanished. Shifting political alliances and extensive trade contacts have been a mark of the region from time immemorial. The Bambara themselves achieved political independence in the seventeenth century, only to lose it to the Fulani about a hundred years ago. Of course, to the ordinary Bambara who culti-

vated his garden in the flood plains of the
Niger, the ebb and flow of political currents
made little difference. Above all he needed
rain for his crops and ancestral help in guard-
ing against misfortune. To achieve these ends,
the Bambara developed a variety of cults in
which masks and figures played a prominent
role. These differ markedly from region to
region within the Bambara territory.

Perhaps the best known of all Bambara
sculptures are the *tji wara* or antelope headdresses (Plate 41). Young men banded together in agricultural confraternities wear these
headpieces in dances held just before the rainy
season. Pairs of carvings—those with curved
horns usually representing the male, those
with straight horns the female—are taken to
parched fields. Then the young men return to
the village, where a dance imitating the leaping of the antelope takes place. Next, all the
villagers form a circle around the leaping
dancers. Sacrifices and further dancing complete the ceremony. Because the headdress
must be seen from all sides, the *tji wara* designs usually make use of much free space and
pure silhouette. The headdresses themselves
are carefully carved, and they are greatly
prized. It seems likely that the style developed out of the three-part animal mask found in
so many parts of Africa. The *tji wara* may in
fact represent a pre-agricultural survival; for
while the rites are performed at a critical

*42   Children's secret society mask. Bambara, West-
ern Sudan. H. 12¹/₂" (Pierre Verité Private Collection, Paris).*

moment in the cultivation cycle, the dancers' movements imitating the antelopes' leaps suggest hunting pantomime.

Other Bambara masks have played various roles in the society. The N'tomo, for example, is a children's organization which protects the youths of the group until they are old enough to join one of the adult societies. The single mask used in N'tomo ceremonies has a fairly realistic face and antelope horns, and sometimes a female figure is carved above it (Plate 42). Decorations of red seeds and cowrie shells often cover the entire face. The N'tomo masks seem to come mainly from the northern part of the Bambara territory. In many ways—particularly in the flattened heart-shaped face—they resemble neighboring Dogon masks and other Sudanese types. The parallel lines on the sides of the face probably represent the three lines, symbols of masculinity, which Bambara men have tattooed from temple to chin.

A number of other masks are used by the Bambara in their Komo, Kono, Kore, and Nama societies; these, however, are of less aesthetic interest. Far more exciting are the figures, some of which depict female ancestors or deities concerned with fertility. Their bodies appear as vertical shafts, and arms and other elements project almost arbitrarily from

43   (Left) Nimba mask. Baga, Guinea. H. 46″ (British Museum, London).

44   Ceremonial mask. Dan, Ivory Coast. Wood with metal, beads, and bells. H. 8¹⁄₄″ (Margaret Plass Collection, Philadelphia).

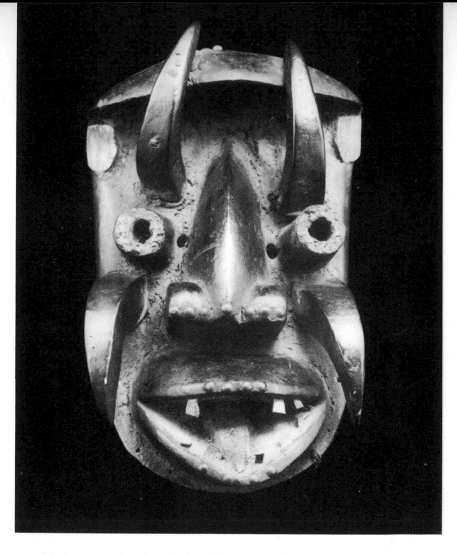

45 *Mask representing the wart-hog. Guere, Ivory Coast. Wood studded with brass nails. H. 28¹/₂" (Elisofon Collection, New York).*

this core. Other sculptures recently discovered among the southwestern Bambara show a more relaxed attitude of the human figure. Here the artists carved horsemen and mother-and-child groups distinctly reminiscent of Senufo carvings. Like the latter, these figures have a marked fluency of technique and a certain flamboyant repetition of sculptural detail.

The Baga

Although they now live on the heavily forested coast of Guinea, the Baga, it is generally agreed, migrated to that area in recent times from the western Sudan. Their way of carving a head is very close to the Bambara technique. But in contrast to this stark geometric treatment of heads, Baga bodies seem soft and spongy. The style is definitely ambiguous.

The finest Baga carvings are those associated with a confraternity known as the Simo society. This group, divided into several grades, uses masks and other objects in ceremonies after the rice harvest and at funerals of its members. No more spectacular object is seen in Africa than the great *nimba* masks worn by one of the grades—a huge female head and bust carving, carried on the shoulders of bearers who are concealed under a long skirt. Women dance around the mask whenever it appears. The *nimba* probably represents the patroness of maternity who is also the wife of Simo Guinea, the Great Spirit of the Simo cult. The swelling curves of the mask contrast with its rigid, metallic decoration. These curves, as William Fagg the English ethnologist suggests, admirably express the idea of ripeness and fertility, the probable intent of the *nimba*. Another important feature is the heart-shaped outline of the face. The pendant which hangs from the nose and a knob at the back of the neck are unexplained. *Nimba*-like faces are carved on drums and figures. Although these are not necessarily used in the Simo cult, they show how strong its impact was on Baga tradition.

The most sacred Simo mask is the *banda*. Worn horizontally by a dancer concealed in a raffia-fiber costume, the *banda* seems to be a composite of several types. In structure it conforms to the three-part tradition so widespread in Africa, but its face and decoration suggest those Sudanese masks that are worn vertically, such as the Bambara N'tomo mask. The Baga mask is the stylized head of a horned crocodile with a human face. It is said to symbolize the complementary relation of water (crocodile) and land (antelope).

The Mende

Moving down the coast to Sierra Leone, we come to another art-producing group, the Mende. Throughout their territory are found small archaeological figures of soapstone which the natives call *nomoli*. When questioned about these carvings, the Mende say simply, "We don't know who made them." *Nomoli* turn up in the vicinity of graves, along with bracelets of iron and brass. The Mende make offerings to these figures, ask them questions, and trust them to give truthful answers. If the *nomoli* lie, they are beaten with sticks. The bringing of good luck and a rich rice harvest are also the work of *nomoli*. The date of these figures is unknown, but the appearance of elaborate costumes, horses, and weapons recalling sixteenth-century Portuguese arms suggests that they cannot be very old. And it should be added that the use of stone as a sculptural medium is exceedingly rare in Negro Africa. Fleshy and sensual, the figures often adopt a hands-under-chin pose. This position and the exaggerated curves of the face, especially when seen in profile, resemble Baga carvings.

Mende masks are associated with the Bundu, a female society charged with training young girls for adult life. Carved of a single helmetlike piece of wood, the masks conform to the heart-shaped tradition. Unlike the *nomoli*, the Bundu masks have delicate features and refined details. They depict the guardian spirit from which the society derives its function and authority. The Mende also use figures known as *minsereh* in connection with a society that divines whether or not a sick person can be cured.

The Dan-Guere

Although culturally diverse, the tribes of the Liberian and Ivory Coast hinterlands form a distinct group artistically. One reason for this is the existence of a unique political institution, the Poro society, which holds sway from Guinea to the western Ivory Coast. For their rites the artists fashion many small masks, usually in human form. Those carved by the Dan tribe are very suave (Plate 44); but the Guere masks, which often depict a wart-hog instead of a human face, are more likely to be grotesque (Plate 45). Both Dan and Guere artists, however, emphasize the eyes and mouth and stress the vertical axis of the face, either by means of a frontal ridge or symmetrical flanking parts. Occasionally a very sharp asymmetry emerges, as in the Dan masks that have noses twisted to one side. These are supposed to help cure facial paralysis. Other Poro masks are used to settle disputes, to interpret omens, to influence battles, and to collect overdue debts. The magic power latent in them also protects pregnant women and aids the owners in dangerous undertakings. In this area it seems that masks have acquired the meanings usually accorded only to cult figures: they are for honoring guardians, venerating ancestors, or simply entertaining members. So intermingled have these roles become that it is almost impossible to attribute any one function to a given mask. An exception is the small mask presented to children as a talisman.

The Senufo

The Senufo, like other tribes that stand between two different traditions, have achieved a somewhat ambiguous style. Their art has some of the softness and naturalistic quality of Ivory Coast carvings, and yet it possesses the violence and abstraction of the Sudanic styles. Among the massive and powerful types, a good example is the "fire-spitter" mask worn at night by members of the Korubla society in their anti-witchcraft rites. Ornamented with wart-hog tusks, antelope horns, and other animal parts, this is a typical three-part mask. A bird or other figure often seen between the two horns is probably a totemic clan symbol. Large bird figures, up to four feet high and similar in every detail to those on masks, have recently been found in Senufo country. They seem to be hornbills which here, as in Nigeria and the South Seas, symbolize the ancestors.

The Senufo have used human figures to commemorate both ancestors and deities (Plate 46); these might serve as oracles to divine the past or future or as protective and fertility devices. Masks have been awarded as trophies in hoeing contests and, completely secularized, attached to chairs and everyday utensils. Almost invariably the heart-shaped face dominates Senufo style.

The Baoule

Of all African sculpture, Baoule carvings are perhaps the most deliberately "aesthetic." And because the style succeeds in being what many people think African sculpture *should* be, Baoule sculpture has achieved widespread fame and popularity. The masks are of several sorts. The realistic

type has the heart-shaped face and numerous details, such as bird forms, that are found in Senufo masks. Another type, representing animals with short snouts, resembles certain Geh masks from Liberia. A third type, which depicts the buffalo or *goli*, is a good example of the three-part horizontal mask.

Baoule figurines usually were treasured as fetishes and commemorative images (Plate 47). In recent times portraits of living persons have even been carved as *objets d'art*. This self-conscious artistry is paralleled in the figures themselves, which show far more selfhood or subjectivity than is usual in African art. With their embracing gestures and inward expression, they seem intent only on self-gratification.

Nigeria

As we move eastward along the Guinea coast away from the Baoule, we encounter increasingly elegant and courtly styles. The Ashanti, from whom the Baoule split off several centuries ago, are among the most aristocratic of African tribes. Especially popular Ashanti possessions are gold weights illustrating proverbs and secular subjects, and handsome robes of woven cloth, once worn only by chiefs and now the national costume of Ghana.

46 (Facing) Spirit figures. Senufo, Ivory Coast. H. 25¹|₄" and 20¹|₂" (Dubiner Collection, Tel Aviv).

47 Detail of standing figure. Baoule, Ivory Coast. H. 18¹|₂" over-all (Dubiner Collection, Tel Aviv).

The dearth of sculpture in this area and in neighboring Dahomey is probably an unfortunate consequence of the warlike interests of the leaders of these people.

When we reach Nigeria, however, we are at last in the center of a major area of traditional African art. Here the heart-shaped, scooped-out face gives way completely to a fully rounded, rather naturalistic conception. The groups whose art invariably has this rounded form include the Yoruba, Ife, Benin, and many Cameroons peoples. Culturally, these groups are by no means similar nor are their styles homogeneous. Nevertheless, their art is unmistakably different from that of the Africans already discussed. This can only mean two things: (1) that the round-faced styles centering around Nigeria are an intrusion into the heart-shaped face tradition that is almost universal in sculpture-producing Africa; and (2) that although more recent than the heart-shaped face, the round-faced style is probably quite old itself, since it has split up into several variations. Fortunately, we have independent proof of the age of the style. Archaeologists working north of the Benue River have turned up numerous terracotta heads from the so-called Nok culture. These heads, always with the rounded face, are dated from the second half of the first millennium B.C. They demonstrate the existence of full-volumed, naturalistic art in Nigeria for at least 2000 years.

The art styles nearest to Nok are those of Ife and Benin. These two styles, scholars agree, are extraordinarily unlike other Negro African art. Outside influence could have come into the cities of Benin and Ife from the northeast by way of the Benue, from the northwest via the Niger, or even by sea around the African coast. Theorists have attributed their art to Portuguese as well as to Greek, Roman, Egyptian, Mesopotamian, Phoenician, and other influences.

Benin

Tradition has it that in A.D. 1280 the king, or *oba*, of Benin sent to Ife for someone to teach his retainers to cast bronze. If this tale is true, it is not

48   Royal head with ornaments showing 16th century Portuguese emissaries. Benin, Nigeria. Ivory. H. 9¹/₂" (Museum of Primitive Art, New York).

readily apparent in Benin art. For the stiff ceremonial style of Benin, with its elaborate detail and interest in costume (Plate 48), is a far cry from the elegant naturalism of Ife. Instead, Benin artists have concentrated their skills on recording the rituals and regalia of courtly life. The dress, weapons, and beard styles of fifteenth and sixteenth century Portuguese visitors clearly impressed the Benin bronze-casters more than the faces of individual Europeans. In this they were continuing a long-standing tradition of symbolic representation of their divine kings. The people of Benin regarded the *oba* quite literally as a living god who had come down to earth. When he appeared he was always dressed in rich garments and beautiful coral, ivory, and metal ornaments. Two attendants, his son on the right and his war chief on the left, flanked him ceremonially and supported his hands with their own. His person was so sacred he could not even be seen by commoners except on the rarest occasions.

The artists of the Benin court used various conventions and devices to magnify the transcendent power of the god-king. Depicted on plaques or in the round, the king is always shown larger than his subjects—as in a kind of hieratic scale. Placed symmetrically on either side of him, the retainers honor the *oba* by their frontal pose and rigid ceremonial attitude. Occasionally two leopards confront

49   *Figure of a king represented as the sea god Olokun. Benin, Nigeria. Bronze. H. 11" (National Ethnological Museum, Leiden).*

one another at his feet. The use of these particular elements is not to be found in any other part of Negro Africa, nor can they be explained as due to Portuguese influence. But anyone familiar with the art of the Ancient Near East will recognize these as frequent attributes of divine kingship in the Ancient Orient.

Among the many striking examples of Ancient Near Eastern influence in Benin art is a bronze mace head in which a figure stands erect upon the back of a miniature elephant. This conception, of the king acquiring extra power and stamina from his "vehicle" or supporting animal, is often seen in Hittite art. Associated with such figures is the plait or guilloche pattern with studs interspersed, a well-known Near Eastern motif. Other connections include the supporting of hands, a ritual gesture found in the Biblical story of Moses and the Amalekites; the rosette; alternating fish and moon crescents; and the snake which encircles the world and holds its tail in its mouth. Perhaps the most convincing of all is the sea-god figure Olokun, whose legs terminate in mudfish heads (Plate 49). This complex figure (from which the mermaid derived) was once popular in the Mediterranean and Near East, where it was often called Abraxas. Sometimes the Olokun figure holds two leopards by their tails on either side of him; this heraldic pose is a well-known symbol in the

50   An unknown king holding the horn and sceptre, symbols of his office. Ife, Nigeria. Bronze. H. 18³⁄₄" (Ife Museum).

51 *Mother and child dance staff. Yoruba, Nigeria. H. 15"* *(d'Harnoncourt Collection, New York).*

Ancient Near East of the mythological figure and culture-hero Gilgamesh.

If further proof of Near Eastern origins of Benin art were necessary, we might consider finally a Benin-like metal figure from Tada, in Nigeria. On the figure's forehead appears a horned gorgon shield and upon its chest a pendant illustrating two animals rearing ceremonially to confront the image of a divine being. Surely the inspiration for this theme can have come only from the Ancient Near East.

The problem still remains: where precisely did these ideas come from? The cluster of motifs we have observed to be Near Eastern in origin do not seem to center upon the more famous ancient societies such as those of Sumer, Assyria, or the Hittite kingdom. Rather, they seem almost to be motifs drawn from various areas and jumbled together without much consistency. Such a pattern of choice reminds us especially of a so-called International style that flourished on the eastern shore of the Mediterranean about 1000 to 500 B.C.: for instance, at Ras Shamra in Syria. That style, created for a market in luxury export goods, was the work of Aramaeans and Phoenicians who traveled extensively. The art of the International style, like that of Benin, consisted almost entirely of *Kleinkunst*—metal work, jewelry, and ivory carving.

Benin influence seems to have been confined mainly to the court itself. However, it is possible that certain styles in the Nigerian area may be attributed to this source. The Ashanti, for example, produced a large brass vessel known as a *kuduo* (used in divination ritual), which is strikingly decorated in the Benin manner. The fighting animals atop these objects also remind us of the Ancient Near East. Other more plebeian forms suggesting Benin influence are the *nduen fobara*, or wooden screens, erected by the Kalibari Ijaw in memory of an ancestor (Plate 38). Representing a chief seated with his wives or retainers, these screens show a hieratic scale and elaborate composition typical of Benin. The same is true of Kwale Ibo pottery groups made to obtain the blessing of the Yam God and placed in his shrine.

Ife

Ife sculpture has been more widely admired than perhaps any other African style. This reputation is fully deserved, and it in no way belittles the Ife artists' accomplishments to point out that the style must have had considerable outside inspiration. More or less as an explanation, several writers have suggested that while the technique of bronze casting may have been introduced into Ife, the motifs are entirely indigenous. But this is as absurd as saying that people can learn weaving without ever seeing cloth. A technique as complicated as bronze-casting must be diffused through the work of a master craftsman who transmits his craft by making examples. These in turn are copied until the original style is modified in its new surroundings. The theory of the independent origin of Ife sculpture also rests on some rather confused ideas concerning the imitation of nature. As we have seen, under ordinary circumstances naturalism has no meaning for the primitive artist. The places where a naturalistic style has appeared in Africa—Lower Congo, Luba, Baoule—are precisely those which have been exposed to Western influence, in some instances for hundreds of years. In the case of Ife, the naturalism of style is bound up with advanced ideas introduced not from Europe but from ancient Egypt (Plate 50).

Close study of a number of Ife heads reveals that Ife portraits were generic rather than realistic. The heads made of their kings are not really individualized but are a sort of official portraiture of royalty. This approach minimizes personal eccentricities, and stresses instead serenity and self-assurance. Only the most minute variations in ornament and proportion occur. The intentions of the Ife artists are exactly the same as those of the late Egyptian sculptors, and the two styles closely resemble each other. The fact that both traditions use such details as lotus buds and rosettes worn on the forehead reinforces this association. Moreover, the left leg of the only full-length Ife figure discovered to date shows a ridge or vertical crease such as was common in all Egyptian sculpture. There can be little doubt, therefore, that Ife style has roots in ancient Egyptian forms.

The Yoruba

The Yoruba-speaking people are the most numerous in Nigeria. Predominantly farmers, they take a lively interest in fertility cults and harvest festivals. The Yoruba look upon Ife as their principal cult site and a center of sophistication. The Yoruba revere Benin also, but make fun of its inhabitants because the latter deny any connection with their less aristocratic neighbors.

Unlike the style of Ife and Benin, Yoruba art enjoys broad popular acceptance (Plate 51). Typical of Yoruba art are masks worn in the public Gelede secret-society dances. The surfaces of old specimens have a beautifully muted tone or blush. The more recent ones, illustrating bicycles, airplanes, and other prestige objects, are usually garishly painted and less refined. Bulging cheeks and crisply defined eyes are used throughout the Yoruba style. They suggest that Yoruba carving, resembling as it does the art of Ife and Benin, may be a folk version of those courtly styles.

Among other important Yoruba sculptures are figures representing the god of lightning, Shango. This deity was probably derived from a historical personage who was invested with the powers of a legendary culture-hero of the same name. Today he is worshiped in cult centers all over Nigeria; wrongdoers are punished by the spirit of Shango. His symbol, the double ax, is a familiar attribute of power and royalty.

Other Yoruba carvings, decorated with elaborate figure groups on top, are carried on the heads of dancers in agricultural rites. Their job is to control and renew the forces responsible for good harvests.

Perhaps the most poignant Yoruba sculpture is the *ibedji*, a small figure carved after the death of a twin. The surviving youngster is taught to take care of the effigy, offer it food, and clothe it. The *ibedji* is a surrogate

52   Mother and child figure. Cameroons. H. 32^1/$_4$″ (Lindenmuseum, Stuttgart).

for the deceased and also protects the other child from harm. The Yoruba feel so strongly about the power of the twin statue that a family might accumulate perhaps ten or fifteen *ibedji* over the course of several generations.

In the Yoruba country and among the related Afo peoples of northern Nigeria, are found mother and child figures similar to those already described in the Lower Congo section. Even these Nigerian versions have the familiar one-hand-over and one-hand-under posture, the suckling child, and some form of seated position for the mother. These too must be derived from the Christian Madonna of Humility theme.

The Cameroons Tribes

Looking at Cameroons sculpture is like being swept up in a dancing throng. Forms pulsate with movement and rhythmic energy. Working with invigorating skill and freedom, the Cameroons artists produce an uninhibited, bold style seemingly far removed from the aristocratic art of Benin and Ife. Nevertheless, the art of the Cameroons grasslands belongs to the round-faced tradition of Nigeria and probably came from that area (in the so-called Tikar migration) a few centuries ago. The treatment of the eyes and the bulbous faces is just like that seen in Nigeria.

In function, most Cameroons sculpture reflects the power of the chief. Just as in Ife and Benin, his office stimulates the arts, and they in turn reinforce and enhance his prestige. Figures of retainers in postures of obeisance are frequently placed on the roof posts, door jambs, and lintels of the chief's house. Other carvings, masks, and ceremonial objects (Plate 12) are set up in his ancestor shrine, helping to ensure the fertility of crops and the good health of his people. In style, Cameroons carving is typically succinct and intelligible to everyone. Colored beadwork (Plate 1) and red ocher are lavishly applied to the surfaces, flouting the usual African tradition of monochromatic decoration. Forms tend to be divided into horizontal zones, not only in figure sculpture but in stools, masks, and dance costumes as well.

53   *Monkey mask. Bacham tribe, Cameroons. H. 26¹/₂" (von der Heydt Collection, Reitberg Museum, Zurich).*

Among the most impressive objects from the Cameroons are large wooden masks and dancing figures (Plates 52 and 54). These figures, used in mourning rites, are perhaps the purest rendering of rhythmic expression that we find in African art. Measured and insistent as the beating of a drum, the pounding reiteration of shapes accords perfectly with the subject's apparent state of complete abandon. In the same way, masks representing human beings and animals discharge a barrage of impulses and feelings. This outpouring of emotion assumes an almost animalistic exuberance and force. No exaggeration, no excess of enthusiasm on the part of the Cameroons carver gives offense. Everything seems to well up from the artist's innermost being. To see and feel Cameroons sculpture is to experience one of the climactic moments of African art.

Homogeneous in form and mutually compatible in function, the art styles of Africa tend to merge and blend with one another. They are tightly bound together by the heart-shaped Megalithic tradition, a tradition broken only by the more sophisticated styles of Nigeria.

Seen in a historical context, the true genius, the achievement, the individuality of the African artist can be better assessed, and his works more accurately measured against the products of his fellow men. Whether or not an object from an African tribe is representative is far less important to us than whether it is unique and has escaped representativeness and the limitations of tradition. In this respect Africa differs from Asia-Oceania and America, where the entire style is usually of the utmost significance. In Africa our admiration and esteem go out, above all, to the single great work—that is, the masterpiece.

54 Big-cheeked mask. Cameroons. H. 27" (Chicago Natural History Museum).

ASIA

NAGA

CH'U

YUNNAN

JAPAN

TAIWAN

BOTEL TOBAGO

MOI

PHILIPPINES

M I C R O N E S I A

PALAU

MORTLOCK NUKUORO

GILBER

NIAS

BATAK

BORNEO

GEELVINK BAY

KANIET

LAKE SENTANI

NEW IRELAND

I N D O N E S I A

ASMAT

Sepik R.

NEW BRITAIN

TAMI

NEW CALEDONI

ENGGANO

LETI

TANIMBAR

TORRES STRAITS

MASSIM

SOLOMONS

M E L A N E S I A

SANTA

NEW HEBRID

AUSTRALIA

NEW ZEALA

OCEANIA

NECKER

HAWAII

MARQUESAS

P O L Y N E S I A

•FIJI

•TONGA

TAHITI

RAROTONGA

RURUTU

MANGAREVA

RAIVAEVAE

EASTER I

CHATHAM

II

The People

The long, rolling waves of the vast Pacific—covering nearly one fifth of the globe—deposit all manner of things upon numberless beaches. Along with plant life and driftwood, these waves have also carried human beings; thousands of people migrating slowly, often sporadically, from Asia out into the Pacific islands. Sometimes the emigrants were refugees fleeing an alien aggressor; sometimes they were highly successful entrepreneurs in search of new territory. All took with them the artifacts and traits of their native cultures. In this way, as time went on, more and more of the sophisticated ideas already developed in India, China, and other mainland areas reached the Pacific area, so that today we find traces of every major Asian culture in the island worlds of the South Seas.

Because it preserves such an enormous variety of cultures and art forms, the Pacific has the same fascination for anthropologists and art historians that a rummage sale or auction has for the antique-lover. In Tasmania, for example, we catch glimpses of a society essentially of the Old Stone Age which survived into the latter part of the nineteenth century. Similarly, Bali is a living link with the Hindu Java of five centuries ago. And art styles that thrived when China was very young still maintain much of their original vigor in the remote islands to the east.

Scholars divide the Pacific into five major areas: Polynesia, Micronesia, Melanesia, Australia, and Southeast Asia, including Indonesia and the mainland peninsula between China and India. However, these divisions are unsatisfactory for the study of Oceanic art, language, or physical types. For instance, the people of the western Torres Straits Islands, between Australia and New Guinea, speak an Australian dialect but are of Papuan stock, and have an art that belongs to still another tradition. The traditional subdivisions actually stand in the way of progress. There is no such thing as "Polynesian style" per se. Rather are there a multitude of styles representing different historical levels of achievement. All of these stem ultimately from Asia.

In the very remote past long before man as we know him had appeared, human-like beings, now extinct, had emerged from an animal state in or near the Asian land mass. Even when *Homo sapiens* finally entered the scene, perhaps a mere fifty-thousand years ago, he had only the simplest of boats, such as floating logs and bundles of reeds, and thus could not cross large bodies of water. Among these early men were Negritos, distant relatives of the African Pygmy, and Australoids, an early Caucasoid stock. Over the centuries, these groups filtered into Indonesia, Melanesia, and Australia from Asia, bringing Old Stone Age technologies and distinctive languages with them. They followed land routes as much as possible, down the Malay Peninsula and out along the Sunda chain, and finally reached dead ends from which there was no retreat. Thus, Australia and Tasmania on the one hand, and the Andamans and Nicobars on the other, preserve some of the oldest stages of Pacific culture and speech.

These earliest migrants had very little art. Their ceremonies, which centered on the placating of spirits, were intended mainly to guarantee adequate food supply. Hunters and gatherers, the Negritos and Australoids conducted their rites in the open, for they lacked even the simplest dwellings. They painted their bodies and ornamented their weapons with earth and vegetable pigments. But these ancient peoples never learned to make masks or figures, although they may have invented a fiber cap of a sort which is still worn by the Warramunga and other central Australian tribes in initiation ceremonies today.

55 (Left) Middle Sepik ceremonial stool with ancestor figure which was beaten with leaves during debates. New Guinea. H. 63³/₄" (Historisches Museum, Bern).

56 (Right) Owl mask used to put children under supernatural protection. Baining, New Britain. Cane and bark cloth. H. 31¹/₄" (Museum für Völkerkunde, Basel).

Next to arrive in Oceania were a more advanced people who, coming in sporadically, brought with them various elements of Neolithic or New Stone Age culture. With their simple dugout canoes, they were able to penetrate throughout Indonesia and Melanesia probably as far as New Caledonia and the Fiji Islands. These first Neolithic invaders brought into the Pacific polished stone tools, improved fishing methods, and various types of agriculture; they do not seem to have had any linguistic unity. For want of any better name, we may call them the Papuans, though this term really only signifies non–Melanesian-speaking Oceanic Negroes. Papuan peoples lived in simple houses near swamps and at the mouths of rivers where they could combine fishing with gardening; many also utilized the sago palm, a source of starchy food. They had no wooden figures and no wooden masks, but they produced effigies and conical face masks made of bark, bark cloth, palm spathe, string, pith, or other flexible fibrous materials. These monstrous creations were used in dances and processions to appease spirits.

The groups described were all early scattered arrivals in the Pacific, quite lacking in group unity. By comparison, the later peoples had at least a major bond: the languages they spoke all belonged to one great family—the Malayo-Polynesian or Austronesian group. Now dispersed over an incredibly wide area extending from Madagascar to Easter

57 Clown mask. Papuan Gulf, New Guinea. H ca. 26" (Present location unknown).

Island, the Austronesians (mixed Mongoloid-Caucasoid peoples) also brought with them a variety of cultural advantages. Foremost among their innovations were large outrigger canoes capable of weathering severe storms and of enduring long ocean voyages. This made possible a maritime way of life—fishing offshore, trading with distant neighbors, and raiding—and enabled the Austronesians to overrun Micronesia and Polynesia as well as Melanesia and Indonesia. With the exception of the inhabitants of Australia, of the Andamans, and the interior of a few of the larger islands such as New Guinea, all Pacific peoples now speak Austronesian languages. Also of Austronesian origin are such innovations as decorated houses, massive wood and stone carvings, and pottery built of coils of clay.

The art forms used by the Austronesians included wood-carved figures and masks representing human-like spirit beings and deified ancestors. Instead of being largely communal, their ceremonies often celebrated individual or clan achievement disguised as public welfare. Concepts of inherited rank or acquired prestige led to social competition and aggressiveness. Austronesian rites were more theatrically staged than those of the pre-Austronesians, with background screens or scaffolding as stage props. Later Austronesian art shows considerable sophistication owing to the influence of higher culture.

58   Detail of canoe ornament. Solomon Islands, Melanesia. H. 32¹/₄" over-all (Museum of Archaeology and Ethnology, Cambridge University).

Where the Austronesians came from originally and how they reached their far-flung island homes is a question that has long perplexed scholars. In 1932, however, the Austrian prehistorian and anthropologist Robert Heine-Geldern brilliantly called attention to the Austronesian adze blade as the best possible migration evidence. This adze or ax blade is a distinctive type generally oblong in shape and rectangular in cross section. Such blades seem to have been introduced into the Pacific from China. Interestingly, linguistic evidence points to much the same origin, for the languages of the Thai and Kadai peoples of the Vietnam-Yunnan border have recently been classified as Austronesian. Although the exact sequence and chronology of Pacific history remains a fascinating problem whose solution will require many years of work, it would appear that ancient China has contributed more than any other source to the development of South Seas cultures.

The Art

The story of Pacific art parallels in its development the rise of the Oceanic peoples. Beginning with the simplest outline sketch or flat geometric painted design, such as we find in Australia, Pacific styles move through the stage of soft ephemeral images to the permanent statuesque monuments of Polynesia. Sometimes these developments were due to a single large-scale migration. In other instances, ideas and motifs spread from one area to another through borrowing, trade, or imitation. We should not, therefore, expect all art forms in an area to originate from the same source. On the other hand, similarities of form, no matter how great the gap in time or space, need more than casual inspection. Canoe figures from Enggano Island off Sumatra and from the Cook Islands, over eight thousand miles away in central Polynesia, provide a striking case in point. That two groups of people working independently could have converged on such similar yet complex forms is highly improbable. Primitive restrictions against novelty and innovation prevent this kind of experimentation. Both examples must depend on a unique, common prototype. Thus, even if we had no other evidence linking Enggano and Cook art styles (Plates 97 and 76), a common source of inspiration would be the most logical and, historically speaking, the most economical explanation we could suggest.

There seem to be at least eight distinct layers in Pacific art. The first,

59   *Rock painting of running women. Arnhem Land, Australia.*
Photographed in 1951.

the Ancient Australian style, lingers today only in the remote deserts of Australia. It consists mainly of geometric and representational designs painted or engraved on two-dimensional surfaces. The second level, called the Old Papuan style, survives chiefly in Melanesia. Among its most important innovations are effigies and conical masks of soft materials, ornamented with large circular eyes, used in initiation rites. The third major influence is that of the Megalithic (big stone) culture. Originating in western Asia during the Neolithic era, this tradition spread over southeast Asia and from there out to Melanesia and other areas. Megalithic culture laid great stress on aggressiveness and fighting. Blocky, frontal, postlike ancestor figures were the particular artistic contribution of the Megalithic tradition.

A fourth influence is that of the Aquatic tradition which now appears only fragmentarily in the Pacific. Aquatic culture introduced masks representing voracious animals, with long snouts, (Plate 65) and related plant, bird, and fish symbols of a composite character. The Aquatic style also laid the foundations for the first truly Chinese art.

The fifth layer of influence stemmed directly from early Chinese art of the protohistoric period, best represented in China in the famous Shang bronzes and bone carvings dated roughly 1500–1000 B.C. Far richer in decoration than the styles previously discussed, patterns in this Sino-Austronesian style tend to be rectangular, symmetrical, and complex. The persistence of Chinese influence in Oceania for over three thousand years should not surprise us; after all, the Australian and Old Papuan styles reflect the survival of ideas much older than any known in China.

Pacific art received its sixth major impulse from a bronze-using culture which appeared in northern Vietnam about 750 B.C. Named for its best-known site, this so-called Dongson influence rapidly spread far out into the Pacific. Its typical motifs include S-spirals organized in parallel rows and a fastidious use of tiny light-dark contrasts. Masks are almost completely lacking in Dongson-influenced cultures.

Somewhat related to Dongson is the seventh layer of influence which emanates from China in the Late Chou period (roughly 500 B.C.). Late Chou art shows modification of the older Shang tradition through the intervention of another Eurasian bronze style akin to Dongson. The main difference is that the former had to blend with the already established Chinese tradition of surface ornament, whereas Dongson penetrated an area in which elaborate decoration was unfamiliar. Influence from the Late Chou

60   *Cult mask. Yuat River, Sepik area, New Guinea. H. 13" (Eckert Collection, Basel).*

tremendously energizes the surfaces, adding flowering spirals and active asymmetrical patterns of extraordinary grace and freedom.

The last wave, brought in with a series of thrusts, carried sophisticated ideas from India to many parts of the South Seas. Indian influence first entered Southeast Asia about the time of Christ, introducing various Brah-

manic, Buddhist, and Hindu sects. Wooden masks as distinct art forms, and figures standing on bases and making meaningful gestures show Indian influence. The Indo-Austronesian movement was distributed irregularly over Melanesia, Micronesia, Polynesia, and almost all of Indonesia.

The eight chief Pacific styles will be discussed in order as follows: Ancient Australian, Old Papuan, Megalithic, Aquatic, Sino-Austronesian, Dongson, Late Chou, and Indo-Austronesian. To make clear the distinctive character of life and art in each of these divisions, we will first consider a single area where one particular style of influence has predominated.

Ancient Australian

The Australian aborigine until recently lived in a manner most of us would think unbearable. He had no permanent home, no crops, no metal, no pottery, and practically no clothing. A hunter and food-gatherer, he wandered in small groups over a vast territory searching ceaselessly for wild game and other food. Even water in that arid southern continent was a daily problem. Although the Australian

61 (Facing) Middle Sepik initiation mask. New Guinea. Wood, feathers, human hair, palm spathe and grass. H. 56" (Übersee Museum, Bremen).

62 Tubuan dancer wearing Dukduk Society costume of bark cloth, leaves, and feathers. Baining, New Britain. Photographed ca. 1910.

had not progressed far in material wealth, long ago he had developed a richly elaborated religious and ceremonial life. According to Australian myth, the world was created by certain semi-human creatures known as the Great Ones of the Dream. They made all living things, and stocked the world with a sort of magical life-essence, concentrating it originally in places such as rocks and trees. Today the aborigine, if he wishes to enjoy a plentiful food supply, believes that he must siphon off some of this essence so that animals may multiply in number. This ambition is accomplished, first, by living in harmony with the precepts laid down by the Dream Ones; secondly, by using rock engravings, bark painting, and other portable ceremonial objects to help achieve his goal. These constitute his sole efforts at art.

In Ancient Australian life an astonishing and important aspect that bears on our subject was the virtually complete lack of private property. Almost all goods belonged to the group. When a hunter killed a kangaroo, the meat was carefully divided according to custom so that the old men received a larger share than the vigorous youths. The hunter often got only the head or the ears and tail. (Similar customs survive from the Stone Age in Europe today: in the Tyrol, for example, the stag hunter gets only the head and horns,

63 and 64 Commemorative ancestor figures. Carved on the male is a tally of his victims, together with his guns. Naga, Assam. H. 71³/₄" over-all (British Museum, London).

just as elsewhere the successful bullfighter receives similar trophies.) The elder members of society thus kept the balance of economic power in their own hands, at the same time insuring an equable distribution of nourishing protein food. If we can judge by such practices, the popular image of the cave man as a cruel, self-centered brute battering his neighbor and seizing everything for himself is probably utterly incorrect.

The lack of any real conception of private property or of commercial value in our sense had a profound impact on aboriginal art. The Australian thought of his art, not as an expression of himself, but rather as a bequest of supernatural power handed down successively since Dream time. To be effective there was no need for such an art to be realistic, and indeed the Ancient Australian style often seems to have been quite abstract, consisting of circles, spirals, and parallel straight or wavy lines. Magical values pervaded even what appears to us to be mere decoration. The designs on the most sacred objects—the *tjuringas* or bullroarer-like wooden or stone slabs—served as memory aids for the elders, who knew their meaning. As a rule, each group attributed its own significance to the various patterns, and related them to the local myths.

Simple as this style is, it illustrates very graphically the interests of the native Australian. Motifs refer to local animals and natural objects having particular relevance for the aborigine. Often represented are life forms, known as totems, from which his group traced its descent, or mythological creatures connected with the Dream Ones. These designs are distributed unevenly over the surface. The idea of organizing large-scale patterns seems to have been lacking in Ancient Australian art.

At the present time, the Ancient Australian style persists mainly in the central desert; other influences long ago penetrated the outer fringes of Australia. In the past the ancient style probably extended throughout Australia and Tasmania. Since the Australians are essentially a Paleolithic people, this style represents a more or less fossilized survival of the art of the Old Stone Age.

Old Papuan

The Baining of New Britain, who typify the creators of the Old Papuan style, would stand out in any gathering. Darker than their Melanesian neighbors, and very primitive in appearance, with kinky hair and short legs, the Baining may well represent a survival of Negrito or Australoid stock. Their language and customs also show great age, harking back to a stage halfway between a nomadic food-gathering way of life and that of full-fledged agriculturists. The Baining earn their living by collecting certain semiwild root crops. Their loosely organized communities, which were sometimes totemic in origin, had no chiefs, special men's houses, or secret societies. However, these people excelled in art. Their masks of bark cloth and other soft materials were made for ceremonies connected with benevolent spirits. Most spectacular and bizarre was the *hariecha* effigy, which consisted of a bamboo pole of up to forty feet in length, surrounded with leaves and covered with painted bark cloth. Constructed in secret, these images represented a friendly spirit believed to be present at combined harvest and initiation rites. At the beginning of the ceremonies, the figure was laid out horizontally in a clearing in the forest; an audience consisting of the uninitiated was at one side. But at the climax of the rite, a man raised the grotesque form to his shoulders and, aided by other men with poles, staggered with it for a few steps; then the effigy was permitted to fall and later to decay.

The significance of these weird constructions is not entirely known. The powerful spirits to which they refer were probably mainly totemic and, therefore, not really ancestral. The monstrous shapes and soft perishable forms of the *hariecha* typify Old Papuan style. Emblems sketched on the surface represented, among other things, betel nuts, sugar cane, shells, eyes, all meaningful to the Baining. Essentially, the *hariecha* ceremony was an attempt to ensure general fertility.

Another Baining mask almost as stupendously effective as the *hariecha* was that used by members of the Dukduk society. Dukduk men wore a conical bark-cloth mask decorated with two large eyes and a tuft of feathers at the top, and a long, bushy leaf costume that covered the wearer to the middle of the thigh (Plate 62). Painted motifs consisted for the most part of irregular circles, looping ovals, and wavy lines of varying size and thickness.

Dukduk rites, as they were originally performed, introduced Baining youngsters to the kindly bush and water spirits venerated by the people. First the boys were abducted and terrorized, and then they were instructed in the secrets of the group. At the culmination of the ceremony, which took place in public but at a special clearing in the jungle, masked figures danced, disguised as the spirit beings themselves. Masks of conical shape with large round eyes known as Tubuan were worn, whereas other more elaborate, tiered masks represented the Dukduk spirit itself. The Tubuan type was older and more important than the Dukduk, which is of a later, somewhat different tradition. The Dukduk mask stimulated competition and hostility between individual members. This may explain why the society degenerated into a sort of Mafia dedicated largely to terrorism and extortion.

Today Tubuan masks, used for benevolent purposes and non-exclusive in function, perpetuate both the functional and artistic qualities of the Old Papuan style. Their simple conical shapes, soft materials, and round staring eyes are typical of this widespread tradition. Echoes of Old Papuan conical masks occur in New Guinea among the Asmat, Mimika, Papuan Gulf, Tami, Iatmul, and Abelam peoples, in the French Islands (Witu) and other parts of New Britain, in Tanga, Nissan, and the northern Solomons, the Banks and New Hebrides chains, and New Caledonia; by some inexplicable quirk, the type even reached Mangaia in the Cook group in Polynesia. The conical shape so typical of the Old Papuan style may well have developed out of the ancient tapered cap or head decoration still worn by the primitive Warramunga and other central Australian aborigines in their initiation rituals.

Megalithic

The outstanding characteristic of Megalithic influence, aside from its massive wooden and stone monuments, is aggressiveness. Nowhere is this trait better illustrated than among the Naga people who live in the highlands of Assam between India and Burma. The Naga, until recently inveterate headhunters, lived in hilltop villages defended by ditches and palisades. Fighting, sex, and social position dominated their interests. These activities were, moreover, interrelated, for the Naga killed in order to acquire the soulessence of their enemies, which in turn enhanced crop fertility. Similarly sexual potency was equated with the capacity to increase food supply, and both abilities were of great esteem. A Naga needed visible evidence of his achievements, and this led to the carving of a variety of forms symbolizing individual success. Among these were such themes as the human head and phallus, circular rosettes representing the moon, and the horns of buffaloes sacrificed in feasts of merit. The commemoration of ancestors, particularly if they were great warriors, helped to imbue future enterprises with the spirit of past greatness. Thus the Naga were as energetic and future-oriented a people as may be found in primitive life. The chance of raising one's status through achievement gave Megalithic groups a highly dynamic quality.

Strangely enough, Megalithic art is extremely static. Simple postlike figures (Plate 63) emphasizing the head and genitalia are common, as are representations of buffalo horns (often placed at gables) and two-pronged forks signifying a triumphant sacrifice of buffalo. Sheer undecorated surfaces and stubby rectangular shapes also characterize this tradition. Stonework, where it appears, is often of colossal size though quite carefully fitted. Megalithic carving shows a preference for frontal views, massive sculptural qualities, and simple heart-shaped faces with slitlike eyes. Isolation of motifs and a tendency toward repetition combine to give a tally-like treatment of forms, with one item told off after another. In these forms the simple juxtaposition of parts reveals some awareness of horizontal and vertical relationships but not of composition in the true sense. The Megalithic artist used universally understood symbols in a very obvious manner. Always he strove to aggrandize individual and clan accomplishments.

From its beginnings in western Asia, Megalithic influence spread widely over eastern Asia and the Pacific, skipping Australia but carrying its message

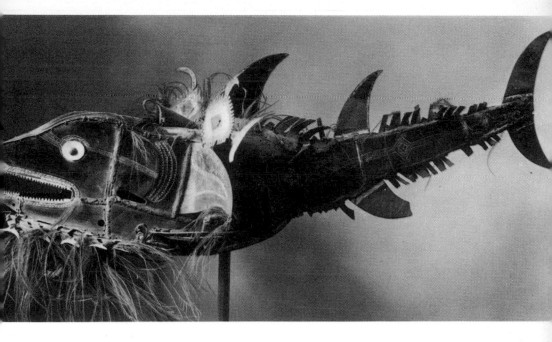

65 Snout animal mask worn to ensure an abundance of fish. Mabuiag, Western Torres Straits. Turtle shell with lime inlay and cassowary feathers. L. 50" (British Museum, London).

of competition and violence into Melanesia, Micronesia and even to Easter Island in the farthest corner of Polynesia.

Aquatic

Thousands of years ago an entirely different culture, unlike any known in the West, evolved in the fringes of the lakes and rivers of eastern Asia. With shellfish-gathering, fishing, and hunting to provide a steady livelihood, elements of this culture spread over the Asian littoral and out to the offshore islands nearby. Now blurred in most areas, a remnant of this Aquatic tradition has been permitted by favorable circumstances to survive near New Guinea in Torres Straits.

The quintessence of Torres Straits life was the sea. Without the abundance of fish, mollusks, and marine mammals taken from the water, even the intelligent, resourceful islander would scarcely have achieved his magnificent ritual art. In contrast to agriculturalists, the Straits argonaut focused his rites, artistic skills, and social customs on the teeming deep. He wore handsome shell pendants depicting marine totems associated with individual clans. On either side of his large sailing canoe appeared a menacing composite creature with a crocodile snout, a stylized body, and a fish tail. So accomplished was the Torres Straits native in sailing that his vessel could carry dozens of men on long trading or fishing voyages and, if necessary, on full-scale migrations. In fact, though they lived in permanent villages, Aquatic peoples probably spent almost as much time afloat as ashore.

Ritual life in Torres Straits aimed to control and increase the supply of food. Along with fish, the dugong or sea cow and the green turtle were highly valued as sources of rich, oily meat. The timid, plant-eating dugong, a large sea mammal somewhat resembling a walrus, had to be captured with nets or by harpooning. Great prestige resulted from the spearing of one of these beasts or the equally difficult taking of a sea turtle. Ceremonies to insure an abundance of marine life often involved dances in front of ancestral mat screens decorated with lozenge designs or on scaffolds

*66   Votive figure. Marquesas, Polynesia. Stone.
H. 6¹/₂″ (University Museum, Philadelphia).*

similar to those used by harpooners. The
Straits people also delighted in dances in
which they wore monstrous turtle-shell masks
of the composite snout animal (Plate 65).
Their intricate use of turtle shell, a material
which like plastic may be steamed and bent
or cut and incised, is virtually unparalleled
elsewhere in the world. The snout animal of
the Torres Straits masks gives an impression
of solidity and weight, but this is lightened by
the attachment of feathers, leaves, seeds, nuts,
paint, and shells that break up the form and
introduce flimsy projections. Round shell eyes
with black wax pupils, lozenges, rosettes, and
triangular patterns enhance the surface ornament. Incised drawings picked out in white
lime often decorate the backs of the masks.
One curious feature often found is the use of
flaring hornlike projections on top of the head.

Several artistic elements in the Torres
Straits Aquatic repertoire deserve special mention. One is the technique of drawing rather
sketchy figures in dynamic poses, often in profile. Sometimes these figures even form groups
that are related through the performance of
a rite or other ceremonial action. A specially
remarkable feature is the presence of a
ground line or base line on which figures and
designs are aligned. This tremendous advance
over the free-floating figures of Old Stone Age
cave and rock paintings and Australian and
Old Papuan engravings was an achievement
of the Aquatic tradition.

67   *War club, detail. Marquesas, Polynesia. Ironwood. H. 50″ over-all (Musée de l'Homme, Paris.)*

A number of important gestures and postures also appear for the first time in incised Aquatic designs. Mainly frontal, these include the so-called orant pose, with the hands raised on either side of the head and a splayed figure with legs outspread. Human figures are used as surface ornament and are often linked together in horizontal bands. Sleek, streamlined animal forms appear also, carved entirely in the round.

The Aquatic tradition which we have observed in Torres Straits disappeared long ago from the Asian mainland. Traces of its influence survive, however, in the earliest historic art of China. The composite crocodile with fish tail occurs on Shang bronze vessels dating roughly 1300–1000 B.C. The complex *koimai* design consisting of concentric diamonds with hornlike projections at top and bottom commonly depicted on snout animal masks (Plate 65) occurs also on ancient bronzes (e. g., a famous vessel in the H. S. Rubens collection). Even the elaborate ancestor screens with their lozenge designs and totem animals are represented on the Chinese ritual containers.

It is very unlikely that the first historic Chinese cultures could have influenced Torres Straits life. If this had been so, we might expect to see evidence of agriculture, of metalworking, or at least some trace of the use of complex Shang surface ornament. But there is none of this in Torres Straits art. The relationship must therefore be reversed. Shang culture, known almost solely through its bronze, bone, and stone relics, must be the child, not the parent, in this case. For every scholar of Asian history agrees that Shang is already a very mature and sophisticated expression of Chinese life, and the earlier vestiges being of perishable materials are simply lost to us. Careful study of Aquatic art forms accidentally preserved in Torres Straits may therefore help to explain some enigmatic Shang designs.

One Chinese motif that has long baffled scholars is the *t'ao t'ieh*, a monstrous face or head made up of parts of several animals. Like *t'ao t'ieh*, Torres Straits masks represent a composite monster with a long snout. Though highly stylized, the *t'ao t'ieh* has numerous details found in the Torres Straits examples. Among these are the hornlike projections at the top, and the shape and size of the eyes. One distinctive artistic device seen in Shang bronzes consists of two animals in profile forming the frontal face of the *t'ao t'ieh*. The same idea is suggested in the strange demonic faces topping many Torres Straits masks. In both instances the mouths are omitted; the existence of a relationship between the two areas therefore seems highly probable.

Sino-Austronesian

While Megalithic and Aquatic influences were spreading throughout the Pacific, in the first historic Chinese culture the magnificent Shang bronzes were being created. The style of these bronzes, or rather that of their wooden prototypes, seems to have influenced a number of peoples in the maritime fringes of eastern Asia. The forebears of the present Austronesian-speaking people eventually carried sophisticated early Chinese traits to the islands of the South Seas. The resulting Sino-Austronesian style is today best seen in the Marquesas Islands of eastern Polynesia.

The life of the Marquesan native revolved around his three main interests — food, warfare, and sex. Because his rugged homeland provided an inadequate food supply, the Marquesan often found that his appetite could best be satisfied by killing and eating a neighbor. The result was constant hostility and feuding. There was no sovereign leader and no supreme deity; authority was vested in the clan and in the family. The Marquesan household consisted of the wife, a paramount husband, and as many secondary husbands as could be persuaded to join in this arrangement. This system of a single wife for several husbands, known as polyandry, is exceedingly rare in the primitive world but seems to have existed in China in Shang times.

Marquesan art has many features characteristic of Austronesian art in general. A preference for hard durable materials such as close-grained wood reflects the desire for permanent status in these societies. Forms tend to be symmetrical and precise in delineation, vigorous and legible in statement. As emblems of rank or badges of authority, Austronesian carvings and ornaments are explicit and emphatic. This explains why objects in this tradition are so completely standardized. For, as Felix Speiser, the renowned Swiss anthropologist observed, Austronesian carving is "static and pedantic."

The Marquesans carved human figures both in wood and in stone. The former were often used to ornament canoes, bowls, stilt steps, and house posts; those in stone were either a part of megalithic walls or free-standing cult images (Plate 66). The typical Marquesan face consists of two large buglike eyes surrounded by distinct socket areas. Noses are generally short with wide-flaring nostril wings. The mouth is marked by clear-cut lips, the tongue indicated by a ridge between. This Sino-Austronesian face may be seen in the gods of the Cook Islands fishermen and, slightly modified, in a

68　*Mortuary banner showing Tree of Life flanked by supernatural fish. Lake Sentari, New Guinea. Painted bark cloth. L. 54³/₄″ (Musée de l'Homme, Paris).*

Chinese sculpture from Ch'u that dates from the first millennium B.C. (Plate 98).

Close scrutiny of Marquesan art reveals a number of art forms and media not previously seen in the Pacific. Bone carving includes ear and hair ornaments, fan handles, strangling-cord handles, and other forms. Stylistically, these tiny, beautifully worked bone objects are exactly like other much larger Marquesan carvings. The ear ornaments, for instance, which interested Gauguin so much that he copied them in huge scale in one of his Marquesan paintings, portray remarkable scenes consisting of two figures in profile flanking a group of headlike forms. The whole conception is complex and un-Polynesian. A clue to the origin of such carvings lies in the use of the medium itself and in the shaping of the ears. Bone carving is typical of the early Chinese culture, where similar ear designs also occur.

Equally impressive are the wooden fighting clubs carried in this area (Plate 67). These show the Marquesan delight in splitting up the body into its component parts so that certain motifs, such as the eyes, heads, and hands, often stand out alone. This splitting up of the forms, probably a magical as well as a decorative idea, permitted the artist to introduce ambiguous double images with the eyes or noses turning into small heads in themselves. This exceedingly sophisticated device, which Western surrealists have long exploited, is comparatively rare in the Pacific. The regions where it occurred—the Marquesas, the Sepik district in New Guinea, Eskimo country, the Northwest Coast, and Middle America—also happen to be precisely the areas most suggestive of Chinese influence.

Another extraordinary item of culture in the Marquesas was the *kapkap*, a sort of doily of pierced turtleshell attached to a white shell disk, worn only by important men. This object is not found anywhere else in Polynesia, although it is characteristic of the Melanesian portions of New Guinea and New Ireland, New Britain, the Admiralties, the Solomons, and the Santa Cruz Islands. Forms related to the *kapkap* occur in the Philippines, in Torres

69 Carving on piling of chief's hut erected over the water. Lake Sentani, New Guinea. H. 33¹/₂" (Museum für Völkerkunde, Basel).

Straits, and among the Naga. All belong to another tradition — that of the Dongson.

Dongson

The Bronze-Iron Age in the Pacific really begins about 750 B.C., when bronze-using nomadic tribes whose original home lay in southern Russia invaded northern Vietnam. Their innovations spread out over most of Indonesia and later into Melanesia and beyond. Today Dongson culture lives on in the vicinity of Lake Sentani near the northern coast of New Guinea.

Known to thousands of American soldiers in World War II when General MacArthur was based at Hollandia, Lake Sentani is only a few miles inland from the sea. The Sentani people are basically Papuans, though they have acquired certain Melanesian art forms from their coastal neighbors in recent times. But long ago Dongson influences made a vast impression on these people. Daily life in the Sentani region followed the typical New Guinea pattern: the women worked in their gardens and fished while the men did the heavy work and engaged in ceremonial practices and warfare. A peculiarity of Lake Sentani society, however, was the existence of a sort of feudal group known as the *ifoi* who served as vassals and retainers of the *ondoforo*,

70 Rare free-standing figure with naturalistic tattooing. Maori, New Zealand. Wood with shell and human hair. H. 17³/₄" (Glasgow Museum and Art Gallery, Scotland).

71 Carving above council house door. Maori, New Zealand. 34″ × 19″ (British Museum, London).

or chief. In return for wives, bride price, and protection, the *ifoi* provided their leader with food and superior housing; when necessary, they fought for him.

Sentani art is fascinating. Attractive images of mothers and children (Plate 69) are common as well as single or back-to-back male images. Hooks for suspending food out of the reach of rats, bowls, knives, and house ornaments are beautifully decorated with magnificent **S**-spiral designs. But the most striking and puzzling Sentani art forms consist of bannerlike cloths painted with elaborate stylized motifs of birds, fish, plants, animals, and humans. Richly embellished and carefully organized, these banners or cloths give every appearance of being paintings in the true Western sense. They are of bark cloth, a thin flexible substance made by pounding the inner bark of certain trees such as the wild fig or paper mulberry until it becomes feltlike. Widely used in Indonesia, Melanesia, and Polynesia for practical and artistic purposes, bark cloth had its highest pictorial expression here in the Lake Sentani region.

What little we know about the paintings indicates that they were worn by women at marriage and on festive occasions. If the woman died young, her loincloth or a banner painted in a similar manner was hung up beside her grave. But it is not clear whether a man or a woman actually painted the designs. At the wedding, the cloth was tied with a special belt given by the mother-in-law to her daughter-to-be, and the newly wedded girl took the name of a recently deceased person.

Membership in special ceremonial groups also passed through the female line in this society. Thus the use of the banners seems to be connected with transmission of rights and the replacement of the departed by new and fertile human beings. It would therefore be wrong to describe the Sentani banners as merely decorative.

Visually, these cloths contain many surprises. Their subject matter includes a menagerie of fish and animal forms ranging from bats, lizards, and wallabies to sucker fish and eels. Most of these creatures are highly mobile or are capable of clinging to other forms. They are generally of aquatic or aerial origin; appropriately, their appearance is fluid, but at the same time the treatment of surfaces is often jagged, linear, and agitated—actively posed figures swim vigorously in their watery world. Other equally arresting forms have a more aggressive appearance, conveyed by shapes that are spiny and protective. These tend to be isolated and self-governing; sometimes they violently overlap other forms, or even break through the surrounding frame. Unlike the clinging forms which anchor themselves to structural elements, these forms move freely over the surface. In such a conception we can discern more than a hint of the feudal system of Lake Sentani, having a dominant being to whom lesser satellite figures attach themselves. Designs of this sort also teem with sexual implications.

What then are the origins of this compelling style? The "S" or reverse spirals, the most common of Sentani designs, repeated over and over, spring definitely from Bronze Age sources. Equally impressive is the representation of the Tree of Life, a stylized plant flanked by two other plants (Plate 68). This motif, of Near Eastern origin, was introduced into Southeast Asia by the Dongson people. And most startling of all is the use of the frame, a form so distinct that its movement can be traced back step by step across Asia. This device, like the ground line, was invented in the Ancient Near East. Used as a means of separating the artistic from the ordinary world, this drawing of a line around forms to isolate them from the field, creates a special domain that is truly aesthetic rather than magical or religious. The frame has no obvious source other than the will of the artist and his decision to differentiate his vision from ordinary and supernatural experience.

Conclusive proof of Dongson influence around Lake Sentani comes from archaeological evidences. A number of bronze axes actually removed from the lake have shape and decoration and show techniques that could only have come from Dongson culture. This proves to be, in fact, the easternmost penetration of actual Bronze Age objects that is known in the Pacific.

Late Chou

Late Chou influence, as we noted earlier, owes its peculiar character to the invasion of China about 600 B.C. by another bronze-using nomadic culture. Onto the strength and asymmetry of the invading Bronze Age style were grafted Chinese elegance and refinement, resulting in an art of almost unbelievable linear grace and movement. For some reason, the Late Chou phase survives best outside of China in the art of the Polynesian Maori of New Zealand.

Today the Maori in New Zealand are probably the best-liked and most admired inheritors of primitive culture. Their present attitude is one of friendliness toward the European settlers; this is a far cry from the way in which the Maori won the respect of their former white enemies by their sheer toughness in all-out warfare.

Unlike other Polynesians, the Maori settled in a climate that is nontropical, essentially temperate, but one wherein warm winter clothing and substantial houses were virtual necessities. He devoted particular attention, therefore, to the construction of an impressive council house embodying representations of great ancestors and more remote protective beings, figures which would lend their wisdom and authority to the deliberations to be held in the building. So strongly bound up with tribal welfare were these carvings that, when war threatened, they were buried in swamps; for the greatest calamity was for the enemy to pull down and misuse the ancestral figures and gable masks. Young men during their period of training received a full course of instruction in the meaning of the various beings represented. Because the Maori did not restrict ritual lore to a small priest caste, they have succeeded in preserving far more of their occult knowledge than have most

72　*Middle Sepik carved group derived from the Gilgamesh image. Iatmul, New Guinea. H. 16¹/₂″ (Museum of Primitive Art, New York).*

73　*(Facing) Ancestor plaque (see also plate 10). Taiwan. H. 36¹/₄″ (T'aitung Prefecture Library, Taiwan).*

other Polynesian groups. Hereditary chiefs ruled with no more authority than that of the head of a large, loosely knit family. Having no very exclusive symbols of status, Maori society, with the exception of slaves, was more or less democratic.

Maori art is extraordinarily virile and dramatic. Usually carved in high relief as part of larger functional forms that range from an adze to a council house, this style reveals a wonderful richness of linear fantasy and a bewildering variety of techniques. The basic material, a soft, easily cut wood, was shaped into canoe prows and stern pieces, house posts, planks, door lintels, and gable ornaments. These were lightly coated with ocher and fish oil, giving them a monochromatic reddish appearance. Maori carvings, which range in size from a few inches in length to fifty feet or more, received added

enlivenment from the iridescent, abalone-like shells inserted to suggest eyes. Mythological beings and ancestors dominate the Maori artist's subject matter. He has singled out the most climactic and dramatic aspects of his subjects, as for example scenes of copulation or birth. His expressive use of figure groups and integrated compositions implies a long and sophisticated visual tradition (Plate 71).

What is most unexpected in the Maori artist's work is his decorative vocabulary. Rows of raised dots framed by double or triple ridges are among the most frequently used phraseology. We also recognize a toothlike deckled pattern, chevrons, and any variety of scrolls, spirals, and cusped leaflike patterns. Spirited and swirling, these designs contrast vividly with the massive closed silhouettes of the figures. Despite some asymmetry, Maori images are basically frontal and bluntly aggressive, though their minute surface treatment tends to be delicate and complex. The tense and violent postures and gestures of defiance such as the long tongue, often seen twisted to one side, seem incompatible with the vagrant, magical quality of Maori surface ornament. But a recent discovery by a Chinese anthropologist sheds a flash of light on this problem. For years New Zealand writers sought Maori parallels in Melanesia and other parts of Polynesia. Then, quite astonishingly, Ling Shun-Sheng, of the Chinese Nationalist Museum in Taiwan, discovered a wooden board carved by the ferocious and still uncontrolled head hunters of the interior of that island (Plates 12 and 73). The board served as architectural ornament in an important ancestor house. So close to Maori carving is this figure composition that there can be no doubt of a direct connection between New Zealand and Taiwan, more than six thousand miles away. The only elements lacking in the Taiwan example are the peculiar surface designs.

If we had asked the Maori to provide a clue to their origin, they could not have left us a better indication than in the intricate, swirling patterns and the extended tongue motifs of their ornament. The latter motif, as the art historian Alfred Salmony recently showed, originated in the West before 1000 B.C. Probably entering China along with the Bronze Age invaders, the long-tongue motif made its earliest documented Eastern appearance in the Yangtze Valley among the Ch'u peoples roughly four centuries before Christ. Wooden protective figures, essentially postlike Megalithic conceptions, display this feature and even such telling details as circles on the tongues and a slight rolling-up at the tip (Plate 98). This elongated curling tongue symbolized the fertility and life-giving power of the bearer. The extended tongue also survives in protective figures from Borneo, a region permeated with Late Chou influences. Maori ornament, with all its lyrical detail, probably drew its inspiration from Chinese sources. The doorway of a Han tomb model (of slightly later date than the Late Chou) beautifully illustrates the whirling spiral design commonly seen in Maori sculptured art (Plate 134).

Most of the important Maori art forms pay implicit homage to Chinese forerunners. Jade pendants known as *hei tiki* ornamented the breast of every Maori of high degree. This refractory material, a medium popular in China, is one of extraordinary hardness; a figure would take months in grinding. Nevertheless, in spite of all the difficulties involved, the Maori mined and worked jade energetically. In function, the pendants assisted in concentrating ancestral power for the protection and guidance of the wearer. Their bladelike shape reflects a ritualistic attitude toward tools and technology characteristic of Maori religion. Clubs, spears, canoe bailers, adzes, digging sticks, knives, paddles, and other implements also acquired a surface enrichment beyond mere physical requirements. This suggests that the Maori regarded his tools as the embodiment of ancestral power and technical accomplishment. Similar concepts existed among the ancient Chinese—as may be seen, for example, in a phallic stone-ax blade which was equated with the written character for "ancestor."

Other Maori subjects that once seemed bewildering now begin to make some sense. On the underside of the rafters of the council house there were painted designs which have virtually no parallels in New Zealand art. But their billowing shapes and complex linear rhythms tally exactly with the cloud motifs so frequent in Late Chou and Han painting and lacquer ware. Here the Maori usage may even help in reconstructing the form of the lost architecture of China. For if the Maori took over the motif from early Chinese ancestral shrines — as seems likely — the painted cloud motif may have existed under the roof in China also. The pattern would then perhaps signify the celestial part of the symbolic heavenly house where the divine spirits dwelt. Although present-day Maori no longer regard the council house with great awe, they still observe food taboos with relation to this special building.

Another long-standing Maori controversy is the problem of the *manaia*. These creatures usually appear in lintel carvings, flanking a central ancestor figure. One group of writers interprets the *manaia* as being stylized bird forms; others regard them merely as human figures seen in profile. Comparison with other Late Chou-influenced carvings from the Sepik River area of New Guinea (Plate 72) indicates that the *manaia* who rise up on either side of the central figure are bird-monsters. Moreover, as can be easily shown, the theme stems ultimately from that of the Ancient Near Eastern hero Gilgamesh, who controls beasts on either side of him.

Some Maori art forms predate Late Chou influence. The council house with its deep, mouthlike, inviting porch reminds us of Naga houses built in the Megalithic tradition. Round stumpy legs, squat wide-stanced figures, and spiraling ornaments at the joints resemble almost exactly those in the twenty-five-hundred-year-old Late Jomon pottery figurines of Japan (Plate

114). Megalithic and Jomon influence converge in Taiwan. But the ambiguity and elegance of the New Zealand linear arabesques point up emphatically the Late Chou as the major source. Late Chou influence now survives mainly in the art of Borneo, Sumatra, the Sepik, and the Maori.

Indo-Austronesian

The last great migration waves, dating after the beginning of our era, introduced Indian concepts into various parts of the Pacific. Initial stimulus for the movement came from the trade and the cultural contacts developing between India and Southeast Asia at this time. Ultimately such exchanges culminated in the building of Angkor Wat in Cambodia and of the Hindu monuments of Java. But Indian influence penetrated in a less obvious form throughout Indonesia and into many parts of Polynesia and Melanesia. Indo-Austronesian art in such instances usually modified and enriched the older traditions, but lacking the support of full-fledged Indian religion it could not supplant them completely. Free-standing statuesque figures in the round (often provided with their own bases), and a smooth glossy surface treatment as well as sophisticated, meaningful postures and gestures, are typical of Indo-Austronesian style. Careful rendering of anatomy, a preference for hard wood, and an avoidance of glaring colors suggest the essentially aristocratic flavor of this art. One area where Indo-Austronesian style is dominant is the island of Raro-

74 and 75 *Tangaroa, supreme god of Polynesia, creating the other gods. (Far left) Rarotonga, Cook Islands. H.27"; (left) Rurutu, Austral Islands. H. 44" (British Museum, London).*

76 *Fishermen's god figure put in canoe prow. Rarotonga, Cook Islands, Polynesia. H. 16$\frac{1}{2}$" (Sainsbury Collection, London).*

tonga in the Cook group of central Polynesia.

Christian missionaries were among the first Europeans to visit Rarotonga. They marveled at the beauty of its high mountains, rocky eminences, and luxuriant valleys, while lamenting the heathen customs of the people. The Rarotongans lived in villages scattered around the island and obtained food by fishing and gathering fruit, root crops, and coconuts. Special rites helped to placate the spirits responsible for food supply. Each clan had its own patron deity. At the head of the leading clan was the paramount chief or king, who ruled the entire island. Members of the king's clan formed a sort of aristocracy while others remained in fixed position on the social ladder according to a strict hierarchy. All the Rarotongans, however, worshiped the patron deity of the king's clan, whose image stood in national shrines all over the island as well as in the king's sacred compound. Upon converting the Rarotongans to Christianity, the missionaries burned most of these carvings.

Perhaps the finest of all surviving Cook Island carvings is a great male image with attached figures, carved out of a single block of almost impenetrable ironwood (Plate 74). Every element of this figure is depicted with absolute clarity and finality. The upper torso and especially the head are rigidly stylized. The eyebrows, lids, and bulging eyeballs stand out from one another; these in turn are

77 *The monkey prince Hanuman. Probably used for sorcery. Tahiti, Polynesia. H. 12^1|$_4$" (Pitt Rivers Museum, Oxford University).*

echoed as a group in the evenly spaced planes marking the lips and tongue. Distinct organic shapes define the nostril wings, and a sharp vertical ridge bisects the face into two lateral planes. Strangely, in the lower half of the body less attention has been paid to structure than to the semblance of softness and elasticity in the visceral parts. An odd zigzag design ornaments the feet. A total of seven small images appear on the chest and arms.

According to a modern museum label on its back, the magnificent Rarotonga figure represents "Te Rongo and His Three Sons." Although it has been frequently reprinted, this information seems to be wrong. Not only is Te Rongo unknown in Rarotonga, but also, since there are seven and not three little figures, the attribution must be incorrect. However, the placement of these amusing miniature forms on the chest and arms of the great effigy does bring to mind similarly conceived demigods depicted on a unique and wonderful image from Rurutu in the nearby Austral Islands (Plate 75). This second specimen is positively identified as Tangaroa, supreme god of Polynesia, and creator of the other deities.

Confirmation that the Cook image does, in fact depict Tangaroa comes when we compare it with other Rarotongan staff carvings known as national gods. Each god-staff averages about twelve feet in length and consists of a long, thin pole of ironwood carved with

78   The monkey prince Hanuman with movable arms. Philippines. H. 20¹⁄₄" (British Museum, London).

147

an elaborate figure at one end and smaller figures and a phallus at the other. Originally these impressive objects were decked with sacred feathers and a shell necklace containing the "soul" of the image; they were then wrapped in literally hundreds of yards of ceremonial bark cloth until a roll several feet thick had been prepared. Of their meaning, little is known, except that they were kept in the great *marae* or ceremonial area and they represented Tangaroa. The national god-staffs resemble the great free-standing figure so closely as to confirm a close connection between the two designs.

The importance of the Tangaroa figure resides partly in its significance for the Cook islanders and partly in its value as a historical document. According to the Rarotongans, before Tangaroa organized the world, all was mere chaos. The idea of crisis and generative force, therefore, dominate the concept of this deity. He is depicted at the cataclysmic moment most expressive of his nature—that is, in the very act of procreating the other gods out of himself. Showing the supreme god in this way, the artist emphasizes the Polynesian idea of phallic creative energy.

As compared with other Cook figures, the great Tangaroa holds a unique historical position. The idea of carving small forms shown emerging from a god belongs to a highly sophisticated cosmological tradition. Stu-

79 *The monkey prince Hanuman in gesture of obeisance. Southern India. Bronze. H. 23³/₄"* *(Government Museum, Madras).*

dents of Polynesian religion have long thought that the cult of Tangaroa was introduced into central Polynesia by aristocratic invaders, eclipsing earlier deities such as Tu, the war god, Tane, the patron of craftsmen, and Rongo, the master of rain and agriculture. The Tangaroa people, evidently great sailors and navigators, to describe their idea of society used the simile of a ship: the hull, for them, represented the people and the land; the chief was the mast; owners of land were the rigging, and the nobility were equated with the outrigger. In addition to sea lore and ritual, the Tangaroa people brought with them a complete system of cosmology and strict social divisions. Everything about this group points in the direction of the peoples of caste-ridden India.

To gauge the extent and impact of Tangaroan (Indo-Austronesian) influence in the Cook Islands, we need only compare the previously mentioned ironwood effigy with other Rarotongan carvings in softer wood (Plate 76); these represent the god of fishermen. Of moderate size, they were placed, according to the missionary John Williams, "upon the fore part of every fishing canoe; and when the natives were going on a fishing expedition, prior to setting off they invariably presented offerings to the god and invoked him to grant them success." Although smaller and more dumpy in proportion, these figures bear a striking resemblance to the aristocratic Tangaroa. That there is an underlying connection seems certain, since the Polynesian craftsman never would have permitted one deity to be confused with another. Apparently the fisherman's god is no other than an earlier and less aggrandized version of the same sea god—Tangaroa! Now the question follows: how do we know this god-figure is older and, if so, what new features have been introduced in the more sophisticated version?

Looking closely at the fisherman's god, its Sino-Austronesian features become evident. The stumpy legs, pot belly, the hands-on-abdomen pose, and the treatment of the tongue resembles the Sino-Austronesian style of the Marquesas. The great Tangaroa figure shows by comparison a sovereign command of medium and amazing technical facility. The elongation of the forms and the almost unbelievable refinement of surface confer upon this image a wonderful quality of elegance. The expression of self-assurance in the great Tangaroa is truly exalted.

Where, then, did the Tangaroa people get their patterns of imagery? Before we can begin to answer this question, we need to know more about other areas where Tangaroa worshipers have left visible traces of their beliefs. Samoa, one of their strongholds, has little relevance in this instance because the Samoans apparently never had a strong sculptural tradition. But the Rurutu islanders of the Austral group, as we have seen, venerated Tangaroa above all other gods. They depicted the latter as tiny beings all over his body, even representing his features as other small figures. But we know almost nothing of early Austral culture, unfortunately, as missionary influence uprooted the old customs without leaving a record of them. Still, Austral art shows strong affinities with Rarotonga and especially with the Society Islands to the north. It is in fact to Tahiti, the hub of the Society group, that we must turn. Here the Tangaroans had a stranglehold on the older culture of Polynesia.

Tahiti

The golden haze that enshrouds Tahiti bedazzled even the earliest European voyagers to this fabulous island. In 1768, the French captain, L. A. de Bougainville, the second Westerner to visit Tahiti, named it *La nouvelle Cythère*. Cythera signified to him, as to the painter Watteau, a magic, misty land of delight, an idyllic world of amorous pleasure and complete social harmony. Tahiti deserved this name, for in no other place in the world save eighteenth-century France were the arts of living and loving so ardently cultivated.

The Tahitians, a small-boned, handsome people, long ago accommodated their social and religious practices to their rather easygoing aristocratic system. The king and priests ruled mostly on questions of national importance such as war, harvest ceremonies, and funeral and memorial rites for important dead chiefs. Otherwise the majority of art forms that were developed in Tahiti, such as feather headgear, elaborate fly whisks, fans, scented and painted bark cloth, and heavily decorated war canoes, were insignia of rank or emblems of privilege and swank.

Carved figures acquired different meanings in Tahiti. Representations of the great war deity Oro—simple clublike pieces of wood covered with wickerwork—probably symbolize the god in his armor. Certain canoe carvings closely parallel the fisherman's gods of Rarotonga; others were household gods. Yet many Tahitian figures apparently served a darker purpose—sorcery. Each magician would call upon his familiar spirit to enter into the image carved in its likeness; from there it would communicate with the sorcerer-priest. Despite some similarities with the fisherman's god of Rarotonga, these figures display many formal variations, closely resembling those of the small images emerging from the Austral Tangaroa. Each one probably represented a unique magical being. One Tahitian image (Plate 77) brought back by Captain Cook particulary compels our closest attention. Set against art styles discussed heretofore, it shows several peculiarities. First of all, it has a distinct personality. One hand is raised to the chin. The ears are long and pressed close to the head, which is covered by a thick form like a cap. The eyes are concealed beneath a beetling heavy brow. The broad-based nose has prominent open nostrils. The upper lip protrudes considerably, whereas the mouth, normally set high in Tahitian figures, is here placed lower on the face. The left arm, lower body, and legs compare closely with Indo-Austronesian Polynesian forms. If a single adjective were needed to describe this figure, "ape-like" or "simian" would probably suffice. Although there are no monkeys in Polynesia, the term is nonetheless accurate

The source of the concept of this remarkable figure, like the origins of the Tangaroa people, must be sought in the vicinity of the Asian mainland. Traveling back through Micronesia, almost the first large islands we come to are the Philippines. And in this area we also find our first major link in the Indo-Austronesian chain.

From the Philippines come several types of figures, one of which exhibits strong affinities with our Tahitian figure. Carved of a highly polished dark wood, the Philippine image (Plate 78) crouches slightly on its integral base. The right arm with its upward-pointing fingers is hinged at the shoulder and can readily be moved. The deep-set eyes, massive nose, and low, almost chinless mouth, dominate the face. As in the Tahitian and Rarotonga carvings, a frontal ridge bisects the head which is covered by a small cap. The long ear shapes cling closely to the skull. Three features deserve special attention: the first is the distinctly ape-like appearance of the figure; the second is the stylized and cubistic treatment of the upper part of the body; and, third, the curious development of the breasts. These features suggest not only a close affinity with Polynesia, where similiar traits can be observed, but also point in the opposite direction toward India.

The arms of the Philippine figure are attached separately and hence movable. If we raise the figure's right hand to its chin, as the direction of

the fingers indicates we should, the image suddenly becomes intelligible. It is Hanuman, the monkey prince, who plays such an important part in the *Ramayana*, the great Indian love epic introduced into Indonesia in the first millennium A.D. Comparison with bronzes and articulated puppets depicting Hanuman reveals numerous points of agreement (Plate 79). Hanuman stands with slightly flexed legs on a circular base. As in most Indian sculpture, the breasts are prominent. Long, close-set ears and headband complete the resemblance. Hanuman's simian features are clearly reproduced in the Tahitian figure. Isolated as the evidence is, this firm connection is sufficient basis for linking the Tangaroa people and the Indo-Austronesia tradition ultimately to Indian influence, transmitted by way of eastern Indonesia.

The impact of Indian culture on eastern Indonesia was mild, we know, compared with that affecting Java and Sumatra. In certain parts of the Philippines, for example, pagan tribes took over Indian script, but only to write love poems. The use of writing was limited in this odd way because Sanskrit was the language of the *Ramayana* love story. The pagans never passed beyond this early stage, while western Indonesians, like the Indians themselves, developed script into a vehicle of

80 *(Above) Funerary mask. Timur Batak, Sumatra. Wood with horsehair. H. 21¹⁄₄″ (National Ethnological Museum, Leiden).*

81 *Ancestor figure with four arms. Nias, Indonesia. H. 29¹⁄₂″ (Royal Tropical Museum, Amsterdam).*

commerce and communication. In similar fashion, high-culture influence tinctured but did not saturate Indo-Austronesian culture. Nevertheless, in their concept of a supreme god—though Tangaroa rather than Brahma, Vishnu, or Siva—the Polynesians owe an enormous debt to Indian theology.

We have at last come to the end of our survey of the major waves of culture and influence that spread over the Pacific. We have seen how the Ancient Australian, Old Papuan, Megalithic, Aquatic, Sino-Austronesian, Dongson, Late Chou, and Indo-Austronesian levels succeeded one another and blended. It remains for us to examine some of these styles in the intermediate areas from which their influence reached into other parts of the Pacific. Three regions immediately suggest themselves: southern Indonesia, eastern Indonesia, and Micronesia. In the first, Indo-Austronesian style predominates; in the second, Dongson influence is strong; in the third, Sino-Austronesian and other currents mingle. As it happens, these areas also constitute the three possible steppingstones to the widely spaced islands of Melanesia and Polynesia.

South Indonesia

In shape, Indonesia resembles a fan, with Luzon in the Philippines forming the grip, and the southern islands from Sumatra through the Sunda chain to Aru the flaring blades. This southern fringe looks as though it had been drawn on the globe with an inky brush. Islands like Sumatra and Java are large and densely populated; as one proceeds outward, the land areas get smaller and smaller until they finally peter out just short of New Guinea. The plant and animal life of this region, distinctly Asiatic in origin, includes rhinoceros, water buffalo, and tiger. In New Guinea and the islands beyond, on the other hand, we find a limited flora and fauna more akin to the life forms of Australia than to those of the Asian mainland.

The people of southern Indonesia have lived mainly by agriculture. Authority is vested in chiefs and village priests, and religious life is focused on control of spirits and veneration of ancestors. Most of these peoples had contacts with Indian art and custom. Some, like the Javanese and Balinese, have absorbed so much of Indian culture they can scarcely be considered primitive; others took only the externals offered by the new religions while retaining all of their own basic beliefs and values. We will look at some of

153

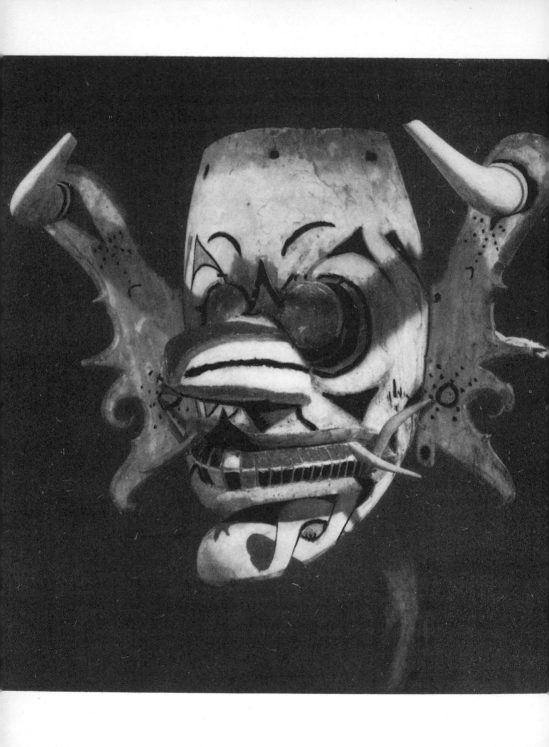

the latter, choosing representative examples from the vast number of island cultures in the area.

Nias

The eighty-mile-long island of Nias lies off the west coast of Sumatra. Reef-fringed and harborless, Nias perpetuates a Megalithic culture, strongly modified by Dongson tradition and overlaid with superficial Indian influences. As among the Naga, aggressive chiefs ruled the villages, engaged in warfare, and commemorated their success with feasts and various monuments. The simplest monuments were no more than carved posts with heads at the top. The two pronglike projections extending up from the head testify to the Megalithic origins of the type. These imitate the wooden fork symbolic of buffalo sacrifice, commonly represented also in Naga art.

But other Nias carvings imply a more sophisticated origin. Included are ingenious ancestor figures, some with as many as four arms (Plate 81). These multiple limbs are distinctly Indian elements, as everyone knows, but are here introduced with little knowledge of their underlying religious meaning. Instead, the Nias ancestor figure continued to serve as the traditional resting place for the soul of the departed. Strictly frontal in treatment and often squatting or seated, these effigies were carved by professional sculptors at the time of a person's death. The more important the person had been, the larger and more elaborate his image. According to Nias belief, the soul migrated from the body in the form of a spider. Thus, when the priest captured one of these little creatures at the grave and placed it on the carving, the soul was successfully transferred to the figure, and the carving was then placed in a special household shrine. On important occasions, such as a marriage or the naming of a child, family members advised the ancestors of the event, addressing the carvings directly. They also consulted or petitioned the ancestors in times of crisis and presented them with delicacies, particularly bits of pork.

Nias carvings often beguile us with the artist's charming attitude toward

82   Dance mask. Borneo. Painted wood with glass eyes. H. 12" (American Museum of Natural History, New York).

scale. Although frequently little more than a few inches high, the figures seem to strive manfully for monumentality. But unlike Polynesian figures, which they in some ways resemble, Nias images also stress attributes of rank and details of costume. A necklace or ring around the neck signified courage or bravery; a beard symbolized the authority of old age; objects held in the hands similarly denoted status or achievement. Certain stylistic details—the treatment of the shinbone and kneecap—indicate a close relationship with the Dongson tradition. If this link is valid we can now better understand certain Nias ideas at one time believed to be the result of Indian influence. Nias thinking divided the cosmos into an upper and an underworld; everything belonged to one sphere or another. The right hand, as in so many societies, was esteemed and associated with the upper world and with the nobility. The rendering of ornaments only on the right side is intended to point to the wearer as a member of the aristocracy of Nias. These ideas probably stem directly from Bronze Age sources.

Nias figures often combine the sacrificial fork of the Megalithic style with Dongson elements, including pointed crests and flamelike topknots. Scroll and leaf patterns add graceful foliate rhythms to the surfaces. Very possibly such decoration represented the Tree of

83-86 Memorial post figures representing various style levels from Megalithic to Dongson and Indian. South West Islands, Indonesia. (National Ethnological Museum, Leiden).

Life, a Nias symbol of birth and regeneration. Branches of this tree supposedly were used in memorial ceremonies where they were said to form necklaces for the nobility.

Wooden masks had only a minor role as a distinct form in Nias art. Although still preserving the heart-shaped face of the Megalithic style, these stilted symmetrical objects give only a faint suggestion of the importance of wooden masks in southern Indonesia and related Indo-Austronesian areas. Unknown in Polynesia, the wooden mask does occur sporadically all the way from the Nicobars in the extreme western edge of Indonesia to the southeastern terminus of Melanesia — New Caledonia. The Nias mask is intimately linked with the ancestors. When a great priest wore the mask, the people recognized in its attributes a new identity through whom contact could be made with the spirit world. By donning the proper guise, the priest temporarily became an ancestor. The Nias mask is probably Indo-Austronesian in origin. The frontal ridge already seen in Polynesia, the long nose, eyebrows in relief, and the long pendant ear lobes all turn up again and again in the wooden mask tradition.

Our pursuit of this Indo-Austronesian style takes us next to nearby Sumatra.

Batak

By most standards, the Batak of Sumatra were hardly a primitive people; they had books used in divination rites, a democratic social system, massive stone carving, and complex architecture. But until the twentieth century they practiced cannibalism, mainly as vengeance for some alleged crime. Naturally, the religious customs of the Batak differed somewhat from one tribe to another. The Timur Batak alone produced wooden masks by means of which the villagers impersonated deceased, only sons (Plate 80). Often, during the rites, mothers kissed the masks. The Batak artist, in making the face carvings, paid careful attention to such features as the teeth shown in the open mouth; he attached real hair to the head and chin. That these masks were at one time used by a secret society, as one writer suggests, seems unlikely, since women touched them.

Masks resembling those of the Batak existed on Timor Island, at Geelvink Bay, and at McCluer Gulf in New Guinea, and further east. The naturalism and simplicity of color and detail in all of these examples indicate that they probably served as substitutes for the faces of the dead. Their public function further implies that the masks were not viewed as dangerous.

Multiple layers of influence enshroud other Batak art forms. Dongson burial customs survive in their bulky stone sarcophagi, though the attached figures are often Late Chou or Indo-Austronesian. Late Chou cloud patterns of the type seen in New Zealand were lavished on the Batak sacred house, and reverse spirals on powder horns and vessels hint of Dongson connections. But for sheer vivacity and shapeliness, no other Batak style could compete with that of the carved magic staffs owned by every important Batak sorcerer-priest. Superbly interlocked figures succeeded one another vertically on these staffs, which, being made of hard monochromatic wood, took a high, glossy polish. Although now modified, these carvings belong to a widespread tradition still extant in the Philippines and in Palau in Micronesia and ultimately probably linked to the totem poles of the Northwest Coast of North America. Like the Batak people themselves, these staff figures are characterized by a sort of languid ease that masks a complex and potentially violent nature.

Borneo

For all their legendary fierceness, the wild men of Borneo spent a surprising amount of their energies on artistic subtleties. Their art and life centered equally on commemoration of ancestors, repulsion of disease-causing evil spirits, initiation of the young, and agricultural rites. Toward these ends, gaudy face masks and monochromatic figure carvings in both grotesque and realistic form were used. Since Borneo is a very large island with a diversity of cultures, the styles of this region are not very homogeneous. Certain rather monstrous masks with bulging eyes, long beak noses, and prominent fangs were supposed to identify the wearer with an ancestral spirit (Plate 82). But probably the underlying aim of most Borneo masks was to achieve supernatural protection for the group in their efforts to repel evil spirits. The function of figure carvings agrees almost entirely with this aim.

A few Borneo masks suggest an older basis of belief. Those depicting animals, usually with long snouts, vaguely resemble Aquatic masks of the sort used in Torres Straits. Employed in hunting pantomimes during har-

vest rites, these snout masks in function may well go back to pre-agricultural days. In style, most Borneo masks have a contrast between the roughness and bluntness of their expression and the intricacy of their surface decoration. This conflict must have a source, and a clue may come from certain wooden protective figures, with long protruding tongues, set up to guard the entrances to villages. This is a Late Chou form also seen among the Maori.

Late Chou influence generated in Borneo perhaps the finest calligraphic lines to be seen in the Pacific. That Sino-Austronesian, Megalithic, and Dongson contributions underlie superficial Indian influence is also apparent. But the bulk of Borneo art, despite its Indo-Austronesian wooden-mask tradition, traces its descent from Late Chou contact with the island. Interestingly, this indicates that the use of masks to instruct the youth in evoking protective supernatural beings may have been earlier than the function of commemorating actual ancestors. For example, while there were no true wooden masks in Polynesia, the Maori gable mask, a pre-Indian form, protected the inhabitants of the council house. From the stationary guardian

87   (Facing) Mask representing supernatural being. Sulka, New Britain. Cane framework covered with pith, carved wooden features, cassowary feathers, and leaves. H. 32" (Übersee Museum, Bremen).

88   Coastal Sepik piggyback figures carved as child's toy. New Guinea. H. 15¹/₄" (Pitt Rivers Museum, Oxford University).

89 (Left) Mask worn
fertility cult rites. Tami,
Guinea. H. 15" (Britis
Museum, London).

90 (Right) Mask wor
celebrate harvest of wild p
Saibai, Northern Torres
Straits. Wild-plum wood
with shell, grass, and fibe
28¹/₂" (Royal Scottish
Museum, Edinburgh).

face mask of Chinese origin, it is but a step, then, to the spirit-revealing mask worn by the Indo-Austronesians. The link between these two is provided by the protruding tongue and will become clearer as we move eastward.

Leti

The little islands of the lesser Sunda group and those to the east, including Timor, Leti, Babar, Damar, Tanimbar, Kei, and Aru, all shared a sort of secondhand Indian culture. Otherwise, life ran in the typical Indonesian pattern. Rice was planted, and spirits were appeased and ancestors invoked. This idyllic way of life has given rise to a mild-mannered, almost introverted art typified by light-brown ancestor figures carved in a soft but close-grained wood. Conspicuous features of Leti style include the compact posture of the body, the absence of relief on the figure (though the bases were liberally decorated), and the cool, restrained treatment of the form. Designed, like

91 (Facing) Funerary mask. Mer, Eastern Torres Straits. Turtle shell with casso-wary feathers and sea shells. H. 16" (Museum für Völkerkunde, Vienna).

92 Mask used in mortuary rites. New Ireland, Melanesia. Painted wood and fiber. H. 17" (Museum für Völkerkunde, Hamburg).

93 Spirit boat with figures representing deceased ancestors, used in funeral rites. New Ireland. L. 19' 6" (Lindenmuseum, Stuttgart).

Nias figures, to serve as a container for the ancestral spirit, the Leti image deliberately inhibits movement, conforming to the shape of the block, with self-embracing or self-supporting gestures that immobilize the limbs. From the aloof, frigid expression of the face, too, Leti figures seem passive and completely self-involved. The posture, with knees drawn up and hands under the chin, may illustrate the flexed burial position probably introduced into Indonesia by the Dongson culture.

The largest Leti figures, representing village ancestors, were set up publicly, and offerings of food were placed in a bowl before them. The post-like concept gives a clear indication of a Megalithic origin (Plates 83, 84,

85 and 86); the same is true of the Naga-like heart-shaped treatment of the face. But the violence of the Megalithic forms yields under Dongson and Indian influence to a new serenity of feeling and relaxation in posture and gesture. Leti female figures seated tailor-fashion with a bowl in their laps have an interesting prototype in images of Parvati, the wife of the great Indian god Siva. Seated cross-legged in her role as the rice goddess, Parvati accepts gifts of the grain bestowed by her people. The custom of returning a portion of the crop to the rice spirits was already widespread among the primitives of Indonesia. Though taking over a deity, decorative designs and sculptural techniques from a higher culture, the people of Leti had no

difficulty in amalgamating Indian elements with their own long-standing traditions of older Megalithic and Dongson origin.

Leti carvers made only one kind of mask. This consisted of a wooden snoutlike animal form decorated with tusks of shell and large shell eyes having black pupils. Crowned with curving shell ornaments and fringed with shell beads, this mask was worn in religious ceremonies. Its bizarre forms bear considerable resemblance to the Aquatic crocodile masks of the western Torres Straits Islands. In nearby Babar island, similar masks represented boars, but nothing is known of their function.

We have now reached the threshold of Melanesia in our study of the spread of Indo-Austronesian influence.

Melanesia

More than any other area in the Pacific, Melanesia is a region of turbulence and violence. Its large and small islands formed around volcanoes, some of them still erupting, which created a rugged natural environment of pestilential swamps, high razor-backed ridges, and deep valleys. The Negroid peoples who

94   (Facing) Ancestor figure of the Uli type derived from the Garuda. New Ireland. H. 63" (Museum für Völkerkunde, Hamburg).

95   Garuda figure, a mythological bird-like creature. Thailand. H. 36" (Museum für Völkerkunde, Berlin).

inhabit this area gain their living largely through fishing and gardening, the principal foods being sago, yams, and taro. The maritime Melanesians succeeded the older Papuan populations on the northern coasts of New Guinea and in the remaining islands. They introduced concepts of chieftainship and competition. Spirit placation and ancestor veneration already existed in the Old Papuan culture, so the newer Melanesian elements simply added further intensity to ceremonial practices. A profusion of materials, ranging from seeds, shells, and fur to cane, cat's-eyes, and cobwebs, enriched the bizarre Melanesian carved wood images and masks. Progressive variations of theme and function make an exciting, if bewildering, panorama of design. Skipping over Geelvink Bay and the Sarmi area, to which we will return later, we stop at the coastal Sepik area, the first region in Melanesia important for the wooden mask tradition.

Coastal Sepik

Along the northeast coast of New Guinea and on the offshore islands within a hundred miles of the mouth of the Sepik there existed an aggressive homogeneous culture which produced monochromatic reddish masks of great beauty and visual impact. Carved with stone tools, these masks usually combine human features with bird or animal elements. Because of their elongation and ambiguous animal forms, coastal Sepik masks often seem especially demonic or terrifying. Yet the frequency of details taken from life—the pierced nasal septum, grass ear ornaments, and the fleshiness of the nose—indicate the artist's genuine interest in depicting the human face. The vertical frontal ridge relates these masks to Indo-Austronesian tradition.

Coastal Sepik masks like most Sepik carvings celebrated the appearance in the men's house of spirits or ancestors associated with various important cults. Some served in public harvest and initiation rites; others depicted the semi-supernatural founders of clans in ceremonies of a more secret nature. Unfortunately, not a great deal is known about these esoteric ceremonies, for until recently the uninitiated—women, children, and outsiders—were rigidly excluded from the most important of them. Despite this hostility, we know that the display of totemic emblems was of major significance. But difficulty in classification arises because several clans employed identical symbols, some regarding them as sacred and stressing one interpretation, whereas other clans might view the same design differently and look upon it as public and profane. In the face of such confusion, which is intensified (1) by the Sepik native's custom of trading complete dance-mask-song complexes up and down the coast, and (2) by our lack of good ethnological information, we must rely mainly on the visual evidence.

The figures of the coastal Sepik very often appear to be wearing masks. In a few examples, in fact, the rounded back of the head contrasts with the flat sharp-beaked treatment of the face. The local belief that the soul of the departed was escorted by or even migrated in the form of a bird helps to explain this peculiarity. Sepik figures have carved birds on their heads or birdlike forms on the face. Similar artistic and religious ideas existed in ancient China.

We will return to these figures when we discuss Middle Sepik art. It is enough now to mention that the coastal style is, comparatively speaking, nonextravagant. Intensity and aggressiveness exist here, but the use of color is restrained, and the forms are relatively subdued. Indo-Austronesian influence probably collided with Old Papuan traits in the coastal area. Without destroying Papuan exuberance, the result was a taming of the older style.

Tami

In the area between Astrolabe Bay and Tami Island in the Huon Gulf, the Indo-Austronesian wooden mask tradition achieved its Melanesian climax. Not entirely homogeneous, this area enjoyed a measure of unity through the use of very large trading canoes and the sharing of similar mythologies, religions, and social customs. In Tami, leaders of clans occupied positions of authority, but the right to make heraldic designs, masks, and other privileges remained the property of the clan. Several kinds of masks were made in Tami. A bark-cloth type known as *tago* was employed in spirit-visitation rites every ten years or so; it probably came to Tami from a Papuan area in New Britain through intermarriage. On New Guinea's mainland, wooden masks, quite stiff and angular in their conception but sharing realistic details such as tongues, teeth, eyebrows, and pendant ear lobes, clearly belong to the Indo-Austronesian tradition. Worn in secret-society rites, they depicted legendary ancestors. As in other Melanesian areas where Indo-

Austronesian art held sway, red, black, and white colors predominated.

Figures carved in Tami and the related area of Astrolabe Bay probably also represented mythological forebears. Several of these wooden hero figures were used as supports for the *lum*, or men's clubhouse, holding the floor on their bulletlike heads or stocky shoulders. The massive, blocky conception of these figures suggests the static, no-nonsense quality of Tami social organization. Yet except for the placement of the head low down between the shoulders, the figures give not the slightest visual suggestion of load-bearing or support. Instead, the arms and legs often seem to bend or contract with a remarkable rubbery appearance. The treatment of the legs in Tami house-support figures resembles the bullet-headed, rubber-legged Cook Islands image of Tangaroa.

Interestingly the aforementioned house was unique among Melanesian men's houses in being plank-built and was probably constructed originally of old canoe boards. The symmetrical confronting bird, fish, and marine-animal designs that adorned this structure and other carvings served to stamp the object with a clan's heraldic crest or coat of arms. Thereafter another clan could appropriate the design only through purchase. Besides offering visual proof of a rigid social stratification, these Tami family emblems suggest

96   Secret society mask worn to ward off typhoons. Mortlock Islands, Micronesia. H. 44" (Museum für Völkerkunde, Hamburg).

a totemic sea-oriented culture still mainly of Chinese rather than of Indian origin.

The wooden-mask style spread over a considerable area. Essentially a very early phase of the Indo-Austronesian tradition, it renders the tongue as a realistic ridge seen in the mouth between two rows of carefully indicated teeth. But the ears with their exact detail and pendant lobes supporting ear weights or earrings are typically Indian (Plate 89). Such details as the projecting beard or the cheekbones, eyebrows, and nostrils receive more or less emphasis depending on the artist's particular intentions.

A glance at other nearby areas reveals traces of Tami contact. For example, in the Admiralty Islands where no masks were used, figure carvings nevertheless show Tami-like faces. The styles of the Sulka of New Britain (Plate 87) and of the Duke of York and French Islands (Witu), although fundamentally adhering to the Old Papuan tradition, still offer in their wooden masks convincing demonstrations of contact with Tami or a related group. If we turn to the south side of New Guinea, to the area of Torres Straits again, we will see just how the Tami (early Indo-Austronesian) style differs from later levels.

Northern and Eastern Torres Straits

The masks of Saibai Island in northern Torres Straits have almost nothing in common with the turtle-shell masks from the western part of the Straits, discussed earlier. Not only are they carved in wood and lavishly adorned with red, white, and black pigments, they also differ tremendously in their stylized naturalism and realistic attachments. Superbly plastic constructions, the Saibai masks stress equally bold painted design and meticulous descriptive detail (Plate 90). These masks played a central part in the *mawa*, a ceremony which took place in September or October after the wild plum harvest. Dancers representing supernatural beings entered the village and spent the night walking about, stealing food and chasing people when they approached, and, finally, after much verbal abuse, they disappeared at dawn. It seems likely that these spirits were benevolent supernatural beings who were first rewarded with food for their help and then sent packing back to the spirit world where the people could be assured of their continuing assistance. As in Tami, each mask belonged to a certain clan. Stylistically, the Saibai masks also resemble those of Tami Island, having even acquired the confronting fish design that occurs frequently in the north.

Quite a different tradition pervaded the eastern Torres Straits islands. Although fabricated in the traditional turtle shell, the eastern mask is far more human in appearance (Plate 91) than is the Saibai type. Actual human hair, pegged in to represent the forelock and beard, adds to the naturalism of the concept. A frontal ridge appears in the forehead. Though not all eastern masks functioned identically, the most realistic type was used to represent the dead in funeral pantomimes. As in the Timur Batak mortuary dances, neither the masks nor the ceremonies were taboo to women; no one feared these objects. Considering their classic simplicity and clarity of form, there seems little reason to doubt that, despite the materials used, these eastern funerary masks belong to the later phases of the Indo-Austronesian wooden-mask tradition.

New Ireland

The climax of Indian influence in Melanesia occurred north of the Tami area in the long, well-wooded, and well-watered island now called New Ireland. The mask style used in this region is characteristic of the red-black-and-white early Indo-Austronesian tradition. But many of the carvings made for the *malanggan* or clan mortuary rites show, in their pierced forms and long tongues, a strong Late Chou influence. Held periodically in honor of the recent dead, *malanggan* rites required quantities of masks, figures, carved house boards, and other objects representing incredible combinations of human, animal, fish, bird, and symbolic forms (Plate 92). These objects were set up, often in special open sheds, or carried around the village and then allowed to rot. Only the most sacred art—the plaited, four-armed yellow sun disks—had to be ceremonially destroyed. Taboo to women, New Ireland *malanggan* carvings commemorated clan ancestors and totem animals (Plate 93). Initiation and circumcision rites conducted at the same time placed the boys under the protection of esteemed clan spirits. The fantastic, bizarre quality of New Ireland masks is the result of the artist's use of pierced elements and gauzy surface designs and of his love of exotic, fragile, or weird materials. Sponge, marine plant life, cockleburs, cat's-eyes, and seeds occur frequently. In his passionate search for new texture, one

New Ireland decorator even centered his designs around a discarded European scrubbing brush!

In the central New Ireland area, a rather different type of figure-carving evolved. Known as Uli, these robust, aggressive images were the subject of a powerful native cult (Plate 94). So sacred and mysterious were the Uli rites that women were never permitted to enter the secret-society house where the Uli figures were enshrined. Ulis did not represent specific ancestors so much as cosmic heroes identified with chieftainship and the moon cult. Upon completion of the month-long ceremonies, Uli figures were wrapped in bark cloth and kept for future use or occasionally sold. Noteworthy Uli features include upraised arms, breasts on otherwise extremely virile figures, and the frequent appearance of a second figure beneath the feet. The strangeness of this conception is heightened by the addition to the figure of winglike flanges under the arms, and of carved ornaments at the wrists, elbows, neck, waist, groin, knees, and ankles. Equally remarkable is the realization of sheer bulk in the carving. Its unprecedented substantiality and sense of weight are superbly expressed in the crouching posture. Despite its symmetrical and heraldic gesture, the magnificent Uli form bulges with masculine strength and energy.

Although the Uli carving stands out as one of the most sophisticated in Melanesia, no one has offered any reasons why this style should have developed as it did nor explained what the image means. But in this instance we have a very specific prototype for the Uli figures. Throughout Indonesia and the nearby mainland, a popular symbol is the Garuda, a birdlike creature given human form (Plate 95). Derived from Indian mythology, the Garuda is often shown with arms upraised and wings at his sides, trampling on another figure below. Every detail of the Garuda is reproduced on the Uli carvings including the knee-length trousers, ankle decorations, and phallic connection with the lower figure. So there is, in short, not the slightest question of the source of the Uli style and the statuesque conception of these figures. Both the theme and detail are ultimately of Indian origin

Mortlock

The only place in Micronesia or Polynesia that the Indo-Austronesian wooden-mask tradition penetrated was the Mortlock Islands (Plate 96).

175

Here the masks, probably introduced from Melanesia, played significant parts in the local culture. Some Mortlock masks decorated the king posts of spirit houses or boathouses. The majority, however, were employed by a sort of secret society. Members wore these masks when they danced on the beach to ward off typhoons and thereby insure a good breadfruit crop. The appeal to the powerful spirit embodied in the mask may be compared precisely to the masks of the people of Saibai in northern Torres Straits.

In style, the Mortlock mask presents an austere black-and-white appearance relieved only by traces of red around the mouth. Stark angular forms and geometric details predominate except in the occasional gull's-wing treatment of the eyebrows or mouth. The extremely unyielding character of the Mortlock mask suggests that the spirit invoked must have been regarded as a highly arbitrary being, one who ordained success or failure with the awesome finality of the dread typhoon. The mustache here, as on Borneo and other Indonesian masks, is a noteworthy detail and a sure mark of Indian inspiration.

We have now followed the wooden-mask tradition to its terminal points. In its earliest forms, such as the Borneo, Tami, Saibai, and Mortlock versions, it seems to be characteristically red, black, and white, to convey a stiff abstract feeling and to be concerned with spirit placation. Although Indo-Austronesian, the development of this early stylized type seems to follow close on the heels of the Late Chou tradition, in which the masks were not worn but buried in tombs or fixed, as in Mortlock, to gables as protective devices. The later wooden masks, as for instance those of the Batak and of the people of eastern Torres Straits, had realistic monochromatic representations of the deceased on whose behalf the ceremonies were conducted.

Having traced the movement of Indo-Austronesian art out from South Indonesia, we must now turn to the older layers of influence in the Pacific. As so happens, there are several islands in South Indonesia which preserve these earlier traditions, and beginning with these will help make our transition easier. One area of pre-Indian survival is the island of Nias, where, as we have seen, a Dongson figure-style exists today. A second region (not

97 *Figure on cap worn by women at harvest rites. Enggano, Indonesia. Wood covered with thin metal. H. 6³⁄₄″ (National Ethnological Museum, Leiden).*

far from Nias) is the island of Enggano lying about a hundred miles off the south coast of Sumatra.

Enggano

Until recently, Enggano has remained almost completely isolated from Indian and other advanced cultural influences. At the time of their first contact with Europeans, the Engganese were without agriculture, weaving, pottery, and metal; they were, in fact, the only people in Indonesia still living in the Stone Age. For their livelihood they fished and hunted, speared wild pigs, and gathered coconuts. Once indefatigable warriors, the Engganese are today so decimated by disease and alcohol that they have almost entirely disappeared. Only a fragmentary record of their extraordinary culture survives.

Enggano art is as remarkable as the culture that produced it. Lacking the restraint of other Indonesian arts, Enggano figure carving stresses bold planes and maximum scale. Bird carvings set atop houses and on canoes emphasize the use of free space. This highly vigorous style shares with that of the Indonesian figures a tendency towards the pure sculptural effects of monochromatic wood carving. But it is in Polynesia, as we have already observed, that the closest parallels to Enggano art lie, particularly in the Cook Islands (Plate 76). Wooden heads placed on the bow of new Enggano canoes at the launching ceremony are almost exactly like the Sino-Austronesian fisherman's gods which were used in much the same way. The Engganese head surely also represents a sea god. The frontal ridge of the Cook carvings, a result of Indo-Austronesian influence, apparently never reached Enggano. Like the Polynesians, the Engganese wore no wooden masks; but they made protective heads with rather short protruding tongues and very distinct teeth that are vaguely reminiscent of the Tami masks which were discussed earlier.

Another exciting form from this amazing island consisted of small wooden caps worn by women in periodic fertility rites (Plate 97). Some

98 Long-tongued protective figure biting a snake. Late Chou period. Ch'u tribes, Ch'ang-Sha, South China. Painted wood. H. ca. 4′ 5¹/₂″ (Peoples' Museum, Peking).

178

represented the sea god; others showed what are probably important ancestral beings. Characteristic of the latter is a special pose in which the elbows. of the figure rest on its drawn-up knees, with the hands placed under the chin. This posture, unknown in Polynesia but common in eastern Indonesia and parts of Melanesia, almost always signifies the protective ancestor. Definitely older than the wooden-mask styles, the knee-elbow-chin tradition probably stems from Dongson culture and hence predates Indian influence in the Pacific. This we see when we return to the southeastern Asian mainland — as we do when we consider the Moi.

Moi

In the interior highlands and jungles of southern Vietnam live other primitive people such as the Moi, who never experienced Indian influence. Pushed into the hinterland in recent times by Annamite invaders from the north, the Moi and other groups traditionally honored their dead and sought the protection of the ancestor for their crops by means of wooden figures carved in the knee-elbow-chin

99 (Facing) Carved head, possibly for canoe prow. Tanimbar, East Indonesia. H. 3¹/₂" (National Ethnological Museum, Leiden).

100 Household ancestor figure. Jobi Island, Geelvink Bay, New Guinea. Wood with cassowary feathers. H. 9" (Museum of Archaeology and Ethnology, Cambridge University).

101 *Image believed to be ancestor figure. Asmat, New Guinea. H. 16¹/₂″ (National Ethnological Museum, Leiden).*

pose. In some cases the ancestral skulls were placed directly on top of these post carvings. Associated with the knee-elbow-chin figures are towering spirit houses erected over the graves of chiefs. These are decorated with pictures of spirit boats and of the Tree of Life. The tree painting suggests immediately the Dongson culture of Lake Sentani. That the Dongson influence in fact carried the knee-elbow-chin tradition down through eastern Indonesia and out into Melanesia now seems probable.

Eastern Indonesia

In the culturally conservative areas of eastern Indonesia, such as the Philippines and Tanimbar, the knee-elbow-chin tradition lives on today. The Philippine examples, like those of Leti, look extremely moody. A few of these well-made ancestor figures are even shown covering their ears, though no one knows exactly why. The meditative quality of these figures contrasts sharply with the extremely warlike character of the people that used them.

The same distinction exists in the Celebes and the Moluccas between a bellicose culture and its delicately conceived, two-dimensional, geometric art. Colorful bark cloth, beautifully decorated with wide-spaced or dense compact designs, and richly ornamented clothing were among the artistic triumphs of this region. In wooden shields from the Moluccas, the artist approached his work in a similarly fastidious manner. Here, however, his taste veered toward black-and-white effects achieved by inlaying white shells or pieces of broken China dinner plates into the dark wood.

South of the Moluccas, in the lovely island of Tanimbar, artists developed a style of almost lyrical fluency. From this area forms penetrated far into New Guinea, perhaps even reaching Melville Island off the Australian coast. Tanimbar versions of the knee-elbow-chin tradition include a figure holding a bowl or other object under his chin, clasping his hands just under the chin, or standing, holding a turtle or shield in front of the body. With large, doe-eyed heads set atop slender bodies, Tanimbar ancestor figures have a feeling of daintiness that is utterly charming.

A handsome head, probably a canoe ornament, from Tanimbar gives several indications why this style seems so fertile (Plate 99). On the headband and ear pendant Indo-Austronesian patterns have been added to the Dongson and earlier traditions. Apparently several of the great styles blended together in this area, their combined form having spread east into nearby New Guinea.

Geelvink Bay

The culture drift from Indonesia which brought new figure styles and decorative patterns to New Guinea greatly enriched the otherwise backward arts of Geelvink Bay at the western end of the island. Ancestor images like those of Tanimbar served the Geelvink people as containers for souls of the deceased. An important adjunct to the family, these figures received respectful attention during the visits of chiefs and at other ceremonial occasions. Attached to many of these *korvar*, as they are called, is a mop of cassowary feathers which accurately reproduces the fuzzy shock of hair widely affected in the Geelvink area (Plate 100). There is something amusing about these earnest little carvings with their alert, quizzical expression and tense postures. Some continue in the knee-elbow-chin tradition; others hold shields and bowls or gently grasp small figures; occasionally, instead of a wooden head, we find the skull of the ancestor placed on top of a carved body or inserted into the back of the figure. The shield, which appears to augment the protective power of the ancestor, displays reverse curves of an almost baroque exuberance. Identical latticelike patterns of Dongson or Late Chou origin appear on neck rests, drums, canoe prows, and other Geelvink carvings. The resulting decorative scheme, in spite of diagonal design and dynamic symmetry, tends to be rather flat and finicky in execution.

A purer Indo-Austronesian style dominates to a very large extent the north coast of Dutch New Guinea, including the Sarmi and Humboldt Bay areas. Lake Sentani, as we have seen, harbors Dongson tradition only partially modified by Indo-Austronesian ideas.

Asmat

The vast swamp where the Asmat people make their home fills the entire arc of southwestern New Guinea from the coast a hundred miles inland or more to the mountains. Although theirs is artistically one of the richest areas in the primitive world, the Asmat remain even today almost unknown except for accounts by the few missionaries, traders, and government officials who have visited these violent, aggressive people. Despite appalling living conditions and constant dread of head-hunters, Asmat artists continue to create objects of enchanting beauty and consummate skill that steadfastly resist final interpretation. What little we know of the Asmat suggests that their greatest artistry was lavished on the *bis*, an enormous canoe-like memorial pole, and similar objects commemorating ancestors (Plate 101). Since these often preserve the knee-elbow-chin posture, Dongson influences unquestionably figure prominently in Asmat style.

The *bis* pole represents a tragedy. Enemy head-hunters having done their ghastly worst, the survivors agree to commemorate the victim with this carving depicting the deceased and other ancestors. The actual carving is performed by in-laws, though the blood relatives, of course, pay for the ceremony. *Bis* poles consist of several superposed human figures (the uppermost grasping a pierced projection) surmounting a miniature canoe-like vessel. Frequently there appear birds' heads—the hornbill, symbol of the beyond, helping identify the human figures as ancestors. *Bis* figures vary in treatment: some have an abstract quality; others with realistic scarifications have a more obviously natural reference. Piercing and openwork occur often, but the free-hand, unstructured character of the designs shows how the Asmat artists have adapted imported patterns to suit their own less rigid traditions. But the projecting flange of the *bis* seems to resemble the stern piece of canoes of the sort used in Tanimbar.

Asmat artists also carved magnificent shields, boldly decorated with stylized human figures and symbolic designs, handsome hourglass-shaped drums, ancestor figures, head-hunting trumpets, canoe ornaments, spears, paddles, and ornate utensils. Depicting all sorts of postures and gestures, the artists further enlivened their pieces with swooping shapes and an active interplay of line. Although comparatively rough in execution and limited in color to the sparing use of red ocher and white lime, Asmat carvings compare well with the finest and most vigorous of Melanesian styles.

To return to Asmat *bis* carvings: it appears that these poles represent ships of the dead. Their erection enabled the deceased to voyage to the far-off land of the ancestors. At this point we are suddenly reminded of the Dongson tradition which seems so important to Asmat art. The Dongson movement originated, as we know, in southern Russia some eight centuries before Christ; but not all of the people went east. Many of them migrated

102   Fishing canoes with houses in background. Botel Tobago, Taiwan. Photographed in 1955.

west and introduced Late Bronze Age culture into Scandinavia. A distinctive type of boat construction involving ribs and planks, once found in Russia, is now typical of Scandinavia. Incredible as it may seem, the Dongson migration probably brought this "Scandinavian" boat type all the way across central Asia to Vietnam and thence out into the Pacific. Boat experts agree that certain Pacific craft involve the same complex construction techniques as those used by Scandinavians in their forays and in ship burials such as at Oseberg and Gokstad. But skeptics will quite rightly ask whether a highly specialized technique of boat construction could possibly survive a migration over six thousand miles of dry Asiatic steppes. The conservatism of mankind when confronted with death supplies the affirmative answer. Once established, the custom of ship burial and idea of the spirit boat is honored scrupulously for religious reasons no matter what the physical obstacles. In the Ancient Near East, of course, vessels had funerary associations. The early Egyptians buried a great sun-boat beside their Pharoah and stocked it with food for his later use. But it was left to the bronze-using nomadic peoples of the north to inaugurate the tradition of burying chiefs and other heroes *inside* their vessels under mounds of earth. Rock engravings depicting soul voyages occur widely in Scandinavia, usually in association with so-called dance- or sun-hills, sites of fertility cults. Comparable representations of ships with the dead en route to the beyond have been found in the Ural mountains and on Dongson drums more than two thousand years old. Coincidence or not, in Lake Sentani the dead are taken on an actual symbolic voyage around the lake. And the Asmat *bis* pole, in design a spirit canoe, is erected on a mound in front of the men's house. The more amazing such connections are, the more we need proof of intermediate stages of linkage. Happily, such a midway mark exists, not far from the point where the Dongson migration first reached the Pacific.

Botel Tobago

A few miles south of the island of Taiwan lies the tiny islet of Botel Tobago, whose population shared many of the aggressive traits typical of the peoples of the main island. These people developed one of the most striking of the many spectacular boat types constructed in the Pacific (Plate 102). Not only are their boats important for their complex plank-built form; they are

103 Canoe prow figure used for protection against shoals. New Georgia, Solomons. Wood inlaid with mother-of-pearl. H. 6¹/₂″ (Museum für Völkerkunde, Basel).

equally remarkable in their beauty of shape and elegance of decoration. The artists who decorated the gunwales, forepeak and stern peak with dots, rosettes, and small orant figures preferred the stark contrast of black-and-white ornament to a more exuberant use of color. From the foremost of little figures there branches out a treelike pattern which carries the eye up into the higher portion of the enframed decorative field. Neatness and repetition of small inserted motifs sum up Botel Tobago decorative schemes.

Perhaps the most astounding feature of these craft is their technical dependence upon the "Scandinavian" tradition. James Hornell, the English boat expert, long ago established the existence of innumerable relationships in structure and detail. As in the Scandinavian type, the Botel

*104   Detail of canoe prow showing attachment of protective figure. Solomon Islands.
H. of figure 13" (British Museum, London).*

Tobago boat also has many oarsmen and a great steering sweep. Interestingly, too, these people also made miniature spirit boats with figures in
them. Details of decoration, moreover, such as the use of the frame and
contrasting monochromatic ornament, lend weight to Dongson associations.

    Bronze Age influence of this sort is equally apparent in Palau, in
Micronesia, where there is found fine shell inlay, wooden swords based on
lost metal prototypes, and plank-built canoes with stylized figures at prow
and stern. Here too we see the Tree of Life represented on the men's house
(Plate 108), and strange animal and human figures in the knee-elbow-chin
pose. In the Moluccas of eastern Indonesia, canoe types, construction details, and shell inlay stem also from this tradition. However, the most aston-

189

ishing yet clear-cut link with Botel Tobago and the "Scandinavian" Dongson canoe type is in the Solomons of Melanesia, where sailing skill long ago carried these Pacific vikings.

The Solomon Islands

During World War II, when Guadalcanal, Bougainville, and New Georgia were in the headlines almost daily, American soldiers had little time to look at their exotic surroundings. Rugged submerged mountains, their coastal grass plains rimmed with jungle and swamp, the Solomons are inhabited by a people with an extraordinary predilection for head-hunting and cannibalism. Yet actually, much of the hostility in Solomons life was dictated by the needs of an aggressive, yet highly sophisticated society ruled over by powerful chiefs. Head-hunting occupied a primary place because no step in life, from the birth of a child to the taking of a name, was considered valid without a bloody sacrifice. Belief in magic and sorcery, veneration of ancestors, and reverence for nonhuman spirits of sea and forest dominated the religion of the Solomons. For rites of various sorts, a few religious objects were manufactured. Yet social needs came first: the bulk of Solomon Islands art served as visible glorifications of the chiefs.

Head-hunting raiders in the Solomons undertook voyages of considerable range in their huge, specially decorated war canoes. Built of planks and having no outrigger, these remarkable canoes are very similar technically and artistically to Botel Tobago boats. At either end of the Solomons war canoe is a shell inlay attached to the high peaks, and at the waterline above the forefoot is fixed a large aggressive head ornamented with white pearl shell (Plate 103). These heads represent guardian beings who were supposed to detect shoals, and probably helped ferret out victims for the head-hunters. Carved with a smoothness and sophistication almost unparalleled in the Pacific, the Solomons head ornaments derive originally from full-length figures in the knee-elbow-chin position. A few of the latter still survive, but it is obvious that the focus of Solomons interest lies in the head. Surface decoration also plays an important part on the exterior of the canoe.

105   Carved head. Northern Solomons. H. 11 1/4" (Museum für Völkerkunde, Basel).

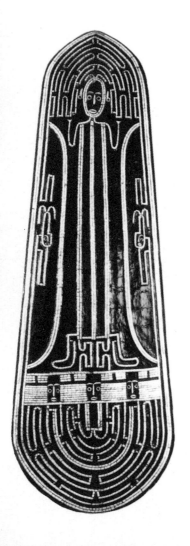

Frequently present are stylized orant figures, one of which, as in Botel Tobago, is connected to the top of the forepeak (Plate 104).

Other Solomons objects reveal an exquisite richness of design calculated to enhance the prestige of the owner. In Isabel, ordinary fighting shields of cane plaited over a bamboo frame, imported from other islands, were covered over with iridescent mother-of-pearl shell squares set in blackish vegetable paste (Plate 106). Presumably purely ceremonial objects, these shields have an almost Byzantine quality with their mosaic technique, stark abstract design, and extreme elongation of the central orant figure. A ritualistic attitude appears to freeze the forms within their symmetrical setting. These shields are admirable objects of elegance. Beautifully inlaid clubs or maces given in Malaita to men who had performed a homicide for their chiefs belong also to this black-and-white category. So strong was the "Scandinavian" Dongson influence in the central Solomons that most of the islands in the group adopted this refined, intricate style of ornament for all their creations.

Massim

Another area having Dongson origins, but where there is no plank-built boat, is the Mas-

106 Ceremonial shield used by chiefs. Isabel, Solomon Islands. Wicker shield covered with nut paste and shell mosaic. H. 36¹⁄₂" (Royal Scottish Museum, Edinburgh).

sim district, which includes the extreme eastern end of New Guinea and the islands offshore. Pivotal in Massim society was the position of the local chiefs—and this was literally demonstrated in the architectural organization of each village. The houses of commoners formed a large circle around the more important areas: the ancestral burial ground and dance site, the chief's hut, and his yam storehouse. The saddle-backed roof of this yam house and its curious ribbed construction suggest the possibility of an evolution from canoe construction.

Similar treatment of roofs in Micronesia and Indonesia among other Dongson-influenced people helps to explain the appearance of sacred buildings—saddle-roofed storehouses and men's houses—which were believed to embody the spiritual essence of the community. Scandinavian mast churches, so strikingly parallel to Batak men's houses, show a comparable dependence on boatbuilding technique.

As for yam houses, interest in yam cultivation in the Massim district is typical of Melanesia, but the high degree of interest is peculiar to this region. Massim languages abound in terms that discriminate between yam flavors or textures. Within his rather bland diet, the Massim man enjoyed nuances and subtle distinctions of taste. The same is true of his art. No masks and few figures were

107 Temple god. Massim, New Guinea. H. 17¹/₄" (University Museum, Manchester, England).

made in this region (Plate 107). Instead, the Massim artist turned his consummate skills to lavish canoe ornaments, mysterious painted shields, dance paddles, sword clubs, and prestige carvings such as neck rests, bowls, and lime spatulas. The use of the knee-elbow-chin, orant, and splayed positions and of Dongson reverse spirals underscores the fastidiousness and complexity of Massim artistry. Avoiding strict horizontals and verticals as much as possible, the artist preferred intricacy, asymmetry, and tireless proliferation. To the Western eye, Massim designs appear almost impossibly enmeshed with one another.

The interlocking character of this art may have originated in the Massim outlook on the world. Closely knit in a ceremonial trading circle that exchanged intrinsically worthless gifts, the Massim area was one of great homogeneity. Exchanging objects probably helped to remind these people of their functional interdependence upon one another. Thus the world, as the Massim man saw it, consisted of interacting elements, linearly connected and not easily detached. This, in turn, perfectly describes Massim art.

Austral Islands

Although the knee-elbow-chin tradition did not penetrate east of the Solomons, there is considerable evidence of "Scandinavian" Dongson influence in various parts of Polynesia. Certain canoe types from the Tuamotus and Tahiti exhibit the high forepeak and stern peak and plank-built construction typical of this tradition. In the Austral Islands, where crescent-shaped canoes sometimes attained great size, we also find paddles decorated with orant figures almost identical with those of Dongson. Evidently ceremonial steering sweeps, these paddles probably honored the great chief whose skill in practical navigation and knowledge of the stars set him apart. One stone image from Raivaevae in the Austral chain (Plate 109) is very similar to the paddle figures but very different from the Indo-Austronesian figure of Tangaroa from nearby Rurutu. Its characteristic kneecap and shin bone and its small pedestal, however, compare almost exactly with those seen in

108   Sacred men's house with Tree of Life on facade. Koror Island, Palau group, Micronesia. Photographed in 1949.

Dongson-influenced figures from Nias in Indonesia. Since the Dongson tradition plays a comparatively minor part elsewhere in Polynesia, it is time to return to the third and last great highway of the Pacific.

Micronesia

The low sandy atolls of Micronesia, including such groups as the Carolines, the Gilberts, and the Marianas lack the rich vegetation of the islands of Indonesia and Melanesia. The Micronesian, having to contend first with drought, then with a typhoon, learns to husband his soil and seed and to remain prepared for sudden emergency. His well-being depends very often upon his ability to sail from one group to another to replenish his food or water supply. As a result, he has acquired great skill in small-craft navigation and carefully conserves this knowledge. The Marshall Islanders, for instance, made rough, gridlike charts from slivers of wood to aid the navigator's memory. Such knowledge, being a gift of the past, could only be entrusted to chiefs or to other important members of the group. Also important for these maritime people are cult boats, wind charms, and sea gods, all of which appear in profusion.

Micronesian art, despite its reputation

109 Aroonoona, god figure that guarded the sacred precincts. Collected in 1826. Raivaevae, Austral Islands, Polynesia. Pinkish volcanic stone. H. 63" (*Pitt Rivers Museum, Oxford University*).

for simplicity, compares favorably with the most arresting Pacific styles. It is extraordinarily diverse and reflects complex levels of influence and a long history of contact with the outside world. Figure sculpture, which may go back to the second millennium B.C. in this area, gives good information on Micronesian prehistory. Once thought almost nonexistent in Micronesia, figures actually occur in every Micronesian group (Plate 110) with the probable exception of the Marshalls. We begin our study of this fascinating area in one of the eastern Carolines.

Nukuoro

Long before Archipenko, Brancusi, and Modigliani, the natives of Nukuoro had achieved a startlingly simplified interpretation of the human figure (Plate 112). Their own images, whether life-sized or smaller—ten to twenty inches tall—utilize the clean-cut, streamlined planes and geometric shapes so dear to many modern artists. This almost industrial efficiency of Nukuoro forms enhances their elegance and sophistication. Although usually highly abstract, a few Nukuoro figures depict facial features but in a rather reticent, unpretentious way. Basically this is an art of pure sculptural values: its materials are form and space, not color and texture.

110   Carved figure. Gilbert Islands, Micronesia. Wood with shell eyes. H. 16^1/$_4$" (American Museum of Natural History, New York).

*III Warrior's shield.
New Britain. Wood and
dyed cane. H. 4' 6³/₄"
(Museum für Völkerkunde,
Basel).*

Functionally, Nukuoro images fit into a familiar pattern. The large six-foot-high carvings represent major cult deities; during seasonal rites priests anointed these effigies with oil. Smaller carvings were probably effigies of minor clan gods. Male and female, the figures often stand on circular bases, their arms hanging free at the sides or attached sometimes by means of struts. This arms-free pose is, as we shall see, an important clue to the origins of the Nukuoro style.

One major controversy surrounds Nukuoro images. Early writers always viewed these objects as purely local products; recent scholars on the other hand regard them as the result of a migration westward from Polynesia. Neither view is, in fact, correct. If we turn once more to Late Jomon figurines from prehistoric Japan (Plate 114), we find an arms-free posture with outward flare of the hands, amazingly close to that of Nukuoro, and indicating the intimate affinity of the two traditions.

On the other hand, certain features of Nukuoro carvings—among them the round bases and sleek surfaces—can only be explained by Indo-Austronesian contacts coming from Indonesia. When we observe the sharp dualism of the Nukuoro figure—the distinction between the stark, abstract head treatment and the softer, more visceral concept of the lower body—the connection is assured. Exactly the same treatment appears in the great Indo-Austronesian Cook Island god figure.

Kaniet

Of the myriad inhabitants of the South Seas, none produced more ingratiating art forms than did the people of the little island of Kaniet just north of New Guinea. Taking their cue from life, the Kaniet artists carved diminutive figures (rarely exceeding two feet in height) which evoke natural forms in a most beguiling manner (Plate 113). With topknots and beards, Kaniet images present a venerable, almost Gothic appearance. That these details were in fact copied from the people may be proven from old photographs of the now almost extinct population.

What little we know of Kaniet figures suggests an ancestral function. In 1875 a German naval officer visiting the island observed a figure of this type over six feet high in the vicinity of a grave. Several post-contact carvings now in the Bremen and Stuttgart museums show the same dependence on life sources. Two of these figures are very clearly the Kaniet carver's rendition of German naval officers. In a third museum example, any first-year medical student could diagnose from the gross swelling of the body a case of elephantiasis. All in all, there is a strong argument for an ancestral role in Kaniet carvings.

In form, Kaniet figures vary from one another scarcely at all. The hands may rest on the thighs or hips; the arms-free pose, as such, does not seem to occur here. But the bland, uncolored wood and the use of piercing with intricate, metal-like designs mark the art of Kaniet as a truly Micronesian style.

Admiralties

A similar situation exists in the Melanesian area of the Admiralties. The physical types, as well as house construction and certain art objects, have links with the north; at the same time the culture of the Admiralties owes much to the Melanesians of the coastal Sepik and Tami regions with whom they have trading relations. The collision of several cultural levels normally would tend to produce a very complex, engrossing art. But in the rather mousy Admiralties style the chief result is inconsistency. Figures of Micronesian type in the arms-free pose often culminate in faces of the early wooden-mask type. The artist's dec-

112 Deity figure. Nukuoro, Micronesia. H. 12″ (Rautenstrauch-Joest-Museum, Cologne).

orative vocabulary is equally limited, being restricted to triangular and circular shapes; his colors are a tiresome reiteration of red, black, and white.

One factor contributing perhaps to the comparative dullness of Admiralty style is its lack of interesting scale. Huge and tiny figures all operate on the same visual scale. Large or small, each part stands in uniform relation to the whole.

Occasionally, however, objects of high aesthetic quality appear in this region. Large wooden bowls with elegant, lacy decoration, finely carved lime spatulas, magnificent *kapkaps*, and stately wooden beds enliven the Admiralties style.

Santa Cruz

A third area skirting the borderline between Melanesia and Micronesia is the Santa Cruz group lying east of the Solomons. Although discovered by the Spanish in 1595, the islands are still inadequately known. The people of Santa Cruz seem to have been somewhat lighter in color than the majority of Oceanic Negroes. They live in round houses and, in their ancestor worship, honor dangerous shark spirits. Chiefs owe their power mainly to their connection with cult spirits.

Santa Cruz art is highly distinctive in style. It has elaborate surfaces while keeping

113   Bearded ancestor figure. Kaniet, Micronesia. H. 32" (Übersee Museum, Bremen).

the sheer shapes and planes of Micronesian tradition. Attached to these sleek shapes are numerous ornaments, including leaves, grass, rings of turtle shell, and other ornaments in profusion. Santa Cruz artists seem to enjoy the contrast between solid sculptural form, often beautifully shaped, and fussy, dangling, or mobile decoration applied to the body. This art expression finds interesting similarities in Melanesia and eastern Indonesia.

Figure carvings (Plate 116) are made at the death of an important man and are kept in the home thereafter by a descendant who serves as the figure's guardian. This person, usually a chief, enjoys the support of the spirit and his social prestige is therefore enhanced. Stylistically, Santa Cruz human images adhere to the arms-free tradition. The somewhat simple, blunted appearance of the face belies the articulate, comparatively fluent treatment of the body. Poised vigorously in space or seated rigidly on a stool, Santa Cruz figures have a very touching and human character. Nearly everyone finds these pert little carvings very endearing.

As for the meaning of these figures, not much is known. Apparently ancestral, they also have to do with a shark cult in which the powerful spirits could catch sharks by using hooks attached to their wrists. Similar figures occur as finial carvings on certain ceremonial houses in the nearby southern Solomons. Like the Santa Cruz pieces, they too have a spritelike, lilting quality and are almost entirely devoid of bulk or weight.

Other Santa Cruz objects of interest include neck rests, dance clubs, extremely stylized human figures known as *djuka* posts, which are venerated as embodiments of spirit power, and a local form of *kapkap*. The latter consists of a silhouette of a frigate bird cut out of turtle-shell and set against a white shell disk. They seem to have been moon symbols. Like most of the art forms of this area, the *kapkaps* of Santa Cruz succeed in giving profound aesthetic impact with great economy of statement. In this respect Santa Cruz objects belong more to Micronesian than to Melanesian tradition.

Tonga

We now turn eastward to Polynesia, where the first area of artistic importance to be considered is the Tonga Islands. First discovered by Captain Cook, the people of these numerous and fertile islands greatly impressed him with their energy, beauty, and social achievements. Warlike and daring, the Tongans had not long before undertaken voyages of conquest and colonization to several parts of Melanesia.

Tongan art includes wooden and ivory figures and hooks, bark cloth, clubs, and decorated utensils. Wooden figures from this area are exceedingly rare, since all but five were destroyed by the missionary John Williams on the converting of the Tongans to Christianity in 1830. Peter Buck, the great Polynesian specialist, located four of these carvings in English collections; one bears a label identifying it as "Household goddess of the Emperor of Tonga and Part of the Dress Worn by him when he worshipped the Devil." Recently the fifth image, spared by the missionaries, has come to light in Scotland in the Aberdeen University Museum. Typically Tongan, the carving vigorously depicts the statuesque proportions of Polynesian women. The very large head thrusts forward from the shoulders and the buttocks extend backward to form rhythmic counterparts of the breasts. Like several others of its type which were mutilated by the converted Tongans, the figure has lost its arms; at the sides it probably had the arms-free pose, indicating Micronesian affiliation. On the back of the Aberdeen figure there is an important missionary label: "Sakaunu, a Great Tonga Goddess."

Other Tongan figures also deserve close scrutiny. One carved in very hard, shiny wood and probably the finest of all is now in the Chicago Museum of Natural History (Plate 115). If the importance of a figure can be partly gauged in Polynesia by its material (as it seems to be in the Cooks), then the Chicago piece may well represent the leading deity of Tonga. Its Indo-Austronesian origin suggested by the very hard wood is confirmed in a third figure illustrated by John Williams. In addition to a round base, the usual arms-free pose and some mutilation, this figure shows a distinct dualism between the stylized head and arms and the softly rounded and organic lower body. On its back is the label: "Goddess of Lifuga hung by Taufaahau on embracing Christianity, Hapai July 1830." These Tongan figures are among the most important remains of Polynesian art.

Fiji

The Fijians are a dark, strapping people basically Negroid in origin. However, from their Polynesian neighbors they have taken over many characteristics, including chieftainship, deity figures, and double canoes.

*114   Figurine. Late Jomon
period. Japan. Ceramic. H. 8"
(Tokyo National Museum).*

Fijian sculpture clearly reflects the mixed background of the people. Rugged figures carved in tree fern—a granular, easily cut material—(Plate 118) bring to mind parallels in Melanesia, especially in the New Hebrides; but svelte ivory figurines in the arms-free position remind us immediately of Tonga. As a matter of fact, some Tongan carvings were actually collected in Fiji, causing ethnologists no end of consternation. Their true origin was only established after comparison with documented pieces. Other Fijian figures in wood, often cruder or more blunted, seem to fall between the Melanesian and Polynesian extremes. In pose these frequently bear a marked resemblance to the carved images of New Caledonia. Some functioned as hook figures in the Melanesian manner; others, used as priest's oil dishes, can only have had a Polynesian origin.

Necker

Far to the north lies another area where the arms-free pose was well known—the Hawaiian Islands. The Hawaiians undoubtedly rose from comparatively simple origins though they later developed much pageantry and ceremony. These humble beginnings are scarcely evident on the main islands, but on the tiny rocky island of Necker, seven hundred miles north-west of Oahu, archaeologists have unearthed fragmentary evidence of the early culture. Our best clues to this culture are a dozen or more strange little figures (Plate 119) carved in porous volcanic stone. Despite a general kinship with other Hawaiian images, the Necker figures remain essentially different. Their origin lies in the Middle (not Late) Jomon tradition of prehistoric Japan.

A very intense animation pervades these Necker images, giving them a sort of demonic energy. Activated by the inflation of the forms, the carving takes on an aggressive, defiant quality. Though frontal and somewhat rectangular, they seem to expand in space, thrusting themselves vigorously upon us. This directness of expression is peculiarly Hawaiian. But the rather democratic attitude of the figures and lack of extreme self-dramatization set the Necker images off from their later, better-known Hawaiian counterparts.

115   Image of a goddess. Tonga, Polynesia. H. 14⁷/₈" (Fuller Collection, Chicago Natural History Museum).

Hawaii

Ever since Captain Cook's discovery of the islands, Western visitors have been awed by Hawaii. That one of the finest and most aristocratic of Polynesian cultures should have evolved in such an idyllic setting is almost too good to be true. To understand this society it is essential to appreciate the tremendous energies the Hawaiians devoted to the glorification of their king. As in other advanced Polynesian societies, a sharp line was drawn between the *akua* or state gods and the *aumakua*, locally important minor or household deities.

Above all, the Hawaiians venerated the war god Ku, official patron of the king; for him they laid out a temple precinct known as the *heiau*. Roughly rectangular in shape, the *heiau* was walled in on all four sides; at one end, in the sacred inner court, stood ferocious-looking images of the war god (Plate 120). Several huts were provided for the storage of religious objects and for the housing of the priestly caste. At certain times the king actually lived in the *heiau*. The god Ku also supposedly resided there during ceremonies. From this description we can readily understand how the *heiau* helped to strengthen the monarchy. Built at the king's command in commemoration of a victory, the *heiau* was in effect a sort of votive offering to the gods. Little

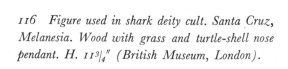

116 Figure used in shark deity cult. Santa Cruz, Melanesia. Wood with grass and turtle-shell nose pendant. H. 11³/₄″ (British Museum, London).

wonder then that the commoners, excluded from participating in *heiau* ceremonies directly, eagerly listened to a description of the rites shouted down to them by a priest standing on top of the wall.

Directly connected with great state cult sites of Hawaii are a number of images of Ku and other figures, more naturalistic in appearance, which were probably royal portraits. The Ku figures of Hawaii are incredibly melodramatic and overpoweringly aggressive. The heavy, full volumes of the body contrast vigorously with the bristling angular forms of the head. This violent dualism underscores the Hawaiian artist's almost expressionistic search for total visual impact. In addition, the tense postures, drastic separation of parts, and rigorous surface definition lend strength. The facial treatment in Hawaiian Ku figures depends heavily on Late Chou tradition, as comparison with Maori sculpture proves.

The artist's use of free space adds further virility to the Ku images. The pent-up volume of air between the arms and the body explodes downward through the narrow constriction at the wrists. By articulating the notably dynamic qualities of its prototype, the Hawaiian artist successfully invested his forms with a maximum of strength and psychological independence—precisely the qualities attributed to the divine king of Hawaii. The flaring treatment of the hands reveals another

117   Image probably representing Rongo, the god of agriculture. Mangareva, Polynesia. H. 38³/₄″ (Museum of Primitive Art, New York).

118 Ancestor figures with sperm-whale tooth pendants symbolizing power. Fiji, Polynesia. Giant tree fern. H. 50"–40" (Royal Ethnographical Museum, Copenhagen).

119 (Below) Sacred precinct figure. Necker, Hawaiian Islands. Porous gray basalt. H. $11\frac{1}{4}$" (British Museum, London).

basic influence in Ku figures: as in Nukuoro, this is the Late Jomon style of Japan (Plate 114). What is more, Japanese temple guardians of the historic period, grimacing like the Ku figures, performed a similar function. However, this is not the whole story. Dongson, Late Chou, and Indo-Austronesian influences appear also to have reached Hawaii.

Figures representing kings and ancestors in Hawaii are often strikingly realistic. Natural details such as white shell eyes, pegged-in human hair, and real tapa loincloths often decorate such figures. The smooth silky surfaces and active postures and gestures further imbue the forms with life. Unfortunately, a large number of these carvings were destroyed in 1819, when Hawaiian culture suddenly began to break up. However, some survived, kept in a sacred mortuary; others, hastily hidden in caves, also escaped destruction.

Another impressive art form of great importance in Hawaiian culture was the feather god, an image of wickerwork covered with lovely red, yellow, and black feathers (Plate 121). These images were carried into battle; many represented Ku and thus served as visible symbols of a chief's power. Hawaiian chiefs often also wore feathered wicker helmets. The emphasis on armor in this area also brings to mind Japan, where since Jomon times warriors have always worn elaborate protective equipment.

Several Hawaiian artistic achievements

120 The war god Ku. Kailua, Hawaii. H. 30¹/₄"
(British Museum, London).

Head of Ku carried as a
dard in battle. Hawaii.
cker framework covered with
and feathers. Shell eyes and
teeth. H. 32" (British
seum, London).

deserve particular attention. These include the royal feather cloak and the short tippet worn by members of the aristocracy. A rare and arduous art, the shaping of feathers into ceremonial costumes requires a comparatively organized society capable of supporting much nonproductive labor. In Hawaii, as in ancient Peru, the craft became symbolic of royalty, red being the color of the gods. Yellow feathers were so hard to obtain that the Hawaiians often set the birds free after plucking them of their prize plumage. There is a similar elegance in Hawaiian bark cloth, widely regarded as the finest in the world.

This brings to an end our study of Oceanic styles related in various ways to Micronesia. To round out the visual history of the South Seas, we must turn briefly to a number of cultures, mainly on the southern side of Melanesia, which we have so far ignored. These areas include New Caledonia, New Hebrides, the Banks Islands, and the Central District and Papuan Gulf regions of New Guinea.

New Caledonia

The Melanesian people of New Caledonia produced a considerable variety of forms on a few simple themes. Particularly interesting are the doorpost and roof spires attached to a

122   War god with crested helmet. Hawaii. Wood with beaten bark cloth. H. 21" (Temple Square Bureau Museum, Salt Lake City).

chief's house, and black wooden masks with
enormous noses (Plate 123). Despite their material and technique, these masks probably
developed out of Old Papuan conical masks.
They were worn by men with thigh-length,
black feather costumes. Believed to represent
water spirits, some of these masks are said to
have originated in the northern part of the
island. Whether or not this is true, we have
strong evidence of Polynesian influence in the
neighboring Loyalty group and southern New
Hebrides. Chieftainship and elaborate wood
carving are apparently fairly recent innovations in New Caledonia. It is therefore noteworthy that many of the black masks bear the
frontal ridge, a sure sign of Indo-Austronesian
influence.

At the same time, the doorposts were frequently decorated with another device—the
long protruding tongue. This Late Chou element forms a link with the Maori on the one
hand and the Sepik on the other. In New Caledonia, the symbolic lozenge pattern below
the faces probably originally represented stylized figure postures. Upon the death of the
chief, these door carvings were sometimes mutilated as a mark of sorrow. On occasion they
were set up to serve as taboo-markers. Roof
spires usually depicted stylized anthropomor-
phic forms.

In most parts of New Caledonia a handsome ax with a green jade blade belonged to

*123 Water spirit mask. New Caledonia, Mela-
nesia. Wood with human hair, string, feathers, and
fiber. H. 40″ (British Museum, London).*

each clan, having been treasured from generation to generation. A sun symbol, it was used to kill human sacrifices and to bring rain.

New Hebrides

The culture of the New Hebrides is distinctly Megalithic in character. The chiefs in this area maintained their superior position by strenuous competition in the arena of life. To acquire status, a man had to accumulate such enormous quantities of wealth that he could afford the necessary feasts and dramatic performances. Each rite symbolized a step upward in grade. With as many as thirty-five different grades to achieve, it is little wonder a New Hebridean man spent most of his adult life climbing the social ladder. For highest advancement, stone carving and stone structures were required. Persons who had outranked everyone else often had separate shrines erected in which ancestral figures, bird-form culture hero symbols, or sacred stones were set up. In the Banks Islands to the north, painted wooden boards showing splayed figures with sun, moon, and bird symbols were also used in ancestral shrines.

124 Demonic figure used in advanced initiation rites. New Hebrides, Melanesia. Cane covered with painted vegetable fiber and boar's tusks. H. 48¹/₂" (Chicago Natural History Museum)

125 (Facing) Secret society mask. New Britain, Melanesia. Painted wood with vegetable fiber. H. 17" (Present location unknown).

New Hebridean art reflects the wild, turbulent character of the culture that produced it. Almost entirely devoid of elegance, the forms are as a rule roughly and hastily executed (Plate 124). Around the dance ground were set up numerous figures of spirit beings fashioned out of tree fern—a material comparable to glued shredded wheat and scarcely more durable. For masks and puppetlike images, the craftsman's usual material was a vegetable fiber modeled like clay and painted with the most garish reds, blues, and whites imaginable (Plate 6). Frequently attached to these masks and effigies were boars' tusks, probably a substitute for horns in an area where cows or buffalo were unavailable. Sacrificial animals in the New Hebrides were not all slaughtered at once but merely tapped lightly with a mallet. This "killed" the boars ceremonially; they could not then be used in subsequent rites.

The only New Hebrides art objects actually carved by a professional sculptor were their slit gongs, which were set up vertically at the dance ground. Their artistic superiority over the homemade products is readily apparent. Many of the latter were hacked out by a man advancing in grade or by his hired relatives. The result is that the bulk of New Hebrides art is comparatively crude and untutored.

The Central District of New Guinea

The people of the southeastern coast of New Guinea paid scant attention to figures and masks. Rather, they excelled in making feather headdresses and ceremonial architecture. The spectacular plumage of the bird of paradise was combined with yellow and red feathers and with *kapkaps* to form ceremonial headgear. In several areas only successful head-hunters could wear these magnificent objects. In architecture, the Central District people concentrated their efforts on the visual elaboration of the men's house. Most of these structures with their elaborate roofs hark back to Indonesia.

Papuan Gulf

The art of the Papuan Gulf region, west of the Central District, consists mainly of decorated shields, boards, charms, and bark-cloth masks (Plate

126). Of the few wooden figures in the round that appeared in this area, one of the finest represents the wife of a mythological hero from whom the people traced their descent. Otherwise, Papuan Gulf art tends to be almost entirely two-dimensional. Repetition of simple design units, such as triangles, spirals, and dentate patterns, leads to a general uniformity of style throughout the area. A lack of vigorous contrasts within the decoration further contributes to the rather monotonous uniformity of style unrelieved by areas of rest or differences in scale. On the other hand, Papuan art is nothing if not bold (Plate 57). Spiky and aggressive shapes as well as surrealistic linkages between the various forms do a great deal to enliven this far from laconic style.

The masks that form the core of Papuan Gulf artistry are of three types: the *kovave*, a conical object worn during initiation rites; the *eharo*, a weird combination of forms intended to be comical; and the *hevehe*, a huge vertical mask of sacred significance. The latter plays a pivotal role in ceremonies for obtaining the blessing of benevolent supernatural beings. Prepared in secrecy over a period of up to twenty years, these masks finally are seen emerging in a procession from the special men's house; they then are carried back almost a month later at the climax of the ceremonies. In form and function they re-

126 Ceremonial tablet from men's house. Elema, Papuan Gulf, New Guinea. H. 3′ 9″ (Museum für Völkerkunde, Hamburg).

semble vaguely the Baining *hariecha* mask and the tall feather masks of Hansa Bay near the mouth of the Sepik. These *hevehe* were constructed by the wearer, who copied a traditional clan pattern. Some represented bush spirits, others marine totems. All in all, they suggest an Old Papuan base (Plate 127) onto which have been grafted certain Megalithic and Indo-Austronesian elements. The typical red, black, and white colors of Papuan Gulf art suggest a dimly sensed connection with the northern part of New Guinea. Despite its many archaic features, this style stands out among those of southern New Guinea areas occupied by Papuans as an especially coherent and pervasive visual tradition.

Having reached the fringes of Torres Straits, we have completed our survey of Pacific styles with the exception of a few areas whose art is so rich with interest that they deserve special consideration. Foremost among these are the Middle Sepik region, Madagascar, and the problem areas— Mangareva and Easter Island in eastern Polynesia. We will begin with the Sepik.

The Middle Sepik Area

From the mouth of the Sepik inland for nearly two hundred miles are several tribes who produced some of the weirdest yet probably some of the most exciting of all primitive arts. Despite the real dangers of head-hunting and the discomforts of insects and diseases, the Middle Sepik people invented and acquired forms and patterns that are much envied by modern designers the world over. The more we look at these objects, the more they impress us as the products of a world gone mad, very nearly, for art. So voracious was the Sepik appetite for spectacular new designs and techniques that warriors used to raid rival villages for their treasured art objects. Of course, behind such behavior lay also an insatiable demand for sources of magical power.

At first glance Middle Sepik art seems to border on hallucination. Its

127   *Totemic fish mask used for clowning during religious rites. Orokolo Bay, Papuan Gulf. Painted bark cloth over rattan with grass. H. 64$^1/_4$" (Pitt Rivers Museum, Oxford University).*

characteristic forms, including figures, masks, drums, shields, painted boards, stools, canoes, men's houses, and modeled skulls, exhibit a fantastic inventiveness of shape and color (Plate 55). Bewildered by the scope and variety of the styles, scholars have generally evaded the question of origins. But despite their complexity, Sepik styles can be treated historically.

The first linkage we observe is with Old Papuan types, especially in masks connected with initiation ceremonies (Plate 61). Scant as the information about these masks is, it appears that many represented totemic ancestors of the various clans and that men and boys wearing the masks performed in front of a palisade said to represent mountains. The latter custom suggests the Aquatic tradition of dance screens noted already in Torres Straits. The most primitive type is worn in the Maprick area during harvest rites; it has the typical fibrous construction, conical shape, and round eyes of the Old Papuan style. In the Iatmul area, the faces are almost always of wood and by their extended tongues betray Late Chou influence. Visually, this wooden type falls between the demonic, monstrous form of Sepik grotesques, and the more human, naturalistic modeling of a real-life ancestor portrait. Still, the over-all conception remains essentially Old Papuan.

128 Crouching ancestor figure from pinnacle of Middle Sepik meeting house. New Guinea. Wood with cassowary feathers, string, and shell. H. 4' 1" (Eckert Collection, Basel).

By an amazing bit of good luck, the Middle Sepik area also intercepted Dongson ideas as these influences moved out over the Pacific. Figures in the knee-elbow-chin pose (which apparently bestowed ancestral protection on the initiation house) were one of several Dongson contributions to Sepik art (Plate 128). But the most astounding of Sepik styles— those involving lyrical surface patterns, extended tongue, and proliferated spiral designs—stem for the most part from the Late Chou. The easiest way to prove this relationship is to examine the wooden doors of a house model placed in a Chinese tomb nearly two thousand years ago (Plate 134). Exactly the same shapes are being carved in the Sepik today (Plate 133).

Other striking wooden carved slabs from the Middle Sepik provide further examples of the rhythmic exuberance of Late Chou style. Concealed within the carved foliage are numerous but almost invisible birds. Despite their weight and great size, these slabs have a lightness and an aerial feeling due to their numerous piercings (Plate 132). These carved slabs were set up in men's ceremonial houses; although usually described as boards or shields, study of the flaring vertical prongs at the bottom indicates that the slabs probably evolved originally out of wooden hooks of the sort often seen today in the Sepik.

The extravagance of Sepik style finds no

129   Middle Sepik hook from men's house. New Guinea. H. 39¹/₂" (Museum für Völkerkunde, Basel).

more impressive illustration than in wooden figures from the region. The artist's uncontrollable impulse to adorn his work appears in the painted as well as in the carved details. Shapes and surfaces conflict violently with one another, touching off an explosion of emotional feeling.

Seldom restrained and never discreet, carved Sepik images do show modification due to other outside influence. Indo-Austronesian style, for example, is responsible for the presence in some Middle Sepik figures of a frontal ridge, monochromatic surface, and hands-on-hips pose. Admittedly reabsorbed by older traditions, such figures do not, of course, look especially Indian. But when they are compared with older styles, the conclusion that they are Indian is borne out.

Perhaps the most spectacular deviation from the Middle Sepik repertoire is the carved wooden figures of the Mundugumor people (Plate 136). Although broadly related to other Sepik styles, these dwarf-bodied, enormous-headed flute figures depart from local tradition in the statuesque concept of the figure and the arms-free posture. Inspiration for this type probably came from Micronesia. In the Sepik area other instances of Micronesian influence also exist. The great clan-owned men's houses are an example. At the base of the gable is a splayed female figure, just as in many men's houses in Palau (Plate 137). The saddle-roof shape of these houses is a ready reminder of the Dongson ship roof seen in Sumatra and Micronesia. According to Carl Schmitz, a German authority on dance ethnology, the beautiful landscaping of the plaza in front of these Sepik houses is also a Micronesian inheritance.

Many Sepik men's houses culminated at the gable peak in a menacing protective mask. With protruding tongue, bold scale, and self-aggrandizement, the Sepik gable mask agrees perfectly with the Late Chou-influenced Maori council house. A variation may be found in the Maprick area where the gable was filled with decorative paintings on palm spathe (Plate 130). Carved figures in these Maprik houses, on the other hand, usually portrayed ancestral beings (Plate 139).

Farther up the Sepik are two areas whose art would draw gasps in any modern art gallery. The Kwoma tribe produced hook figures and paint-

130 Facade painting from men's house. Abelam, Sepik area, New Guinea. Painted palm spathe. H. 71" (Brooklyn Museum).

ings that literally beggar description. Pulsating with energy and vitality, these figures employ a bizarre palette of acid green and pale pink tones to enhance their otherworldliness. The second area, whose unearthly style was only recently identified, is that of the Arambak. In their eerie and fantastically wrought style, disembodied parts form stylized human figures. Yet all in all, it is the Iatmul style that really is the culmination of the astonishing Sepik world of forms. For the huge, unbelievable Iatmul initiation mask from the village of Angoram proclaims what words cannot say (Plate 138). It testifies to the great faith the Sepik man places in his spirits and shows why, when he thinks of these spirits, he always sees them in the form of masks.

Madagascar

If the Sepik River area seems complex, Madagascar, the world's fourth largest island, which lies three hundred miles off the east coast of Africa, is unresolved chaos. The island is populated by dark African Negroes, but the languages they speak are very definitely of Austronesian origin. Furthermore, the area is one that has been neglected both by anthropologists and art historians. The following is therefore by no means a complete account of Madagascan art but merely a sample of the riches to be found in this fascinating area. Most important from our point of view is the fact that certain groups—especially the Merina and Betsileu of the interior and the Mafahaly in southern Madagascar—produced a remarkably Indonesian-Polynesian sort of art. This style we must analyze in detail.

As its base, Madagascan art seems to be strongly Megalithic. Buffalo horns, memorial carvings, protective gable ornaments, and postlike figures appear frequently (Plate 140). These have the typical static frontality and heart-shaped faces of Megalithic sculpture, together with a monotonous repetition of symbols. Another familiar Megalithic theme seen in Mada-

Facing:
131   Middle Sepik cult mask with small figure on chin. New Guinea. H 33¹/₄″ (Museum für Völkerkunde, Hamburg).

132   Middle Sepik ceremonial board derived from hook form. New Guinea. H. 7′ 8¹/₂″ (Eckert Collection, Basel).

gascar is the crocodile climbing a post. Equally prominent, however, are motifs derived from the early Sino-Austronesian tradition. In Madagascar we find, for example, numerous horn scrolls, lozenges, four-pointed crosses, andmoon and sun symbols like those thought to have existed in pre-Shang Chinese art. Interestingly, many of these elements appear in the art of the Admiralties with which Madagascan style has striking affinities. One link between the two areas is the making of great wooden beds decorated with realistic and stylized incised designs.

Architectural forms and basketry shapes seem to parallel certain early Chinese art forms. And many of the carved figures show the hands-on-stomach pose believed to be a Sino-Austronesian convention.

More important than their origins, however, is the light that Madagascan sculpture sheds on the Shang period in China. For many of the Madagascan wooden objects perpetuate the form of perishable containers developed originally in China and now known there only through later bronze reproductions. Tripod vessels and love charms from Madagascar show that similar Chinese vessels must have been supported by three tusks or horns. Other objects probably reproduce the prototypes of the three-legged *ting* and the tall, slender *ku*. Most important of all, the miniature wooden houses erected over the tombs of Madagascan kings explain through their mortise-and-tenon construction certain "decorative" devices used by Chinese artists. In such early Chinese vessels as the *fang i*, we see translated into bronze a wooden model of a house; every detail down to the tenon lugs, bulging roof, and flaring gable shape survives today in Madagascan sculpture. With its emphasis on ancestor veneration, sacrifices, and hierarchy, Madagascar provides a glimpse into the foundations of historic Chinese culture.

Mangareva

Some one thousand miles east of Tahiti lies a compact cluster of islands known as Mangareva. Though high and reef-fringed, these droughty islands

133   Middle Sepik dance drum decorated with hornbill and face mask showing protruding tongue. New Guinea. Wood with skin tympanum and string. H. 21¹⁄₃" (British Museum, London).

134 *Design painted on doors of ceramic house-model from tomb.
Han dynasty (first century A.D.) China. H. 52" over-all (William
Rockhill Nelson Gallery, Kansas City, Missouri).*

support little vegetation. When first encountered by Europeans, the Mangarevan people
did not even have good canoes; they had to
use rafts for their inter-island voyaging. But
Mangarevan art bears clear evidence of influence from the Indo-Austronesian Tangaroa
culture.

Although the Mangarevans were converted to Roman Catholicism over a hundred
years ago, enough of their images have survived—along with identifying records—to give
us a more nearly complete account of Mangarevan sculpture than of any other area in
Polynesia.

Thanks also to the foresight of the missionary fathers, we can now see exactly what
form the Mangarevans attributed to Rongo,
Tu, and Rao, among others of their gods. The
agricultural god Rongo, of whom there are
several images, was depicted as a free-standing nude figure carved in a highly realistic
and organic manner (Plate 117). The smooth,
naturalistic surfaces of the deity's lower body
have a spongy, visceral character; his face,
however, seems rigid, reduced to essentials.
The free volumes of the figure and its alert,
open pose sustain the sense of humanity and
actuality of the image. Arresting in their technical accomplishment, the Rongo carvings
put Mangarevan style among the highest levels
of Pacific art.

A second type depicts Tu, the breadfruit

135 *Middle Sepik puppet with movable limbs.
New Guinea. Painted palm spathe. H. 59" (Übersee Museum, Bremen).*

deity. Somewhat stockier and shorter than other carvings of the style, the statue of Tu is four-legged. The model for this conception surely must lie in the Indian-influenced styles of the South Seas.

A third type clinches the Indo-Austronesian element in Mangarevan style. This figure is identified as Rao, the patron deity of turmeric, an herb used variously as a dye, a foodstuff and, ritually, as a magical medicine. The Rao image shows a frontal ridge and a topknot, as well as an extreme version of the dualism already noted. The upper body is in fact the most abstract conception found in all Polynesia. Tapering radically from the knees upward, the trunk apparently re-emerges in the topknot. The limbs consists of a horizontal band, with two streamlined shapes attached vertically which serve as arms. On either hip appear lozenge-shaped projecting lugs which reproduce almost exactly the size and shape of the ears.

No exact prototype for this Mangarevan sculpture has yet been found in Oceania. However, the comparison with Indian images illuminates the process by which dualism may have developed. Many Indian bronzes imported into Indonesia were regarded as charms and passed from hand to hand until, upon reaching remote areas, their ceremonial content was forgotten. Some of these charms seem to have been rubbed or kissed until the face was worn away almost completely. Copied in wood, primitive carvings then perpetuated this tradition and helped carry it further into the Pacific. Both the dualism and the frontal ridge, major hallmarks of Indo-Austronesian art, can be seen in certain of these minor bronzes, some of which are so completely worn away that Indians themselves would be hard pressed to identify their subject. Thus through changing circumstance and altered environment, a new and glorious imagery arose in Mangareva. That this Indo-Austronesian style has its immediate origins in Indonesia is only part of the story. The Indonesian forms themselves derive from Indian sculpture which in turn stemmed from Greece by way of Gandhara. The early missionaries who thought they were destroying an utterly debased primitive art would indeed be surprised to learn of its ultimate classical origins. Yet this best explains the naturalism of the Indo-Austronesian style.

136   Middle Sepik cult figure inserted in end of sacred flute. Mundugumor, New Guinea. Wood with cassowary feathers, turtle-shell, cowrie, mother-of-pearl, and rattan beard. H. 16" (Eckert Collection, Basel).

Easter Island

The easternmost inhabited island of Polynesia, Easter Island is not nearly so mysterious a place as writers would often like to have us believe. The language, people, and culture are closely related to those of other Polynesian islands. Study of the art forms discloses numerous affiliations with Oceania. Despite the spray-drenched *Kon-Tiki* voyage and the ingeniously contrived theories of Thor Heyerdahl, there are few if any direct connections between Easter Island and the Western Hemisphere.

Until their culture was virtually destroyed a hundred years ago by Peruvian slavers, the Easter Islanders shared a precarious existence on their reefless and sparsely-wooded volcanic home. Lacking breadfruit, large canoes, and all but the poorest paper mulberry trees for tapa cloth, the islanders turned to the only sculptural material readily available in their area—stone. Their achievements in the easily cut volcanic stone of Easter Island were little short of miraculous (Plate 141).

The art of Easter Island includes, besides stone, wood, and bark-cloth figures, petro-

137   Roof support with female figure from open gable of Middle Sepik men's house. New Guinea. H. 11″ (Franklin Collection, Los Angeles).

138   (Facing) Huge Middle Sepik mask of a supernatural being, worn collectively by initiates. Angoram, New Guinea. Painted palm spathe. L. 16′. Photographed in 1912 by Dr. Roesicke (From Herbert Tischner's Kulturen der Südsee*).*

glyphs, paddles, masklike headpieces, and written script. Long a mystery and the focus of heated controversy, the Easter Island script seems at last to be yielding its secrets. The story is a fascinating one. Early visitors to the island discovered that ritual tablets and other pieces of wood were sometimes inscribed with strange characters for the use of priests. Several investigators in the late nineteenth and early twentieth centuries attempted to find the meaning of the script, but before a consistent record of this writing could be obtained the last knowledgeable priest died. So numerous fantastic theories arose, including the belief that the few thousand Easter Islanders could have achieved such a major step as writing entirely on their own. In the 1930's, however, a Hungarian ethno-linguist, Guillaume de Hévésy, published a sensational theory that linked the insular script with the undeciphered language of Mohenjo-Daro, a culture that flourished four thousand years ago halfway around the world in northwestern India. Immediately scholars split into two camps: a few accepted the theory, others rejected it utterly. Later a third theory, actually a refinement of Hévésy's views, was put forward by Robert Heine-Geldern, a Viennese scholar. He argued that the script stemmed ultimately from the Ancient Near East but by way of China; in his theory the Easter script came from southern China and is not directly linked with early Shang dynasty writing, the archaic forerunner of present-day Chinese.

In the last decade the problem has been brought to the point of solution through the brilliant, painstaking work of Thomas Barthel, a young German linguist. Barthel's book, besides capturing the spirit of the language, provides extensive reference material and observations on syntax. He finds that the language is not mere picture writing but expresses ideas, poetic images, and sometimes sounds, through varied but regular meaningful combinations of its one hundred twenty-odd basic characters. This writing is therefore essentially ideographic, having a fixed relationship between the ideas the scribe puts in and those that can be read out. Easter script is not merely a memory aid or an exact visual equivalent of speech, as is our writing. Barthel compares it to a very terse telegram where much can be said and suggested without word-for-word transcription. He further proves

139   Ancestor figures shown in sacred men's house. Abelam, Sepik area, New Guinea. Photographed in 1956.

that Easter Island script entirely accords with Polynesian traditions and cannot be therefore an entirely local development.

Visual analysis of the script supports Barthel's conclusions and at the same time points further west. The majority of figure poses and animal types are those of the Austronesian tradition; the orant and splayed postures are especially prominent. Moreover, the form of these ideograms closely resembles tree carvings made by the Moriori, a group of Polynesians living on Chatham Island off New Zealand, whose art and culture predates that of the Late Chou-influenced Maori. And finally, it is now possible to show structural and visual connections between Easter Island and Shang Chinese characters. For example, a tattoo mark on the chest of an island native compares almost exactly with the Shang ideograph *fa*, meaning "to cut" (Plate 143). In each we see a conventional version of the human form viewed from the side, but in both instances lacking the usual head. Instead, at the neck appears a pole-ax consisting of handle, blade, and counterbalance, the latter angled away from the blade. The scene depicted in the Chinese character is literally that of human sacrifice, as the excavations in Honan Province have shown. Immolation of

140   Memorial post made for someone who dies childless or far from home. Madagascar. Wood with large cattle skulls. H. 10' 10" over-all (Musée de l'Homme, Paris).

141   (Facing) Clan ancestor figures. Easter Island, Polynesia. Volcanic stone. Photographed in 1958.

human victims was also practiced in Easter Island and other parts of Polynesia.

So far we have discussed only the mysterious Easter Island script. By comparison, the art forms seem relatively intelligible. Certain rather bizarre headdresses and figures, for example, are made of bark cloth stuffed with bulrushes. The figures are ancestral protectors of the house and probably have some connection with Old Papuan effigies (Plate 142). Bark-cloth headdresses, on the other hand, with both their sloping eye sockets and button noses, remind us very much of the Maori and Hawaiian styles. Spirit faces, either above or below the human form, are found in New Zealand, Hawaii, Taiwan, and other Late Chou-influenced traditions.

One Easter Island art form—the well-known skeletal wooden figures—is unique indeed in Pacific art (Plate 145). Representing the mummified bodies of ancestors, these were worn by their owner, who danced with a string of them around his waist during harvest festivals and in times of great stress. At other times, the owner wrapped the figures in bark cloth and cared for them tenderly. On top of the figure's head a lizard was carved, and much attention was paid to anatomical details

142 (Facing) Protective ancestor figure placed outside house. Easter Island, Polynesia. Painted bark cloth. H. 15¹/₂" (Peabody Museum, Harvard University).

143 and 144 Designs representing beheaded human figure with sacrificial ax. (Above) Easter Island chest tattoo; (right) Shang pictograph, China, ca. 1000 B.C.

such as the ankle and wrist bones. In their emaciated appearance, Easter Island statues find a parallel in the crude carvings of the Moriori of Chatham Island off New Zealand. There, too, ribs are shown prominently. But the smooth wood and sleek naturalistic style of the Easter Island figures, not present in Chatham, probably stems from Indo-Austronesian influence.

We must now consider the art form for which Easter Island is most famous—the large stone heads and half-length figures. In the Pacific, stone figures of such great size are found only in eastern Polynesia. This fact led Thor Heyerdahl to undertake the *Kon-Tiki* voyage by which he hoped to prove a Peruvian origin for Polynesian civilization. But in truth the Easter Island figures fit entirely into the Indo-Austronesian tradition. Erected on hillsides and funerary platforms, they seem to represent clan ancestors or important guardians rather than national gods. All look very much alike. The lips are pursed, the long nose is slightly articulated, and the eyes are deep shadow cavities beneath the massive brow. A reddish stone hat often tops the shallow skull. Occasionally a frontal ridge appears on the chin. Easter Island stone figures show traces of dualism.

That the oldest stonework on Easter Island consists simply of great blocks carefully cut to form walls would suggest that the

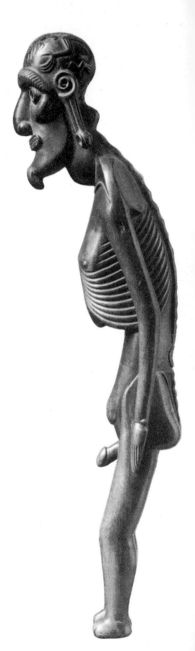

145 Ancestor image suspended from dancer's waist during harvest rites. Easter Island, Polynesia. H. 17¹/₄" (British Museum, London).

earliest Easter Islanders came from an area of Megalithic influence. What led them to begin carving figures in stone was not, therefore, a lack of wood so much as a long-standing interest in stone itself. Why, we may ask, did this shift take place? Every Easter Islander knows the story of the "Long Ears," an invading group that arrived not too many centuries ago. Supposedly after a long struggle they lost control of the island. Who the Long Ears were we may discern from looking at the stone and wooden statues the invaders are said to have encouraged in Easter Island. These carvings always include long, pendant ear lobes and heavy ear decorations. Moriori skeletal figures, probably reflecting an older style, have no such ornamentation; but in every Indo-Austronesian area, pendant ears are found. Taking these facts into account, the Long Ears must be identified as the bearers to Easter Island of the Indo-Austronesian tradition.

The penetration of Asian art into Oceania is one of the most exciting chapters in the unwritten history of man. How Indian influence reached Tahiti and Easter Island we cannot now say. But it did. And Chinese styles are distributed even more widely. Did these waves of inspiration stop short in the islands or did they continue on to America? That is the question we will try to answer in the next chapter.

ESKIM

BERING STRAIT

ESKIM

ESKI

KAMCHATKA

ALEUT

Amur R GILYAK

A M E R I C A

ESKIMO

ESKIMO

LINGIT

TSIMSHIAN

BELLA COOLA
KWAKIUTL
NOOTKA
SALISH

HAIDA

PLAINS

NORTHEAST

IROQUOIS

ADENA

PUEBLO

SOUTHEAST

SOUTHWEST

KEY MARCO

AZTEC
TLATILCO VERACRUZ
OLMEC
MONTE ALBAN MAYA

ARAWAK

NICOYA SAN BLAS
COCLE
VERAGUAS QUIMBAYA BUSH NEGRO
CHIBCHA

WITOTO MAUE MARAJAO
TUCUNA

Xingu R.

MOCHICA CHAVIN
CHIMU INCA CHIRIGUANO
TIAHUANACO

ARAUCANIANS

III

The High Culture Problem

The primitive peoples of the Americas produced an astonishing variety of art forms. But despite apparent diversity of style, there is an underlying unity to this art. With a few exceptions, such as Northwest Coast and Eskimo art, almost all primitive styles in America are influenced directly or indirectly by the high cultures of Mexico and Peru. Thus, although the Maya, Olmec, and other pre-Columbian art styles lie somewhat outside the scope of primitive art, their contribution to tribal styles makes it essential that we include them in our discussion. If we are to understand the nature of primitive tribal efforts, we must have some grasp of the origins of the more advanced American styles.

When high culture art was rediscovered a little over a hundred years ago, the monumentality of its forms and its intricacy of surface detail won the immediate admiration of the Western world. But observers were at the same time puzzled by a problem: how could this sophistication have developed among otherwise not very advanced aborigines? How could Indians who knew nothing of the plow, the wheel, and draught animals conceivably have erected such ingenious structures? And so the marvels of Yucatan were attributed to one of the lost tribes of Israel or to a band of wandering Egyptians. Superficial similarities helped sustain these theories for a while. But then archaeologists began to discover that sites had been occupied for hundreds of years, passing through successive phases of development. Careful analysis of the earliest material revealed that the ancient Americans were Indians, and did not differ greatly from present-day aborigines.

The Indians themselves, scholars now agree, did not originate in America. Of Mongoloid descent, they must have come, it is thought, from northeastern Asia by way of the Bering Strait, from some twenty-five thousand years ago on. Pushing southward in search of game, they finally infiltrated the entire Western Hemisphere. According to the most widely accepted modern view, migrations to America then dwindled to an insignificant trickle. After centuries of living at a food-gathering level, Indians are supposed to have independently developed agriculture, highly organized societies, stone architecture, elaborate cosmologies, writing, and also advanced mathematics (Plate 149).

Within the last decade or two, this orthodox theory has been challenged by another point of view. For scholars of this persuasion, American Indian development appears to have been less isolated than the majority view would indicate. They suggest that small groups of people, perhaps no more than a few boatloads at a time, may have crossed the Pacific directly from Asia or Oceania and influenced the natives. Thus, without imposing Asian patterns on the Indians, these people may have stimulated the development of American cultures. Of course, everyone agrees that there are marked differences between the two areas; whether or not the similarities are sufficient to prove contact is the point of disagreement.

The problem of high culture origins is indeed a crucial question. Either there were significant contacts with Asia, or the influences were trivial and America achieved high culture independently. If American cultures did develop independently, similarities can be explained as the result of parallel development.

The importance of this issue for the whole science of history cannot be overestimated. American isolation and independent development are always cited by historians trying to show that similar phenomena may arise in different areas without any connection between them. But if the American comes to be seen as related, and not merely parallel, to outside develop-

ments, the argument for purely independent invention evaporates. And with it go a large number of pet theories. The followers of Jungian psychology, for example, which has called attention to many interesting similarities in the myth, art, and religion of different cultures and has attributed these to the collective unconscious or race memory, will have to find more down-to-earth explanations for the diffusion of man's ideas.

The whole subject of the development of American culture is fraught with such explosive overtones. The best we can hope for is that the evidence will be tested and weighed before a conclusion is reached.

Having described the general problem, we must now define the question to be considered. But first we must agree to examine high culture art on its own grounds, i.e., as art. Only then can we arrive at a valid judgment. For art, as we have already seen, is susceptible to more rapid change than language, physical types, or culture as a whole.

Pre-Columbian styles, largely ceremonial in purpose and authoritarian in outlook, naturally reflect the outlook of ruling classes and powerful institutions for which there was no exact Asian parallel. It is astonishing, therefore, to note that there are certain clusters of motifs and ideas in American cultures which do have strong affinities in Asia. Even more surprising is the fact that although these stylistic traditions lagged slightly behind Asian developments, they follow the Asian sequence *exactly*. Perhaps the best way to appreciate this relationship is to study the American developments in chronological order.

Mexico

The first inhabitants of the Western Hemisphere were hunters and food gatherers who knew nothing of agriculture, pottery, or metallurgy. Their lives were completely taken up with the ever-pressing quest for food. However, in the middle of the second millennium B.C., there appeared in central Mexico a people who made pottery and figurines of clay, grew

146   Inlaid plaque. Coastal Tiahuanaco, Peru. Shell inlaid with semi-precious stones and gold. H. 2¹/₄" (Oechsle Collection, Zurich).

crops, and practiced extended rituals. Where they came from no one quite knows, but scholars agree that the early Mexican cultures of El Arbolillo and Tlatilco (roughly 1500–800 B.C.) mark a drastic change in the Indian's way of life.

If we turn to the clay figurines of these people (Plate 147), we are at once aware that theirs was a fully developed style. Stressing body volume and costume detail, these charming little objects are posed vivaciously, though their faces seem frontal and archaic. A few smile gently. Eye forms vary but in the early period they often slant diagonally. Except for elaborate head ornaments and jewelry, the figures, usually female, are nude. Some stand with their arms hanging free at their sides; others sit with their legs splayed or with their hands to their breasts. Pottery bowls and tripods were also made in this period. The legs of these vessels take the form of female breasts or perhaps of sea shells.

This style may have developed from earlier and as yet unknown American beginnings, or it may represent a modification of an Asian style. If we examine, for example, Middle and Late Jomon figurines (Plate 114) dating from 3000–1000 B.C. we note in this early Japanese style the arms-free posture, wide hips, decorative attachments, slanting eyes, frontal attitude, and splayed legs and hands-to-breast positions also seen in Mexico. There

147   Votive figure. Tlatilco, Mexico. Fired clay. H. 5" (American Museum of Natural History, New York).

are differences; but even the way the hands of many Tlatilco figurines flare outward can be matched perfectly in Jomon images. Tripod vessels, effigy pots, and bowls with faces on the lip can also be found in Oriental traditions of the second and third millennia B.C. It is tempting, therefore, to connect these two cultures despite the tremendous distances that separate them.

148   Feline bowl figure. Chavin, Peru. Stone. H. 7¹/₂″ (University Museum, Philadelphia).

Peru

The next major development in American culture history took place far to the south, in Peru. Not long after the introduction of pottery (*c.* 1200 B.C.) and maize agriculture (*c.* 1000 B.C.) in the dry river valleys at the foot of the Andes there appeared the beautiful art of Chavin. Named for a cult site, this style differs markedly from all earlier New World art. Characteristic of Chavin style were a highly formalized decoration, complex animal and human representations, and elaborate, monumental architecture in stone. The leading spirit-beings venerated in the Chavin cult were animals made up of feline, serpent, bird, and fish forms, sometimes combined with the human body (Plate 148). These amazing composite creatures were reproduced over and over again with only minor variations. The few carvings that show human features have round eyes, thick lips, and wide bulbous noses, all roughly comparable to certain masks from the Northwest Coast of America.

By far the most common Chavin motif is a feline monster with a projecting snout, the end of which curls backward onto the face (indicated by lines on the face or, when seen in the round, a ring). Almost all Chavin animals have prominent fangs and fantastic features such as eyebrows, tongues, or hair tipped with tiny heads. Double scrolls, crosses, and spirals enrich the otherwise stiff rectilinear shapes. Except for the curling tails of serpents confronting each other, the blocky shapes of Chavin carvings usually emphasize the cubic form of the stone on which they appear. Chavin artists also used a feline creature with a human body and other ornate standing figures in profile. Thin metal masks, stone and bone inlay, and engraved sea shell call attention to the suavity and richness of Chavin style. Ceramics from Cupisnique and from later Peruvian cultures testify to the continuing vitality of Chavin visual ideas a long while after the culture itself had vanished.

The elements of Chavin style—its dominant themes, spatial concepts, and methods of building designs—coincide almost exactly with those of Chinese art of the second millennium B.C. as we have described it in Chapter II. The same intricate surfaces, the same postures and gestures, and the same animal demonism appear in both regions. The Peruvians, it is certain, did not take the style to China. They were not great sailors, nor

49 Stele. Monte Alban,
Oaxaca, Mexico. Stone.
Photographed in 1960.

is there anything in Asian art to suggest that such peoples might have spread out across the Pacific. But Aquatic and early Sinitic peoples already had canoes with which they could have crossed the ocean and thus might have brought a new inspiration to American art and culture. The earliest Chinese styles have deep old roots, whereas Chavin art flowered suddenly and inexplicably in a virtual desert. The question remains: how could the advanced visual ideas of Chavin art have burgeoned overnight without leaving any evidence of its prior development? Similar achievements in Asia required a cross-fertilization that can be traced through period after period.

The influence of Chavin art penetrated far beyond its origin. Objects from the Esmeraldas culture in Ecuador, the Chibcha in Colombia, the Cocle in Panama, the Marajao of Brazil, and perhaps even certain Olmec art forms from Mexico reveal some effects of the artistic eruption at Chavin.

Yucatan

During the first millennium B.C. in Mexico and Yucatan, art forms changed considerably. The so-called Olmec people, for instance, developed beautiful jade figurines and mosaic pavement inlays in which the main motifs are human faces, an upturned snout, and a jaguar

150   Maya maize god. Copan, Yucatan. Limestone. H. 28¹/₂" (American Museum of Natural History, New York).

mask. These changes signalized a restlessness and a stirring among the old cultures that eventually culminated in the achievements of the Maya of Yucatan.

Mayan art, quite naturally, builds upon earlier foundations. In recent years, excavation has brought to light numerous older pyramidal structures and styles—pottery types, motifs, and designs—especially among the Olmec, that foretell Maya accomplishments. But if it no longer appears that the Mayas were so unique or unprecedented as they once seemed, they nonetheless achieved distinct advances in art that are explained by no earlier styles. Surprisingly enough, these aspects of style include the extended tongue and exuberant, curving ornamentation.

An important structure for the study of Maya achievements is the inner temple at Uaxactun to which archaeologists have given the unromantic name of E VII Sub. Apparently the earliest Mayan building of its kind, Temple E VII Sub. dates probably from the third or fourth century A.D., and certainly no earlier than the time of Christ. It consists of tiered stages, rather like a wedding cake, of stucco, stone, and rubble. Unlike later Mayan temples, E VII Sub. had no permanent building on top; a wooden hut, now lost, crowned the edifice. The chief decorations of the pyramid were eighteen large masklike faces affixed at the various levels. Eight of these represent serpentlike forms, the rest human faces with animal elements. From several of these masks a long tongue-like form, sometimes forked, extends downward below a zigzag line of teeth. On either side of the upturned snout are scrolls forming eyes. The stark stare of these faces gives them a belligerent, awe-inspiring appearance.

There is a marked resemblance between the E VII Sub. masks and Late Chou art of the Pacific. The long-tongued, grotesque architectural masks of the Maya recall the council-house masks of the Maori of New Zealand and the gable masks of the Sepik River people. Moreover, in Late Chou Chinese tomb figures we note the same squarish treatment of the forms, and similar hornlike ear scrolls and triangular teeth designs. That there is some relationship between these areas seems certain. What is more, Mayan bowls (thought to date from somewhat later times) from the Ulua Valley in Honduras find striking parallels in Late Chou bronzes. Both in decoration and in spatial organization the resemblances are extraordinary.

Another point of relationship can be seen in early Mayan religious architecture. For instance, at Temple II at Tikal—an expression of profound religious belief—the temple rises steeply to form an elevated platform reached by a stairway, and this platform supports a separate house of stone crowned by a high roof crest or comb. Similar houses with high crests raised on platforms are found in India, Java, Cambodia, China, Vietnam, and other parts of southeast Asia. They symbolize the celestial residence—the home of the gods. In Middle America a temple consisting of a house elevated on a mound has exactly the same cosmic significance.

Many Mayan motifs are highly reminiscent of the art of India and the Hindu cultures of Java and Cambodia. The Maya and other Middle American peoples, for example, carved great open-mouthed serpent-monsters on either side of the foot of the great stairway leading up the face of pyramids. Occasionally, as in Copan door lintels, these monsters rest on the heads of human figures. These symbolic figures mark the entry into the supernatural world. In Indonesia and India, similar devouring monsters known as *makara* serve exactly the same purpose. They too are sometimes supported by human figures. Such resemblances between America and Indian Asia are an argument in favor of some long-forgotten flow of influences across the Pacific.

We have now noted many influences in Maya art that can have come only from Late Chou, Dongson, and Indian sources. By the time of the Maya period in America, these traditions had become so mixed in southeastern Asia that they ceased to be distinct stylistic entities. This may be seen in Java where grotesque protective masks of Late Chou origin grin menacingly from above the entrance of Hindu temples. Similarly, recent discoveries in the Chinese province of Yunnan (Plate 151), not far from the Vietnam border, disclose an amalgam of Late Chou, Dongson, Central Asian, Near Eastern, and Indian elements. Dating from about 175 B.C., these art forms include great bronze drums decorated with processional scenes that resemble, extraordinarily, Peruvian and Mexican art of a few centuries later. As in Mexican art, long-tongued dogs, and people carrying water jars appear along with hunting views and scenes of human sacrifice.

Central America

In Yucatan, new influences from southeast Asia were imposed on a rather advanced culture derived from Mexico. But in Central America and

254

northern South America from Nicaragua to Ecuador, newly introduced art forms had no previous tradition on which to build. As a consequence there is the curious situation of relatively primitive societies producing gold and jade work although they had no prior monumental architecture or little stone sculpture. Such peoples were the creators of the Nicoya style in Costa Rica; the Chiriqui, Veraguas, Venado Beach, and Cocle styles in Panama; and the Chibcha and Quimbaya styles of Colombia. Except in Costa Rica and Colombia, which border, significantly, on the high culture areas, none of these peoples achieved monumental sculpture. They all excelled, however, in the very difficult *cire-perdue,* or "lost-wax," metal-casting process. The question this poses is how these Central American tribes could have evolved such a complicated technique without having a more developed culture of their own. If we look at Central American art, we are immediately impressed by the number of times we find S-spiral designs or a frontal human figure grappling with two flanking animal figures in profile. Common, too, in Peru are figures in the orant or splayed position, the use of frames, and representations of boats with dragon heads as prows at either end. The forms remind us sometimes of the Solomons style, sometimes of the Austral Islands or Nias traditions. But always the Dongson style is brought to mind. Even though we cannot date the American pieces very accurately, there is every reason to believe that they were made between A.D. 100 and 1500; this was long after the Dongson people first reached the Pacific.

Resolving the High Culture Problem

The story of high culture art in America only begins with the styles we have been describing. It goes on to the brilliant phases of the Chimu and Inca in Peru, and to the Toltec, Mixtec, and Aztec in Mexico. But the outlines for all pre-Columbian arts are sketched in the earlier traditions. We have seen the emergence of the single frontal human figure in the round in clay, and the monumental fanged composite animal carved in stone. Then emerged the idea of the mask, and of space, interrelationship, and frame, and finally the realistic ceremonial figure in metal adorned with emblems of rank. It is instructive, therefore, to note that this development follows exactly the sequence of a similar development at a slightly earlier date in the Orient. Is this, then, a natural evolution through which both cultures progressed independently? Probably not. The history of art in the Far East is by no means accidental, as we have been able to show. Art in China passed successively through its Aquatic, Shang, and Chou phases precisely because a contact with outside ideas and influences broke down old traditions and opened up new vistas for the artist. Left to their own devices, the pre-Columbian Indians would probably have perpetuated their old styles. Instead they followed an irregular zigzag course of stylistic change. Scholars who believe that pre-Columbian advances took place in isolation must explain why such developments occurred in precisely the Oriental sequence; even more, they must show how this course could have been followed without access to the sort of outside ideas that transformed Far Eastern art and civilization. On the face of it, this would appear to be an impossible task.

Marginal Groups

Far to the south of the high culture area lived numerous food-gathering societies left almost untouched by the impressive developments in Peru. Among these marginal peoples were Patagonian tribes such as the Yahgan and Tchuelche. Earning their precarious livelihood left them little time for artistic work; so, except for simple conical masks of bark and warm skin robes decorated with fret designs, there is little art in the lower peninsula of South America.

151   *Rubbing of bronze drum (detail). Shih Chai Shan, Yunnan Province, China. H. of detail* ca. *4″ (Peoples' Museum, Peking).*

Overleaf:
152   *Karaja sacred masks kept in hut forbidden to women and worn with skirts (foreground) in fertility rites. Araguaia River, Central Brazil. Feathers and vegetable fibers. Photographed in 1960.*

153   *Tucuna spirit mask worn by men during girls' puberty rites. Upper Amazon, Brazil. Painted inner bark and resin. Photographed in 1958*

Slightly to the north, in Chile, however, were the Araucanians who, though they accepted little from the high cultures of the Andes did have several advantages over the primitive southernmost tribes. The Araucanian practiced agriculture, performed elaborate rituals, and loved a good fight. For him war was not, as in the high cultures, part of an imperial scheme; it was simply a natural means of settling feuds and acquiring human victims.

Araucanian customs are rather similar to those of other Megalithic peoples, especially those of the Marquesas. In both areas, as Jose Imbelloni, a South American anthropologist, has shown, the word *toki* means "ax" or "adze." The Araucanians also called their war chief *toki*, and a ceremonial ax, symbolic of his martial role, was brought forth at the outbreak of war. In Polynesia, Toki was the name of a deified chief whose symbol was also an ax blade. The fact that the Araucanians lived in palisaded villages, took heads, and performed dances on stilts suggests further similarities with Megalithic culture in various parts of the Pacific.

In art, the Araucanians limited their efforts to large post figures and human-like face masks. They marked graves with a wooden column, the very top of which was carved into a face. Apart from repetition of simple rhythmic shapes, there is little attempt at

154 and 155 Male and female Witoto ancestor figures. Putomayo River, Colombia. Wood with bark cloth. H. 71–79" (City of Liverpool Museum).

ornament in these figures; they remain very much in the wooden Megalithic tradition. The masks, on the other hand, are much harder to classify. Somewhat similar in appearance to Cherokee face carvings from the southeastern United States, they are used at festive gatherings. But it is not clear whether these Araucanian masks are deeply rooted in the old culture or are later innovations introduced by the Spanish.

Amazon Basin

The Amazon River drains a huge area of tropical rain forest and grassland extending over most of western Brazil. The people of this hot, humid region rely on the river and its tributaries for transport and communication. West and south of them were the high cultures, but the towering Andes Mountains stood in the way of any high culture exchange program. Thus, though geographically close to the high culture peoples, the Amazon folk had more contact with the primitive cultures of coastal Brazil and the Guianas than with advanced civilizations from Peru. Their culture still remained therefore at a fairly low level, resembling somewhat that of the peoples of the southern marginal regions.

Hunting, fishing, and some agriculture provide a living for the Amazon Basin people. They live in airy, often wall-less huts, and wear a minimum of clothing. For ceremonies, the Amazonians construct masks, drums, and musical instruments (Plate 152). These they have decorated with incised geometric designs and rectangularly organized patterns. Their masks are of wood, fiber, feathers, or bark cloth. Wood masks, the rarest type, were used mainly in the upper Xingu River region. Carved out of a flat piece of wood and given crude human features, these nevertheless represented animals. A dancer wore the mask in secular plays intended merely for the amusement of his village. Possibly at one time these masks had a deep religious significance, as the angular designs painted on them sometimes have a symbolic meaning.

Another tribe that has produced wooden masks is the Chiriguano, who live southwest of the river in the Bolivian foothills of the Andes. The arresting wood masks of the Chiriguano are believed to have played a part in rites in which masked men, pretending to be nature spirits or ghosts, invade a village, collect food, and leave; the village elders then publicly lament their departure. The plastic strength and aggressive style of this Chiriguano mask suggests a more cultivated origin than the Amazon Basin. Stylistic influences from the Andes, seen also in the impressive pottery of the Chiriguano, may help explain the mask's sophistication.

The bark-cloth masks appear sporadically throughout the vast Amazon region. Those from the northwestern Amazon, made by such people as the Tucuna, Cubeo, and Witoto, stand out aesthetically and deserve pride of place (Plate 153). Usage varies widely. Among the Cubeo, masks sometimes represent a crop-destroying demon who has to be propitiated; others portray animals, birds, and mythological spirits who hover around at mourning ceremonies. In the latter type, the masked figures help to reassure the villagers of the continued benevolence of the gods by expelling the spirit of the deceased from the camp. Among the Tucuna, masks are required at puberty rites. Upon completion of the ceremonies, Amazon masks are usually destroyed. Stylistically, each group makes its own variation on the central design. The Witoto and Cubeo masks, which are of bark cloth and are conical in shape, bear a strange resemblance to the Dukduk masks of New Britain.

Figure sculpture is quite uncommon in the Amazon Basin. One example collected among the Maue of the central Amazon over a hundred years ago suggests the existence of a skilled ancient tradition, based perhaps on ceramic prototypes. Carved wooden figures are found in the Yagua and Witoto areas of northwestern Brazil. Some made only recently seem crude and highly simplified in style; but others obtained long ago in the Witoto country would be triumphant technical achievements in any primitive society (Plates 154 and 155). According to the army officer who collected them, these two carvings represent "a god and goddess from a Tribal House"; ethnologists who have worked among the Witoto declare, however, that the figures are really memorials to deceased ancestors. In spite of the hard tropical wood in which the figures are carved, there is a sympathetic concern for the human image. Details such as the thick calves, the loincloths, and body decoration are reproduced from life. Male and female body types are clearly distinguished from one another. The faces are diamond-shaped, with deep-cut eyes, odd tablike ears extending to the sides, and a thin mouth flanking the broad-based triangular nose. The body posture, with hands held between the breasts or on the upper abdomen, resembles that seen elsewhere in the Amazon—for example, among the Maue. A more distant linkage can be found with the art of the Arawak tribes of the Caribbean.

Caribbean

The first European in the Caribbean who left any record of his voyage was of course Christopher Columbus. Erroneous as many of his ideas were, Columbus was quick to note a strong similarity among various peoples he visited. Anthropologists now agree completely with Columbus and recognize a common tradition extending throughout the Caribbean islands and around its fringes. Today the Caribbean peoples have all but lost their old culture; fortunately, from surviving art objects and other records, we know something of their former customs.

The most interesting Caribbean people were the Arawak. Living in the lush hills and drier savannah country of Cuba, Puerto Rico, and the smaller islands, they enjoyed a remarkably elegant and courtly way of life. The Arawak introduced agriculture, permanent villages, the idea of an aristocracy, and ceremonies involving the use of images. To ensure continued blessings, they made images of wood, stone, bone, shell, and clay which they often decorated with gold (Plate 156). These images belonged to individuals, who felt that they conferred specific powers upon them. Some helped the hunter, farmer, or fisherman; others could produce children or foretell the fate of raiding parties. The owner set the figure in a niche or on a table and took an overdose of snuff to induce hallucinations. These visions, he believed, were messages from the supernatural world. Offerings of food placed on the figure guarded the owner constantly against the displeasure of the spirits.

Arawak figures are amazingly realistic. The rendering of cheekbones, brows, nostril wings, and eye sockets show the artist's awareness of natural structure in the face. In the body the rib cage and vertebrae are often visible. All points of articulation, such as the ankles, elbows, and the muscles of the upper arm and chest, are vigorously depicted. As in Witoto figures from the Amazon, the calves of the leg are large; and as in the Amazon male figure, the phallus is erect. For some unknown reason the legs of Arawak figures usually diverge sharply, making a sort of inverted Y of the body. Ear pendants and decorative headbands enhance the figures, but the gold ornaments rarely remain, owing to the greed of treasure hunters.

Arawak figures in wood form a distinct link with those of the Amazon, even though there are differences between them. They also recall gold and gold-alloy objects from Quimbaya in northern Colombia and Veraguas in Panama. There is, in Central America and the Caribbean, a similar emphasis on ear ornaments, knee articulation, and on holding cylindrical objects in both hands. Figures may be standing or seated, but a ceremonial posture is invariable. If we are correct in believing Central American cultures depend to a considerable extent on those of southeastern Asia, especially Dongson, finding parallels with such areas as Nias should not be difficult. And indeed it is not. Stone seats from Costa Rica resemble, on the one hand, Nias stonework and, on the other, Arawak wood carvings. Figures with prominent knee articulation, holding objects in both hands, and wearing ear pendants, add further evidence of the relationship. Even the Ancient Near Eastern myth of the World Tree from which all people are descended (a major theme in Nias cosmology) finds an exact parallel in the Caribbean region. And in Costa Rica and Honduras, figures are known that employ the Dongson knee-elbow-chin pose. An American variation in which only the left arm is raised may also be seen in Indonesia.

The Guianas

An area of minor importance is the Guiana region. Although ideas were acquired from neighboring groups, Indian culture remained rather meager.

Most interesting are the crisply carved, rectangular wooden clubs; these were used over a wide area. They have a ceremonial purpose and, appropriately, a very formal sort of ornamentation. Guiana people also produced brilliantly colored feather headdresses, tiny figures carved in soft wood and tan-and-black basketry of considerable interest.

Apart from the Indians, another group of primitives live in the Guianas; these are the Bush Negroes, who first came from Africa to America as slaves in the seventeenth century. During periods of political unrest, many of these Negroes escaped from their harsh masters and fled into the bush, where they re-established a primitive way of life. Having more advantages than the Indians, the Bush Negroes flourished in the Guianas and evolved a highly specialized and unique art. Contributing to their style are numerous West African elements, including incised designs on combs and stools, very much like the Ashanti art of Ghana. At the same time, American Indian patterns of form and decoration occur in the Bush Negro's carved canoe paddles. A third contribution to this art was made by European culture: Dutch strapwork of the sixteenth and seventeenth centuries is the source of much of the decoration that the Bush Negro now applies to his furniture and utensils.

156   Arawak god figure. Jamaica. Wood with shell. H. 27″ (Museum of Primitive Art, New York).

Panama

Few Caribbean and Central American tribes have escaped Western influence or conquest during the past five hundred years. One group of people who did not capitulate, however, are the Cuna, a stocky chocolate-brown tribe now living in the remote jungles of Panama. Although often hard pressed to get sufficient food, the Cuna nevertheless possessed certain luxury goods—wooden seats, pottery, braziers, and other objects—that suggest high culture origins. Another striking feature of Cuna culture is a written picture language, although it is used only for memory purposes. Attempts have been made to relate this script to the writing of the Easter Islanders and the Chinese.

When their food wants have been satisfied, the Cuna through their shamans concern themselves with the control of disease. These shamans dart about curing illness or recovering souls stolen by evil-doers. Each important shaman owns a carved staff and a *nuchu*, a small figure that symbolizes his individual magic power. Large balsa wood effigies belonging to famous shamans are used in public rites designed to halt epidemics. With their postlike bodies, sloping shoulders, and flat faces, they resemble the wooden figures used by the Araucanians.

Western Mexico

High culture civilizations held sway over the entire area from Honduras to the central highlands of Mexico; the great empires of the Maya, the Toltec, and the Aztec swallowed up primitive tribes and overwhelmed their simple art. But beyond the mountain chain that splits Mexico into two areas lived people who were insulated from all but the strongest high culture influences.

The people who created western Mexican art are familiar to us almost solely through their ceramics. Were it not for the imaginative yet realistic effigy pots and figures that they buried with their dead, we would scarcely

157 Pottery effigy buried with the dead. Colima, Western Mexico. H. 12″ (Stavenhagen Collection, Mexico City).

know these people had existed. There are no buildings or stone sculptures of importance in the area, nor are there records or traditions of the sort found in the high culture areas. Fortunately, the ceramic art is explicit and descriptive and thus, to a large degree, tells its own story.

Illustrated in the art of western Mexico are many scenes of daily life: a woman making tortillas, grotesque images such as hunchbacks, ceremonial sports, animals, and house groups (Plate 157). In the latter, numerous little figures sit in or around a house where funeral ceremonies, phallic dances, or healing rites are going on. Almost unparalleled in the Americas, except perhaps in Peru among the Mochica, these ceramics resemble complex bronze groups from Yunnan Province in southern China.

In style, western Mexican sculpture derives its basic format from the early art of central Mexico as seen in El Arbolillo and Tlatilco. The use of clay, the simplification of shapes, and the down-to-earth subjects chosen reflect this origin. At the same time there is a fluidity of surface and a spatial freedom in the western style that distinguish it from all its forebears. A figure twists on its axis, raises an arm, or gesticulates violently as if under psychological pressure to express its feelings. The force and directness of these figures is nothing short of incredible. Even when depicting deformed creatures, a spirit of gay, irrepressible fantasy and good will pervades the artist's work. In contrast with the grim, authoritarian styles of Middle America, the style centered in western Mexico is exuberantly physical, warmly human, and often exceedingly funny.

These spirited works of art are so unlike other Mexican styles that it has been suggested this sculpture represents a genre or folk art devoid of religious content. This interpretation ignores the connotations of the figures and stresses only the obvious joyousness and playful character of the style. But certain themes are repeated over and over as though they were visual chants intended to perpetuate the status quo. Continuity in life and survival after death appear to be the underlying ideas behind the seemingly irreverent art of western Mexico.

The Southwest

The art of the Indians north of Mexico, complex and diverse though it unquestionably is, probably derives from three distinct main sources.

First, there are numerous signs of influence emanating from northern Asia; these probably came across by way of the Bering Strait over a long period of time. Secondly, many high culture ideas have entered the area from the south. Some penetrated the New Mexico-Arizona area via the deserts of northern Mexico. Other influences straggled around the Gulf Coast or came up through Florida from the Caribbean islands. The third major source that the North American Indian artist drew upon was art introduced by Europeans. From the sixteenth and seventeenth centuries on, European designs gradually assumed an ever-increasing role in Indian art, introducing first French and later, English, Spanish and American motifs. Today there is probably not one Indian art form still practised in the United States which has not been affected by Western standards and motifs.

Thanks to extensive excavation and scholarly work, the story of Indian art in the American Southwest has now become clear. About two thousand years ago in the sparsely vegetated, dry plateau country of New Mexico, Arizona, Colorado, and Utah, a distinctive Southwestern people first emerged. Naturally, the earlier peoples developed slowly, first acquiring basketry and agriculture, then creating many spectacularly beautiful pottery styles. In their prime, some eight hundred years ago, they built the famous cliff palaces

158   Ahayuta, one of the twin Zuni war gods. Southwestern United States. H. 27¹/₂″ (Dockstader Collection, New York).

of Mesa Verde and Montezuma's Castle and the great apartment dwelling, Pueblo Bonito. Descendants of these people, such as the Hopi and Zuni, still live on the plateaus and mesas, sometimes even in villages of very great age.

The more advanced the peaceful Pueblo people became, the more they seem to have put their trust in a democratic social community. They have always avoided an aristocratically organized state of the sort that evolved in Mexico. Their houses are still similar to one another, and all clans continue to have access to rituals. Despite long contact with Christianity, Pueblo religion has vigorously resisted change; contemporary rituals are therefore extremely helpful in the interpretation of archaeological discoveries. Pueblo spiritual life has apparently always centered on the need for rain. Ancient mural designs painted in the great *kiva*, or underground ceremonial centers, depict clouds, lightning, and water, in symbolic form. Though ritualistic in appearance, these delicately balanced Pueblo murals have none of the heavy ornamental burden of Middle American wall paintings. The *kiva* artists usually anchored their designs to a ground line and to a vertical central axis with figures symmetrically placed on either side. Forms are outlined in black, then filled in with flat areas of color. Characteristic of these paintings, and indeed of all Southwestern art, are the dry, dusty hues of blue, red, yellow, and white and an intricate geometric subdivision of the surface.

In recent times, the Pueblo have made much use of Kachina masks and dolls. Both represent spirits. The masks are worn in religious ceremonies and remain sacred; but the less important dolls are given to the children to help them recognize the various supernatural beings in the Pueblo pantheon.

Far more sacred were the wooden figures of war gods of the Zuni (Plate 158). These were made in secret and, after the traditional ceremonies, were placed in a war shrine and allowed to decay. In most examples, a funnel-like helmet surmounts a crude, Megalithic face and nondescript body. From the center of the stomach protrudes a carved staff known as a feather cylinder. These sticks represent the figure's navel and by analogy the center of the world and all life-giving power.

About seven hundred years ago, tough nomadic tribes from the north invaded the Pueblo area bringing crude forms of art. But like the Romans who, upon conquering Greece, adopted Hellenic culture, the vigorous Nav-

159   *Pipe figure. Adena
Mound, Ohio. Stone. H. 8"
(The Historical Society,
Columbus).*

aho and the proud Apache, chief descendants of the invaders, took over many ideas and art forms from the docile Pueblos. Today, Navaho blankets, jewelry, and sand paintings, all borrowed from their neighbors, are among the finest of surviving American Indian products.

Sand painting plays a vital role in Navaho healing rites. After smoothing a flat area on the floor of the octagonal ceremonial house the medicine man strews five colors of sand in angular, geometric, and elongated representational designs. These symbolize deities, birds, animals, and various heavenly bodies. His drawing stresses four compass directions, which occupy an important place in Navaho thought. North, south, and west are potentially dangerous, while the east is the source of great benefits. Such a belief, transferred from Mexico, agrees precisely with a widespread Asian tradition. In both areas, certain colors and phases of time are symbolically related to the four directions. The harsh drama of these sand paintings offers a ready proof of the artistic genius of the alert and unfettered Navaho mind. Noted for their sheepraising and commerce, the Navaho are today the fastest-growing Indian population in the country and are well on their way toward

160   *(Facing) Breast ornament. Oehnaville, Texas. Shell. Diameter 5¹/₂″ (Museum of the American Indian, New York).*

161   *Ceremonial pipe showing warrior beheading victim. Spiro Mound, Oklahoma. H. 9³/₄″ (Museum of the American Indian, New York).*

achieving a new cultural synthesis combining the advantages of modern technology with elements of the older, indigenous way of life.

The Southeast

Between the Ohio and lower Mississippi valleys lies a large section which may be called the Southeast. In this region, where a warm, humid climate encourages abundant plant and animal life, Indian culture, despite brilliant beginnings, crumbled away quickly as the European intruders penetrated. By the nineteenth century most of the tribes were in retreat or were suffering terribly from disease and dying out. What little we know, therefore, of the Indians of the Southeast we owe to the archaeologist's spade and to the scattered records of the early contact period.

Of the countless art objects recovered in the Southeast, those from the late or Mississippi period, dating perhaps A.D. 1000–1700, have the greatest aesthetic interest. They clearly derive their complex symbols and advanced formal designs from the art of the high cultures. Even earlier, in the Adena and Hopewell cultures, objects of a distinctly Mexican appearance crop up constantly. A perfect example is the magnificent Adena pipe excavated in southern Ohio (Plate 159). Other pipes from this phase, representing birds and other animals, are simpler and more naturalistic. The Adena and Hopewell people also erected many of the mounds popularly ascribed to the "Moundbuilders". Designed as burial places, the outlines of these early mounds often resemble birds, snakes, or other animals. Other mounds constructed in the succeeding Mississippi period were more pyramidal in shape and were intended as symbolic platforms on top of which ritual houses were built. Here, too, a Mexican origin is likely. The purpose of these temple mounds seems to have been to reproduce the cosmic idea of the celestial mountain. As understood in Mexico, the piled-up layers of the temple mound represent the universe in its various levels and the house on top symbolizes the home of the gods.

The Mississippi period saw the climax of a gruesome series of rites known as the Southern death cult. Human sacrifice and other ritual horrors spread over the Southeast, and with them as favorite motifs in art the human skull, trophy heads, axes, and eagle warriors. Among the most revealing artifacts are circular breast pendants made of shell and incised with

274

figures, both human and animal, often in violent action (Plate 160). Some warriors appear to be running or dancing; others paddle boats, brandish clubs, or exhibit trophy heads. The active postures of the figures and their elaborate costumes are strongly reminiscent of Middle American art. And if we look closely at the forms, we also perceive many indirect connections with southeastern Asia, especially with Late Chou and Dongson. Strange feline monsters with protruding tongues and central figures flanked by two snakes also occur in the art of the American Southeast. The shell pendants on which these designs appear resemble remarkably the *kapkaps* of the Pacific, even having double-S spirals or a square shape inside an eight-pointed star. The human hand with an eye on the palm, a well-known Southeastern symbol, is another link with Asia. But the immediate inspiration for these designs must have its sources in the south. The revolving spiral, spider on disk, double-bladed ax, arabesque, S-spiral, and other related motifs are especially prominent in the Southeast. Parallels to most of these designs can be found in Mexico, Central America, the Caribbean, or in the Mochica, Tiahuanaco, and Chimu styles of Peru (which also reflect the Dongson tradition) (Plate 146).

Besides shell-work, the Indians of the Mississippi period also mastered the art of carving figures in stone (Plate 161). One of the most interesting examples shows a kneeling man holding sticks in one hand and a disk-like stone in the other. He is playing a game, well known in the Southeast, in which a disk is bowled across a field and a stick is thrown after it. The object of the game is to have the stick land as close to the stone as possible. From an artistic point of view it would be hard to conceive a more sculptural interpretation of the human figure. The same is true of wooden masks found preserved under layers of mud in Key Marco, Florida. Painted with white, creamy pink, and bluish-gray pigments, the Key Marco masks belong to one of the most expressive and elegant of American art styles.

The Northeast

The people of the northeastern part of North America received far fewer impulses from the high cultures. But they seem to have acquired many ideas from northern Asia, including stamped pottery, ground-stone tools, semilunar knives, and socketed and stemmed copper weapons. Otherwise their lives differed little from those of Indians in the Southeast: they planted corn, squash, and beans, and hunted small game in the dense forests. Archaeological materials from this area usually lack aesthetic interest, and most of the objects made in recent times borrow heavily from European art. We will therefore discuss only one native tradition, that of the Iroquois, which persists to the present day in western New York State and parts of Canada.

Where the Iroquois came from has long puzzled anthropologists. Some see them as Indians who occupied their historic homeland for centuries; others regard them as recent migrants from the south. Whatever their origins, the Iroquois had a genius for political organization; the loose confederation of tribes they founded is thought by some scholars to have been a model for the American Articles of Confederation.

Iroquois art consists mainly of wooden masks (Plate 162). Strikingly different from the placid features of Southeastern masks, the faces show great animation and expressiveness. This hyperdramatic intensity points in the direction of northern Asia where Aleut and Japanese masks often depicted strong emotions. Moreover, if we turn to the function of the Iroquois masks, we find further suggestions of northern Asian shamanism. Members of the Iroquois False-Face Society

162   Mohawk mask representing supernatural helper. Northeastern United States. (Made ca. 1750.) Wood with tin and horsehair. H. 12" (Museum of the American Indian, New York).

wear their masks during protective and healing rites. The masks represent various mythological beings or spirits who help the owner. Certain types occur again and again. With their twisted mouths and noses and deeply wrinkled brows, most Iroquois masks are truly grotesque. Round metal disks form the staring eyes, and the hair is a hank of horsetail. Other than the wide cheekbones, there is no attempt to depict the handsome features of the typical Iroquois face.

South of the Iroquois were the Delaware Indians, who periodically warred against and then made peace with their powerful neighbors. In this way the Delaware acquired knowledge of Iroquois ways. Many of the carved objects they produced seem to reflect Iroquois inspiration. One of these is a wooden center-house post carved by the Delaware after their forced removal to the Indian Territory (now Oklahoma). Representing the supreme god, Mising, and probably serving as protector of the house, the post with its forehead grooves still retains echoes of the Iroquois style (Plate 163).

The Plains

It is ironic that the Plains horseman, the stereotype of the American Indian, is a late-

163   Delaware Indian house post showing Mising, the supreme god. (Made in 1874 after the Delaware migration to Oklahoma.) H. of face 20" (Philbrook Art Center, Tulsa, Oklahoma).

277

comer to aboriginal history. The war-bonnet-
ed, wild-riding warrior attacking buffalo
herds or wagon trains or sitting in front of
his famous tepee really did not appear until
the end of the eighteenth century. Before that
time he lived a settled existence in the quiet
river valleys and along the clay bluffs of the
prairie country. Lacking the horse (which
was introduced by the Spanish), these Village
Indians, as they are called, could not lead so
freely migratory a life as the later Plains
Indians.

The art of the Plains Indian revolved
around his wandering way of life. And since
this started so late, his art tends to be almost
entirely borrowed from outside sources, Indian as well as European. Synthesized during
a long period of migration and trade, Plains
Indian decorative art achieved a measure of
power and ornamental sophistication. Tepee
covers, shields, and clothing received a rich
appliqué of color and design. Geometric patterns were the work of women, but the more
dangerous naturalistic forms belonged to the
men. The latter recorded their exploits on
vividly painted buffalo-skin robes, using a lit-
eral, graphic style of illustration (Plate 164).
Because the victorious warrior was sometimes
a less than gifted artist, Plains Indian painting often looks naive and unskilled. And no
doubt it often is. All the more tragic, therefore, is the fact that this art stemming from
so self-confident a people did not survive the
terrible settlement wars of the nineteenth century. Decorative and pleasing as contemporary Plains art may be, the style has somehow
lost its proud reason for being.

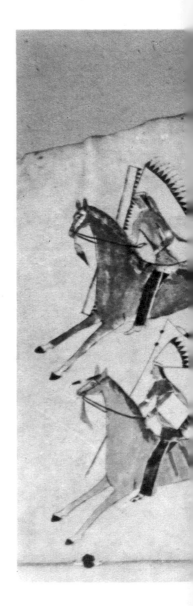

278

Detail of Cheyenne warrior's robe depicting his exploits. Plains area. (Made ca. *1865.) Painted buffalo skin. (Denver Art Museum).*

Northwest Coast

Living along the tattered fringe of land between the Rockies and the Pacific from Puget Sound to southeastern Alaska, the Indians of the Northwest Coast reached astonishing heights in mythology, art, and drama. They carved the towering wooden columns every school child knows as totem poles. And yet these remarkable achievements were attained without the aid of agriculture, useful metals, or domestic animals other than the dog. How the Coast Indians, despite such handicaps, developed the raw materials of nature into a rich and vigorous expression of life is a fascinating story.

The world of the Northwest Coast native consisted basically of two elements—wood and water. From the countless islands, hills and mountains, he hewed the wood—cedar, fir, alder, and yew—for his material goods. The myriad inlets, sounds, and rivers provided the bulk of his food and his highways of communication. Although cultivation was unknown in the area, every spring the Coast inhabitant harvested a "crop" of salmon and other fish that surged into the sheltered waterways to spawn. Sea lions, porpoise, and whales were harpooned or stranded almost at his doorstep. The sea provided such an

165 Salish spirit post figure. Puget Sound. H. 50″ (Washington State Museum, Seattle).

166 (Facing) Kwakiutl performers wearing hinged animal masks in dancing house. Vancouver Island, British Columbia. Photographed ca. 1900.

abundance of food that the Northwest Coast Indian could enrich his material and ceremonial life far beyond that of any other food-gathering people. For the means of this enrichment he turned to the inexhaustible and easily worked raw material nearest at hand—wood.

Wood and its by-products played as conspicuous a role in the life of Coast inhabitants as did the buffalo in Plains Indian culture or the coconut palm in that of central Polynesia. Houses, canoes, clubs, boxes, traps, fishhooks, armor, tools, and a host of household objects all were made from cedar. Blankets, hats, baskets, and rain capes were fashioned from plaited bark, fiber, or tree roots. And for impressive theatrical displays, trained specialists carved wooden masks, cleverly conceived noise-makers, magical apparatus, and gigantic ornamented poles (Plate 166). The pretext for making these carvings was usually a mythological story in which fantastic animals and other supernatural beings influenced the natural world or the lives of the people.

As in all societies where day-to-day survival has ceased to be the chief concern, the possession of objects in the Northwest Coast fulfilled other than mere physical needs. Almost all belongings, including even food, served ultimately to express the owner's social status. Moreover, since theirs was a competitive, aristocratic society, every Northwest Coast chief had to vindicate his superior position with proof of worldly success. To amass riches became the driving force in the lives of nobleman and commoner alike, the end being the same—to achieve prestige.

Besides birth and wealth, Coast society approved of another route to high status that penetrated into the realm of the supernatural. The Coast Indian paid scant attention to remote gods; he placed his faith in the acquisition from his personal guardian spirit of a magical commodity known simply as "power". Sometimes the Indian went into partnership with his "power," and all that was necessary to gain esteem was to demonstrate the existence of the relationship. In other instances the owner became in effect a shaman and actually used his magic power for private and public ends such as curing the sick, increasing the food supply, winning in battles, and, on the negative side, malevolent sorcery against unwitting victims. The successful shaman enjoyed fat fees and also enormous prestige. It it small wonder, therefore, that many gifted but socially insignificant individuals deliberately went in quest of and achieved "power" from the supernatural world.

*167   Long-visored Aleut hat worn by chiefs to ensure success in hunting. Alaska.
Painted wood, incised ivory, beads, and sea-lion whiskers. H. 8" (Museum of the
American Indian, New York).*

Such a striving for ostentatious displays of wealth are peculiar to the
tribes of the Northwest Coast. Even the earliest European visitors arriving
in the middle of the eighteenth century noticed this; they called attention to
similarities between the Coast people and those of Kamchatka in eastern
Siberia. Scholars used to assume, therefore, that there once was a fairly
close relationship between the two areas, and that the linkage had been
broken by the influx of the Eskimo into Alaska. But archaeologists recently

excavating along the southern part of the Coast were amazed to discover that the oldest artifacts they found bore a startling resemblance to those of the Eskimo. Remarkable as this may seem, we will find yet further indications of Eskimoid influence in many parts of the Coastal region.

Historically the people of the Northwest fringe, though isolated from the main continent, had knowledge of one another. Each tribal group or "nation" shared a distinct language and unique culture, though none achieved political or economic unity. From south to north these groups include: the Salish-speaking people around Puget Sound and the Gulf of Georgia; the Nootka of western Vancouver Island; the Kwakiutl who occupy the rest of the island and nearby mainland; the Bella Coola who are found on the inner reaches of Burke and Dean inlets; the Haida of the Queen Charlotte Islands; the Tsimshian of the Skeena and Nass riversheds; and the Tlingit of southeastern Alaska. Of these, the Tlingit, Haida, and Tsimshian clearly belong together; the Kwakiutl, Nootka, and Bella Coola form a unit, though with ties both to the north and south. The Coast Salish, by no means a homogeneous group, participate only marginally in Coast culture. Since language, art, and custom vary widely among the "nations," it is well to discuss them singly.

168 Salish shaman's mask with animals encircling the face. Fraser River area, British Columbia. H. 18" (National Museum of Canada, Ottawa)

169 Nootka wolf mask worn during abduction of children for initiation rites. Vancouver Island, British Columbia. Painted wood. H. 7¹/₂" (American Museum of Natural History, New York).

The Coast Salish

The Salish are a rather amiable and likable people. Unlike other Coast groups, they have been comparatively democratic. Except for slaves who were in effect family servants, all adults enjoyed considerable freedom. Chiefs owed their positions to good fortune, personality, and wealth as well as to birth. They gave advice and distributed food and valuables at festivals known as potlatches: these affirmed the chief's paramount status and drew attention to his people's achievements. Potlatching around Puget Sound never became so violent or competitive as it did in the north. Similarly, art objects made by Salish craftsmen exhibit little in the way of aggression. Contained within crisp closed silhouettes, the forms are usually reticent and discreet.

The most impressive Salish wood carvings are shamanic wands, masks, post figures, boards, and grave images. The motivations underlying the form and decoration of these pieces were in part religious, in part social. Every important Salish person, chief and shaman alike, had a personal spirit guardian who gave him magical power and the right to display-privileges, including a song, dance, mask, or design. The intent faces on shaman's wands and figures—typical of carvings displaying the owner's power—admirably express their purpose. Some show the shaman actually grappling with demonic animals that symbolize his familiar spirit; others, where the animal is omitted, indicate constraint by means of linear tensions or a self-embracing gesture. In addition, the squareness and angularity of the forms intensify their effect of arbitrariness. The stiff poses and insistent rhythms of the figures seem to abstract them from everyday reality.

The Salish people have only one kind of mask, the *swaixwe* (Plate 168). The owners of these masks are supposed to have acquired from supernatural beings the right to wear them. Dancers wore the *swaixwe* in public rights commemorating the birth of a child, the giving of a new name, or at marriage celebrations. Although the donning of such masks conferred prestige on the wearer and on the person paying for the ceremony, the underlying purpose of the *swaixwe* was religious. This may be seen from the feathers worn with it—a costume typical of shamans—and from its various sculptural details reflecting the acquisition of magical power. The strange animals, for example, that form the features of the face are identical with those symbolizing the shaman's familiar spirit. The straining peg-like eyes and square, downward extending tongue contribute also to an otherworldly appearance of this mask. Worn at a slight angle in front of the face, the mask was made by a professional sculptor, but the owner painted it himself to accord with and express his visionary experience with the supernatural.

According to native informants the Salish mask originated in one particular area up the Fraser River, not long before the coming of the first

170   Kwakiutl wild man mask. British Columbia. Painted wood with horsehair. H. 12″ (Provincial Museum, Victoria, British Columbia).

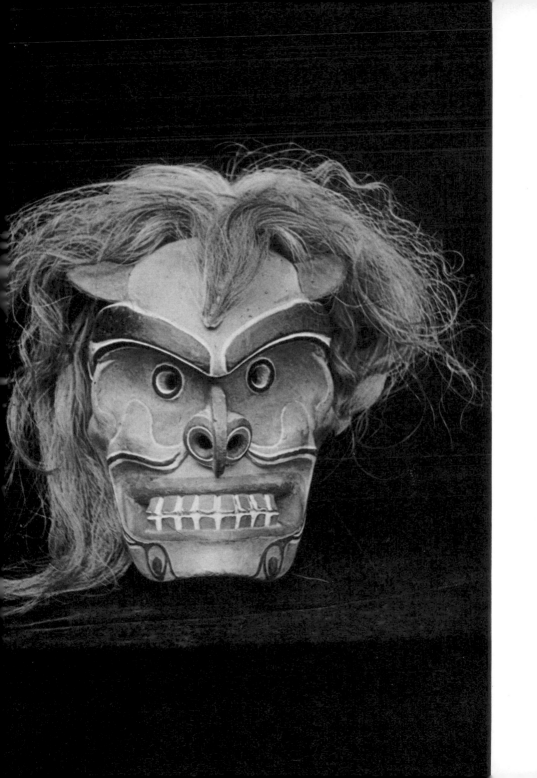

white explorers. Later its use seems to have spread north to Vancouver Island and up the mainland as far as the Tsimshian country. Because the type is so distinctive, it probably has some unique explanation; one writer, detecting functional similarities, suggests that the form may have come from the Nootka. Visual evidence will carry us even farther, for Salish masks bear a striking though submerged resemblance to certain Tlingit and Eskimo masks. Worn also by shamans, these frequently have small animals converging from the sides toward the nose just as in the *swaixwe*. The deep eye sockets and sea-lion whiskers ornamentation help corroborate this relationship.

Nootka

The Nootka of Vancouver Island's western fiords were a rugged and provincial people noted for their daring pursuit of whales and other sea mammals. As in so many other parts of the world, seafaring in this area involved a proper observance of religious tradition, both ashore and upon the sea. Nowhere is this more graphically illustrated than in the land-based imaginary whale hunts which they enacted. Central to this Nootka whale ritualism was a secret sacred shrine where statues of supernatural beings and skulls of dead ancestors

171 Kwakiutl chief holding his bloated stomach. British Columbia. H. 45" (Leff Collection, Uniontown, Pennsylvania).

were hidden. Properly approached, these spirits would cause dead and living whales to come ashore. The figures set up in the shrines characteristically show a rather crude conception of the human body. The forms and technical details, such as the preference for unpainted wood, strongly resemble Eskimo memorial post carvings, some of which were also used to control whales.

Other Nootka figures served as welcoming images in potlatch ceremonies and as interior architectural decoration. Their sturdy naturalism seems well suited to these static public occasions. Movement is depicted rarely, but when it is, as in the case of two figures grasping a bowl, the artist works vigorously and directly to achieve a straightforward solution. Tilting the faces, he produces a sense of expectancy in the figures. The curves of their backs and the vertical lines of the chests give vivid expression to the idea of a vessel—that is, a void that needs to be filled.

The Nootka artist also carved masks of various shapes and sizes. The largest and most handsome represented realistically carved human faces and were used in potlatches. These over life-size heads with their open mouths and eyes seem to represent a suddenly stimulated awareness. Since Nootka potlatches were a means of establishing the legal right to certain privileges—and participants in the ceremony functioned more or less as expert witnesses to the owner's claims—the alert expression of the masks is entirely appropriate.

In most other Nootka carvings little attention is given to fineness of surface: In some masks a rough-hewn quality is emphasized even to the point of stressing tool mark imprints. One type, made of four flat boards shaped like a box, seems almost anti-aesthetic. Other animal masks, worn on the forehead at the conclusion of the Wolf ceremony, often have broad conventional features (Plate 169). Both types are worn in the same manner as the mask-like Eskimo and Aleut hunting hats (Plate 167).

The Wolf Dance masks owe their visual character to certain attitudes peculiar to the Nootka. Everyone participated in the Wolf rites. Children pretended to be initiates, and were "kidnapped" by commoners dressed as wolves. Then the rest of the people, including chiefs temporarily demoted during the ceremony, rescued and helped to purify these newly instructed "victims." Masks used during and after the ceremony show little or no subordination or domination in their elements. In a way this reflects the democratic character of Nootka society.

Of Northwest Coast tribes only the Nootka produced many masks of

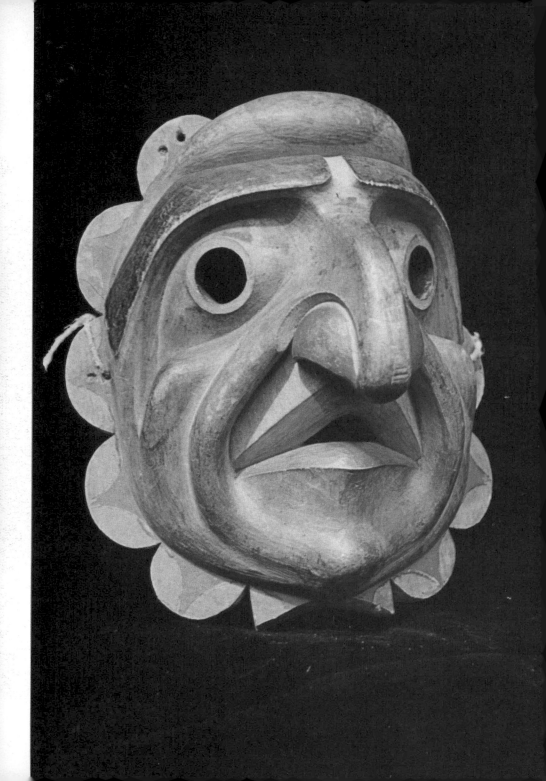

172 *(Facing) Bella Coola mask used in winter ceremonials. British Columbia. H. 9″ (Provincial Museum, Victoria).*

173 *Bella Bella moon mask from shaman's burial house. Kwakiutl. British Columbia. H. 14¹/₂″ (Provincial Museum, Victoria).*

whalebone; but this, interestingly enough, was a common medium for masks among the Eskimo. The Nootka also made wooden masks to wear over the face; more realistic than the animal headpieces, these masks still have no great refinement of shape and little interest in contrast. Because of their moderate scale and lack of bulk, the forms seem sometimes expressionless and aesthetically inert. But the best Nootka carving is truly articulate on two levels that are often ignored in other Northwest Coast areas. The use of vigorous texture distinguishes this art as that of a craftsman; secondly, in contrast to the extravagance of other Pacific coast art, there emerges from Nootka work a quality of honesty and directness and an economy of execution. This lack of pretension is probably due to historical conditions. Compared to the Salish craftsmen, carvers in the Nootka area seem to be fully conversant with the Eskimo tradition. Nootka art and culture, in fact, spring almost directly from this style.

Kwakiutl

The Kwakiutl were without question the most self-dramatizing and arrogant tribes in the entire area. Even today the Kwakiutl are notoriously thin-skinned, and when dissatisfied with the respect shown them will simply stalk away in as haughty a manner as possible. Pride in prerogative and accomplishment was of central importance to a Kwakiutl and a prime motive in his works of art. Quantities of ritual objects were produced for the use of dancing groups, or secret societies, as they are sometimes called (Plate 166). Dance societies convened during the winter months to initiate new members with the aid of masks, songs, and distinctive ceremonies. Some rites involved violence and destructiveness; others were as peaceful as the excitable participants would tolerate. The plot of dance-society performances was quite simple: members re-enacted some past successful quest that had conferred privileges on the ancestors of the novice. A spirit-being entered the village, kidnapped the protagonist and gave him special powers. The hero then returned to the village and displayed the prerogatives which his forebears had given him. So overpowering was the influence of the spirit within him that he at first stormed about in a frenzy, pretending to bite people and destroying property. The public seizures and eventual purging of the spirit took place at night before flickering fires. Awesome sound ef-

292

174 *Tsimshian realistic face mask. British Columbia. H. 17″ (Museum of the American Indian, New York).*

175 Tsimshian mask with naturalistic face painting. British Columbia. (Made ca.
1800.) H. 9¹/₂" (Museum of the American Indian, New York).

fects, weird cries, and sudden prearranged appearances and disappearances
added to the theatricality of the ceremony. Puppets flew back and forth on
concealed strings, droning voices came out of nowhere, and sleight-of-hand
tricks mystified the viewers. The sequence was repeated for several evenings,
until at last the assistants succeeded in taming the irrationality of the novice.
Dramatic changes of pace and disheartening relapses frequently occurred.

The masks worn in dancing rites by members as well as by the novice
depicted monsters, fabulous animals, and various spirit beings of human

appearance. Because of the great secrecy and danger surrounding such objects, only skilled members of the society, working always in seclusion and under strict supervision, were allowed to make them. To prevent any improper usage, the leaders of the society sometimes destroyed the masks at the end of the season. Correct handling of the carvings during the ceremonies was absolutely essential, since any inappropriate act or gesture on the part of a dancer might require the death of the culprit.

Kwakiutl art in its boldness of scale and excess of feeling mirrors the aggressive and assertive tendencies of the people. Bulbous projecting forms contrast with textured or hollowed surfaces. Painting dramatizes both the magical and supernatural character of the themes. Departing from reality through simplification and intensification, Kwakiutl carving achieves a truly expressionistic form.

The compulsiveness with which the artist approached his subjects may be seen in old photographs showing the long beak masks associated with the "cannibal ceremony." For the carver, the quintessence of these forms was their incredible elongation and voracious expressions. He therefore exaggerated the mouth, eyes, and nostrils—the organs most suggestive of sensory experience. Representations of human subjects are no less arresting. Especially when rendering "wild" people, the artist has modeled the forms in space as recklessly as he dare. Insisting on protrusion and recession even where it is scarcely necessary, he has charged his images with an inner freedom and vitality. So powerful and assured is this treatment that the forms seem almost to determine their own shape and expression. The impact of the mask derives still further vigor from the pigments that are applied; and these may enrich, articulate, or even deny the integrity of the solid form beneath.

There appear to have been two major traditions in the Northwest Coast, intersecting one another in the Kwakiutl territory. The southern Kwakiutl artists like the Nootka and Salish usually adhered to a static but eloquent style of a rather positive character. Those from the northern subdivisions shared with the Haida, Tsimshian, and Tlingit a preference for sensitive and sophisticated delineation. In the one, public symbolic representation dominates; in the other, expressiveness and aesthetic feeling come between the viewer and the overt meaning of the object. Northern Kwakiutl style combines the directness of the south with the subtle animation of the second tradition (Plate 173.)

295

One type of mask delighted all of the Kwakiutl — the movable mask, an ingenious arrangement of hinged parts and concealed strings. At the proper instant, the dancer or his assistant pulled the strings, causing the parts to wiggle, gyrate, or fly apart, to the feigned amazement and consternation of the spectators. The changing forms of the mask helped to convey certain dramatic qualities depending on the nature of the movement and the theatrical potentialities of the situation. Eye motions might suggest sleepiness, tension, or irrationality. If the mouth gaped, speech or animation or aggression might be expressed.

Of all Northwest Coast carving, perhaps the most impressive is the revelation mask wherein one face suddenly splits open to disclose a new form within. Used for instantaneous transformations, these bewildering masks often represent mythical creatures that assumed new guises or moods in the course of a dance. They thus provided amusement and surprise.

The figure carvings of the Kwakiutl, some of high aesthetic quality, represent the achievements of great chiefs; others (Plate 171), set up at potlatches, heap ridicule upon rivals. A man with a hugely inflated stomach illustrates the fate of a skeptic who doubted the ability of his competitor to provide enough

176   Tsimshian dancing shaman figure. British Columbia. Wood with abalone shell eyes and horsehair. H. 24" (Leff Collection, Uniontown, Pennsylvania).

177 Haida house with attached totem poles and commemorative post with bear on top. Skidegate, British Columbia. Photographed ca. 1878.

food. Gross and exaggerated though it may be, this type of lampoon often attains a level of true caricature.

Kwakiutl art is among the most impressive creations of primitive man. In its astonishing variety of forms and consummate technique, it can take its place among the great expressive styles of history.

Bella Coola

The Bella Coola, a small, close-knit tribe, live at the head of two fiords, cut off from the coast by intervening Kwakiutl peoples. They are in many ways an unusual group. Linguistically they differ from their neighbors because they speak a Salish dialect, though there are no other Salish tribes within two hundred miles. Either the Bella Coola must have migrated from the south, or the Kwakiutl, moving in later, blocked them off from the other Salish-speaking groups. In such a situation many tribes would have been intimidated and would have yielded completely to the more powerful Kwakiutl. But the Bella Coola, regarding the Kwakiutl as interlopers in their territory, managed to retain their identity and unique style.

Certainly the Bella Coola did not always carve and paint as they did in historic times. Whatever Salish forms they may originally have had they threw over largely for art in the Kwakiutl pattern. And yet the Bella Coola artist refused to be entirely taken in by the bombastic approach of his new neighbors. His masks are only partly decorated (Plate 172). Opaque red, azure blue, and dull black contrast vividly with the natural reddish-white hue of the cedar. Comparable to the use of unpainted wood among the Salish and Nootka, this choice probably reflects a conservative Eskimoid outlook.

Painted designs in Bella Coola art are also unlike those of the Kwakiutl: they rarely outline or underscore basic sculptural features. Instead, patterns swirl over surfaces as if possessed of a life of their own. This sets up a tension in Bella Coola style between structure and decoration which remains unresolved. But the artist avoids the formal antagonisms that make the Kwakiutl style so oppressive.

The Bella Coola ceremonies also differed from those favored by the Kwakiutl. Less addicted to posturing and to strutting, this small group displayed inherited rights and enacted dramatic stories of encounters with spirit-beings. The pervasive theme of these ceremonies was the harmony and solidarity of the tribe.

The attempt at unity in Bella Coola society parallels almost exactly the character of Bella Coola art. Although superficially vigorous and expansive, the style at the same time shows signs of timidity. A feeling of apprehension and uneasiness clings to these masks like fog to a Northwest

Coast mountain-top. How are we to explain this curiously ambiguous attitude? Perhaps the answer lies in the cultural dislocation of the Bella Coola.
Originally a simple, village-oriented community of people, they found themselves suddenly confronting masks with which they were ill at ease. In-
hibited by a lack of knowledge, they nevertheless tried to achieve a Kwakiutl
level of expression in art. No wonder their style shows so much tension and
conflict. It seems logical to conclude that this appealing, somewhat anxious
art style is the direct consequence of the Bella Coola's reaction to the very
difficult situation thrust upon them by aggressive neighbors.

Tsimshian

To the north of the Bella Coola in the Skeena and Nass River valleys are
the Tsimshian, a proud, independent people, widely known for their skill in
wood carving. Unlike previous groups, the Tsimshian belonged to the more
northern coast tribes, and their art consequently reflects the complex social
patterns of that region. Combined with the elaborate pageantry of the south,
this makes Tsimshian carving exceedingly rich in symbolic form and pro-
fuse in detail.

On the whole, Tsimshian masks tend to be naturalistic; many of these
carvings served as crests or heraldic symbols of privilege. Included are
animals, mythological spirits, and human figures such as a Russian trader,
or even strange objects—e.g., the white man's dog, a palisade fortification,
or a wagon road, all of which became crests of the man who first saw them.
The most important thing was that each crest represented an increase in
the power of the owner. Yet because of the high artistic standards of the
Tsimshian, when the artist publicized the owner's triumph he used all the
means at his disposal. The Tsimshian artist strove always for accuracy of
form and directness of expression. The result is a wonderful naturalism of
style combined with an immediate visual impact.

Tsimshian masks are remarkably sculptural: the deep backward thrust
of the cheek planes give an appearance of complete heads rather than flat
face masks (Plate 175). Similarly, the artist's interest in fleshy surface and
bone structure contributes a three-dimensional feeling to the whole. Muscu-
lar tensions in the mouth further enhance the feeling of dramatic realism.
A complete aesthetic integration of form and color is a hallmark of the style.

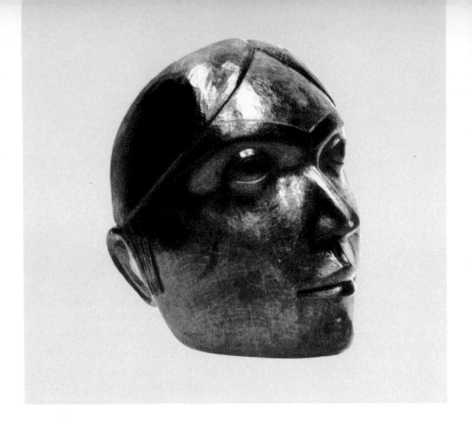

178   Haida carved head. British Columbia. H. 8³/₄″ (Pitt Rivers Museum, Oxford University).

Figures in the Tsimshian area took several forms (Plate 176). Medicine men used small, dynamic wooden figures and intricate rattles in performing their magic rites. The animal and human forms combined in these objects were evidence of the sources of power controlled by the shaman, and he was at pains to display them as boldly and effectively as possible.

The totem poles of the Tsimshian people are another story. Theirs is essentially, as Paul Wingert has shown, a contained "classical" style. Each figure stands out clearly, and each group contributes equally to the total organization of the design. At the base there is usually a single large figure; above, there is a narrower band of small figures, then comes another large figure, and so on. A careful spacing of intervals and strict separation of parts make Tsimshian art one of wonderful clarity and vigor.

Haida

Of all the Northwest Coast people, the Haida were the most aggressive and the most adept at carving. The totem poles they made are familiar the world over as masterpieces of design and technique. But we must now consider the totem pole not only as an art form but also as an object of historical significance. There is agreement among scholars that the northern region, especially the Tsimshian and Haida areas, was the center of the carved column. That the tradition was of long standing is proved by the description of Étienne Marchand, a French explorer who was there before 1800 (Plate 177). Marchand described the house entrance pole thus: "It imitates the form of a gaping human mouth, or rather a beast, and it is surmounted by a hooked nose about two feet in length, proportional in point of size to the monstrous face to which it belongs... over the door is the figure of a man carved in the attitude of a child in the womb... and above this figure rises a gigantic statue of a man erect which terminates the sculpture and the decoration of the portal; ...on the parts of the surface which are not occupied by the capital, subjects are interspersed, including carved figures of frogs, toads, lizards, and other animals." Marchand was so impressed by the Haida poles that he adds: "Everywhere on the Queen Charlotte Islands appear traces of an ancient civilization; everything indicates that men with whom they have had the opportunity of being acquainted have belonged to a great people, who were fond of the agreeable arts and who knew how to multiply the production of them."

Marchand's theory of a high-culture origin for Northwest Coast art has been most sympathetically received by several anthropologists, including Leonhard Adam and Robert Heine-Geldern. They believe that the complex surface patterns and rich animal symbolism of the Northwest Coast derive from the Shang period in China. While Shang influence is indeed probable, a more likely source is perhaps the Late Chou period. The evidence for this lies in the familiar long tongue, a symbol frequently found along the Northwest Coast, and particularly so in the Haida area. The shape of the nose and treatment of the eyes is exactly that seen in Late Chou carving. Even such details as the stick that the beaver chews find exact parallels in Chinese wood sculpture of the fourth century B.C. (Plate 98). Rectangular jade ax-blades, simultaneous frontal and profile images involv-

179 *Tlingit shamanic figure. Alaska. H. 25″ (American Museum of Natural History, New York).*

ing animals, and paired animals flanking human beings all occur in China, so the chances of a direct link with the Northwest Coast seem to be very great. Canoe types, bone carving and shell inlay, and specific mythological themes and artistic motifs lend further weight to the connection.

Of all Northwest Coast arts, none is more famous than the tall wooden columns that are called totem poles, although they were not actually totemic in function. These columns were carved for several purposes: to commemorate a social event, such as a marriage, birth, or the inheritance of a name; to dignify a house, mark a grave, or provide a container for the remains of an important man; and, representing crests, to tell mythological stories connected with the patron. Always behind the public purpose lay the artist's overpowering urge to express individual and group prowess. This is why the totem pole, though a traditional art form, flourished mainly in the nineteenth century when wealth from fur trading had intensified the struggle for status. For these great columns were as conspicuous a method of consuming money as anyone could possibly devise. The carving of wood posts as memorials extends virtually throughout the entire Americas from the Salish to the Araucanians. It also occurs among the Eskimo and in

180 Ceremonial blanket worn by Chilcat chiefs. Alaska. Mountain goat wool. L. 53" (American Museum of Natural History, New York).

many parts of Asia: for example, in the Gilyak region of Siberia. Usually the heart-shaped face predominates (Plate 165). Probably the idea is very ancient and is ultimately associated with the wooden Megalithic tradition.

Shifting our attention from the Haida totem poles to painted house facades, we are again struck by Chinese elements in the design. One splendid example, illustrating on a colossal scale the face of a bear, is enough to show the use of the double image; small heads form the eyes and mouth — an artistic conception we have also seen in the Marquesas (Plate 67) and in Peru and Mexico. Surely such a complex idea bears some relationship to the Chinese tradition.

The stunning beauty of Haida carving and the technical skill of the Queen Charlotte artists is particularly apparent in masks and other small-scale objects. Although they used only a few masks, the Haida created some of the most impressive examples on the entire Northwest Coast (Plate 178). Their treatment of an old woman's face is extraordinarily fine; and no reflection on the Haida genius is made in saying that remarkably similar interpretations of the face occur in the Late Chou period in China.

Tlingit

The northernmost Northwest Coast tribe were the Tlingit. Their importance as a group derives from the strong control over the inland fur trade routes which in the nineteenth century made them the richest tribe in the north. In the interior lived peoples who spoke the Tlingit language but who differed culturally from those along the coast. This curious situation actually sheds light on the past, for it suggests that some erstwhile interior groups migrated down to the shore and acquired there the technological procedures necessary to a maritime way of life. Thus the cultures of the coastal and inland Tlingit split rapidly apart from one another while their languages remained virtually the same.

In art the Tlingit reveal that they were eager, if not always judicious, pupils of their neighbors. The Tlingit totem poles, shorter and more slender than in other areas, combine elements of Haida and Tsimshian styles with a somewhat fussy, nervous character of their own. Forms tend to be less monumental and relationships comparatively unsophisticated. This is particularly true when paint has been applied to the surfaces.

Mask carving for the Tlingit had a special function. Worn by shamans during their healing dances, the faces indicated the supernatural powers controlled by the wearer (Plate 179). The more masks he could put on and take off, the greater the shaman's chances of effecting a cure. Consequently, the Tlingit produced an enormous number of these masks and loaded them with symbolic details. Little animals coming out of the cheeks and nostrils, for example, were supposed to intensify the use of the senses and their ability to ferret out disease. Franz Boas, the greatest authority on Coast cultures, long ago observed that the use of small animals in Tlingit masks is a distinct point of contact with the Eskimo. This connection becomes even stronger when we compare Tlingit masks with those used by the Salish. The *swaixwe* mask of the Salish, which we believe is related in origin, consists largely of bird and animal heads (Plate 168).

In addition to masks and totem poles, the Northwest Coast Indians also carved handsome wooden hats and animal plaques which they wore on their heads, together with ermine tails and sea-lion whiskers. These maskettes, as they are called, did not conceal the wearer's identity; they seem rather to have placed him under the supernatural protection of his clan animal. Similar masklike coverings appear often in Late Chou art, and even in modern China on babies' caps representations of the mysterious monster known as the *t'ao t'ieh* provide protection from evil spirits.

Northwest Coast carving techniques triumphed in the making of ornaments and such utilitarian objects as bowls and boxes. Equally impressive as works of art were some valuable metal sheets known as "coppers." Functioning as objects of prestige, these sheets were made of local surface copper until the European sheet metal was brought in. Their origins are obscure, but the design elements engraved on the surfaces clearly imply Chinese sources. The same is true of another art form made in Tlingit country—the famous Chilcat blankets (Plate 180). Women wove these and the similarly designed aprons, following a wooden pattern board. The board, made by a man, helped the weaver to lay out the field design of the blanket. Naturalistic art thus remained a masculine prerogative, the women being quarantined, so to speak, from its power.

Viewed as a whole, the art of the Northwest Coast gives an impression of tremendous power and vast accomplishment. Building on an Eskimoid base, there came a strong wave of Megalithic influence, as a result of which competition and boasting were intensified. In the north in particular, this

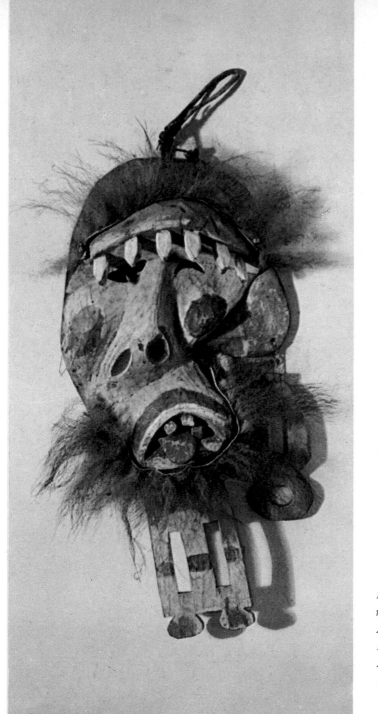

181 *Grotesque Eskimo mask. Kuskokwim River, Alaska. Wood with fur. H. 13" (Museum of the American Indian, New York).*

wooden Megalithic tradition gathered increased strength from the historic arts of Shang and Late Chou China. Of all American groups, the Northwest Coast people were the least influenced by the high cultures of Middle and South America. Yet numerous resemblances, especially in the arts, exist between these widely separated areas. The long tongue, the double-headed feathered snake, the orant and arms-free pose, the figures flanked by animals, the curled snout, the double image, the splitting up of the face, monster masks worn on top of the head, and many other artistic devices come to mind. Barring direct contact, the best explanation for such similarities is a shared prototype. In Asian art of the first millennium B.C. we find precisely that common origin.

Eskimo

The Eskimo people can claim a special distinction: they and their offshoot, the Aleut, have successfully mastered one of the most hostile environments known to man and have developed a fairly comfortable and happy way of life. Where few Europeans would be able even to survive, the Eskimo achieved a stable food supply, an optimistic outlook, and a marked aesthetic accomplishment. Far from being a marginal or arrested culture, Eskimo life stands as a monument to human adaptability and resourcefulness.

The Eskimo spread out around the Arctic Sea from the tip of Siberia as far west as Greenland. But even when they moved into southern Alaska, they always remained in close touch with the sea. In the past, scholars generally held that the Eskimo were part of a continuous ethnic tradition extending around the Pole and including the Lapps of Scandinavia and the northernmost peoples of Russia. Present-day theorists, however, call attention to the unique aspects of Eskimo life: their dependence on sea mammals for their food and their use of an advanced technology to cope with a hostile environment. If the Eskimo are unlike other peoples around the North Pole, the question remains: where did they come from? Ancient cultures in the Lake Baikal region of Central Asia show some points of connection, but the similarities with Eskimo culture in that region are really comparatively few and unimportant. The same is true of the Arctic coast of Siberia, which lacks sea mammals. The northeast Asian Pacific coast is therefore the most logical place to look for a sea-oriented, harpoon-using culture. And Russian archaeologists working between the Amur River and the Kamchatka Peninsula have recently discovered Eskimoid sites that date back to the third millennium B.C.

In the modern period, Eskimo art centers in the lower Yukon and Kuskokwin River areas. Similar to the older Bering Strait styles, this art consists mainly of masks carved from pieces of wood gaily painted in a profusion of colors (Plates 181 and 183). For public rites, the shaman wore a special mask that represented the spirits seen in his dreams. The Aleut shaman who wished to foretell the future also wore a mask while communing with his familiar spirits. Other Aleutian masks were buried in caves with the dead. But by far the most frequent Eskimo masks are those worn in the "inviting-in" feast, a ceremony that resembled a potlatch. The ostensible purpose of this joyous occasion was to obtain the blessing, in future hunting expeditions, of totemic guardian spirits represented by the masked figures. But in fact the person sponsoring the ceremony also acquired great prestige.

Bizarre and absurd though they may seem to us, Eskimo masks used in these feasts usually had a specific purpose. For example, often the human face seen in the stomach of an animal actually honors the *inua* or inner spirit of the beast. Sometimes hands or flaps would cover this face until at a dramatic moment the dancer could pull a string to reveal the concealed *inua*. As in the Northwest Coast transformation masks, such dramatic changes helped amuse and amaze the spectators. In some instances the masks were deliberately comical, descending even to the level of gross caricature.

Eskimo mask designs relied on the addition of pieces of wood attached to an armature rather than on solid carved sculptural forms. Feathers, hide, ivory, bits of wood, and flat areas of paint were preferred. Despite a certain timidity in plastic shaping, these masks disclose a truly artistic sense of linear play and asymmetrical balance. If the face should be lopsided, the features are adjusted to compensate for this imbalance. When distortion or exaggeration is required, the artist produces the desired effect but with a lightness and sureness that redeems the form from grotesqueness. However fantastic and inane Eskimo masks may seem, they all preserve the gentleness and ingenuous character of the Eskimo himself.

The attempt to place Eskimo art and culture in a historical context yields some extraordinary results. This art style is unlike that of any other American group, with the important exception of the peoples of the North-

182   Tupilak, Eskimo evil spirit sent by sorcerer to kill his enemies. Angmassalik, East Greenland. H. 2¹/₄" (Pitt Rivers Museum, Oxford University).

west Coast. And, compared with the Eskimo the southern styles, particularly the Nootka, show the most similarities. As a matter of fact, because of their remote location, the Nootka seem to preserve a remarkably archaic form of Eskimoid culture, one that appears old fashioned even when compared with the now extinct Okvik, Ipiutak, and Old Bering Sea cultures (1st–4th centuries A.D.), which represent the high point of Eskimo development in the Bering Strait region. Nootka art is in some ways closer, therefore, to the earliest Eskimo cultures than is the archaeological Bering Strait material which already bears some mark of high culture Chinese influence. Thus any discussion of Eskimo origins ought to take into account the evidence provided by the Nootka.

With the aid of archaeology and ethnology the origins and development of the Eskimo can now be reconstructed with some accuracy. Thousands of years ago, long before the rise of Chinese civilization, the eastern littoral of Asia must have been occupied by primitive fishing peoples. As their skill increased, their implements became more efficient and more specialized. They developed heavy harpoons and sturdy seagoing craft. These permitted them to catch large marine mammals, which in turn contributed greatly to their prestige as a group. But at the same time they were committing themselves more and more to a precarious form of live-

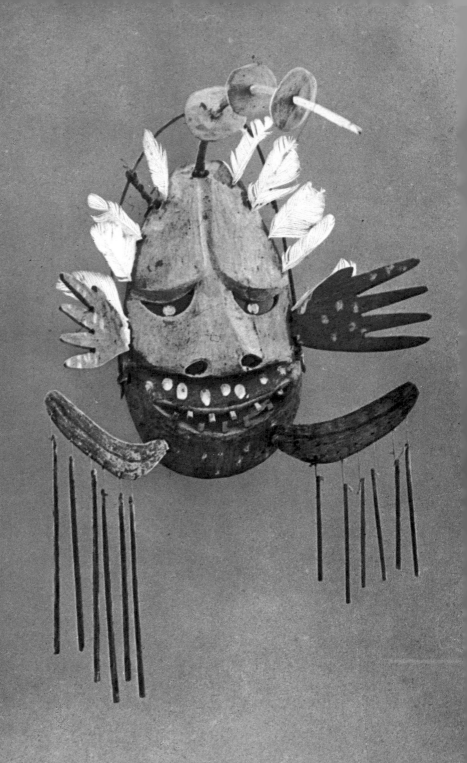

lihood, for as the population increased, sea mammals became steadily less plentiful. Small bands of hunters could pursue the retreating animals north toward the Arctic Circle; the remaining population had to give up its way of life, not having a flexible, adaptive economy or technology.

If this theory is correct, the Eskimo represent the flowering of the Aquatic tradition. This, as we have already shown in Chapter II, is one of the main indigenous traditions underlying historic Chinese culture. To test this theory, we should compare the Aquatic tradition, as seen in Torres Straits, with its survivals in eastern Asia and with the oldest strains of Eskimo culture preserved for us in various areas. The large hunting harpoon, the basic tool in both the Aquatic and the Eskimo cultures, is unknown in Melanesia except in the Torres Straits area. But the shape of the barbed harpoon head used in Torres Straits is found in prehistoric Japan and in present-day Eskimo territory on seal harpoons. Even the foreshafts, in their animal decoration and method of attachment, show close resemblances. A mythological marriage between a woman and a dog, and similar funeral dance patterns, are found in Torres Straits and Eskimo cultures. Stone spinning tops, peculiar in Melanesia to the Torres Straits area, occur also among the Eskimo. The latter people, for as yet unsolved reasons, had a crocodile-like creature as an ornament on either side of their boats, though surely there are no crocodiles in the Arctic. Two crocodiles appear on Eskimo masks, the open mouths meeting at the lower part of the face; exactly the same motif may be seen in Torres Straits. And the eight-pointed rosette occurs at the back of Straits masks, whereas a similar star-like design ornaments the same place on Aleut hunting hats (Plate 167). That the finest of these hats, magically conferring hunting prowess, were worn only by leaders suggests the possibility of their having originated from horizontal masks of the snout type. Nootka masks probably represent earlier, more naturalistic versions of the same idea. And their comparison with Torres Straits animal masks reveals numerous points of agreement. The upturned crocodile snout has become, in the Nootka type, a wolf's nose; but the same articulated jaw, voracious teeth, and side flanges are present. What is more, in both areas a human face is sometimes placed diagonally above the animal head.

183   Eskimo feast mask worn in animal fertility rites. Kuskokwim River, Alaska. Wood with feathers. H. 22" (Museum of the American Indian, New York).

Nootka bird masks and Torres Straits bird carvings are, in design and color, almost indistinguishable.

Similarly, the great totemic screens of the Northwest Coast that separate the chief's apartment from the commoner's dwelling-space seem ultimately to refer to the ancestral screen as known in Asia. How else can we explain the fact that in one of the wettest climates in North America these walls are still known as rain-inducing screens? The screens of Torres Straits supply an answer; there the dances held in front of ancestral screens were intended to bring rain, not because the Straits people were agriculturalists, but because they had long before observed that the supply of fish and other sea creatures increased sharply with the return of the winter monsoon.

Ordinarily it would seem sheer fantasy to look for Eskimo-like cultures in Melanesia. But one exists there. The links between Torres Straits art and that of the Eskimo make it abundantly clear that both had their common origin in the Aquatic tradition of eastern Asia.

Viewed from afar, the art of America appears to be a panorama of styles. The variety of materials and the skill of these artists is little short of amazing. Yet when we examine these styles closely, there emerge patterns and relationships laden with significance. The same motifs—fanged animals and human figures with caps or masks representing long-tongued protective monsters—occur again and again. The same heavy ornaments, the same complex surfaces appear in examples beyond count. Taken as a whole, then, the art of the Americas forms a fairly compact unit in contradistinction to, say, the art of the South Seas. And the unity it possesses comes not only from the conservative character of the American Indian but also from the fact that he had only spasmodic and filtered contact with outside ideas. Occasionally open to exchanges then shut off from them, these American Indian cultures have a sort of inherent asymmetry—advanced in one respect, retarded in another; sophisticated in Mexico and Peru, backward in less favored areas. Similarly, the artists of the Americas, ranging in technique from the untutored to the most accomplished, have worked along lines appearing to be essentially chaotic. Artistic solution in one group does not lead to the conquest of another problem. Achievements may be set aside or even discarded. All in all, the development of American art can only be explained by sporadic trans-Pacific inspiration stemming from the high cultures of Asia.

SUGGESTED READINGS

Where no reference is cited, the reader should consult the general books at the beginning of each section.

Introduction

L. Adam, *Primitive Art*, London (1940) 1954.
F. Boas, *Primitive Art*, New York (1927) 1955.
R. Firth, 'The Social Framework of Primitive Art,' in *Elements of Social Organization*, London, 1951.
R. Linton, 'Primitive Art,' in E. Elisofon & W. Fagg, *The Sculpture of Africa*, New York, 1958.
M. Smith, ed., *The Artist in Tribal Society*, Royal Anthro. Inst. (in press).

Africa

GENERAL:

E. Elisofon & W. Fagg, *The Sculpture of Africa*, New York, 1958.
C. Kjersmeier, *Centres de style de la sculpture nègre africaine*, 4 vols., Paris, 1935-38.
H. Himmelheber, *Negerkunst und Negerkünstler*, Braunschweig, 1960.
E. Leuzinger, *Africa*, New York, 1960.
D. Paulme, *Les sculptures de l'Afrique noire*, Paris, 1956.
M. Plass, *African Tribal Sculpture*, Philadelphia, 1956.
W. Schmalenbach, *African Art*, New York, 1954.
E. von Sydow, *Afrikanische Plastik*, 2 vols., Berlin, 1930, 1954.
P. Wingert, *The Sculpture of Negro Africa*, New York, 1950.

SPECIFIC AREAS:

Bambara: R. Goldwater, *Bambara Sculpture from the Western Sudan*, New York, 1960.
Baoule: B. Lindholm, *Les portraits baoulé et leur base sociale*, Etnog. Mus. Goteborg, 1955-56.
Benin: P. Dark, *Benin Art*, London, 1960.
Bushman: R. Summers, ed., *Prehistoric Rock Art of the Rhodesias and Nyasaland*, Salisbury, 1959.
Bushongo: E. Torday & T. Joyce, *Les Bushongo*, Annales Musée Congo Belge, Brussels, 1910.
Cameroons: W. Bascom & P. Gebauer, *West African Art*, Milwaukee Public Museum, 1953; R. Lecoq, *Les bamiléké*, Paris, 1953.
Dan-Guere: P. Vandenhoute, *Classification stylistique du masque Dan et Guéré de la Côte d'Ivoire Occidentale*, Med. Rjiksmus. Volkenk., Leiden, 1948.
Dogon: M. Griaule, *Masques Dogon*, Inst. d'Ethnol., Paris, 1938.

313

Ibo: K. Murray, *Masks and Headdresses of Nigeria*, Zwemmer Gallery, London, 1949.
Ife: K. Murray, *The Art of Ife*, Lagos, 1955; F. Willett, 'Ife and its Archaeology,' *Jour. African Hist.* 1, 1960.
Kota: E. Andersson, *Les Kuta*, Stud. Ethnog. Uppsala, 1953.
Kwele: L. Siroto, *Masks and their Uses among the Bakwele*, Columbia Univ., Ph. D. (in press).
Lower Congo: O. Nuoffer, *Afrikanische Plastik in der Gestaltung von Mutter und Kind*, Dresden, n. d.
Luba: F. Olbrechts, *Les arts plastiques du Congo Belge*, Antwerp (1946) 1959.
Nigeria: W. Fagg, *Nigerian Tribal Art*, London, 1960.
Pangwe: G. Tessman, *Die Pangwe*, 2 vols, Berlin, 1913.
Pende: L. de Sousberghe, *L'art pende*, Brussels, 1958.
Senufo: B. Holas, 'Note sur la fonction rituelle de deux catégories de statues sénoufo,' *Artibus Asiae*, 20, 1957.
Sudan: F.-H. Lem, *Sudanese sculpture*, Paris (1948) 1949.
Teke: R. Hottot, 'Teke Fetishes,' *Jour. Royal Anth. Inst.*, 86, 1956.
Yaka: M. Plancquaert, *Sociétés secrètes bayaka*, Brussels, 1932.
Yoruba: W. Fagg, 'De l'art yoruba,' *Art nègre*, Paris, 1951; U. Beier, *Sacred Wood Carvings from a small Yoruba Town*, Lagos, 1957.

Asia-Oceania

GENERAL:

T. Bodrogi, *Oceanian Art*, Budapest, 1959.
A. Bühler *et al*, *Oceanien und Australien*, Baden-Baden, 1961.
R. Heine-Geldern, 'L'art prébouddhique de la Chine et son influence dans l'Oceanie,' *Revue des Arts Asiatiques*, 11, 1937.
R. Linton & P. Wingert, *Arts of the South Seas*, New York, 1946.
C. Schmitz, *Oceanic Sculpture* (in press).
F. Speiser, 'Versuch einer Siedlungsgeschichte der Südsee,' *Denkschr. schwitz. naturfor. Gesell.* 77, 1946.
H. Tischner, *Oceanic Art*, New York, 1954.
P. Wingert, *Art of the South Pacific Islands*, New York, 1953.

SPECIFIC AREAS:

Asmat: A. Gerbrands, *Asmat Art in its Context* (in press).
Australia: A. Elkin & R. and C. Berndt, *Art in Arnhem Land*, Melbourne, 1950; F. McCarthy, *Australian Aboriginal Rock Art*, Aust. Mus., Sydney, 1958.
Baining: R. Parkinson, *Dreissig Jahre in der Südsee*, Stuttgart, 1911.
Borneo: C. Hose & W. McDougall, *The Pagan Tribes of Borneo*, 2 vols., London, 1912.
Botel Tobago: T. Kano, *An Illustrated Ethnography of Formosan Aborigines*, Tokyo (1945) 1956.
Cooks: P. Buck, *Arts and Crafts of the Cook Islands*, Bishop Mus. Bul. 179, 1944.
Easter Island: A. Métraux, *Ethnology of Easter Island*, Bishop Mus. Bul. 160, 1940,

T. Barthel, *Grundlagen zur Entzifferung der Osterinselschrift*, Abh. Gebiet Auslandskunde, Hamburg Univ., 1958.

Enggano: J. Keuning, ' Holzschnitzereien von der Insel Enggano,' *Nachr. Gesell. Natur-Völkerk. Ostasiens*, 83, 1958.

Fiji: K. Larsson, *Fijian Studies*, Etnog. Mus. Goteborg, 1960.

Geelvink Bay: T. van Baaren, *Korwars and Korwar Style* (in press).

Hawaii: P. Buck, *Arts and Crafts of Hawaii*, Honolulu, 1957.

Kaniet: H.-H. Petri, ' Ethnographika von Kaniet, ' *Veröff. Übersee-Mus.*, Bremen, 1, 1956.

Lake Sentani: S. Kooijman, *The Art of Lake Sentani*, New York, 1959; P. Wirz, *Beitrag zur Ethnologie der Sentanier*, Nova Guinea, 16, Leiden, 1928.

Madagascar: J. Faublée, *L'ethnographie de Madagascar*, Paris, 1946.

Mangareva: P. Buck, ' Mangarevan Images,' *Ethnologica Cranmorensis*, (Chislehurst, England) 4, 1939.

Maori: A. Hamilton, *Maori Art*, Dunedin, 1896–1901; R. Firth, ' The Maori Carver,' *Jour. Poly. Soc.*, 34, 1925.

Marquesas: K. von den Steinen, *Die Marquesaner und ihre Kunst*, 3 vols., Berlin, 1925–28.

Moriori: H. Skinner, *The Morioris of Chatham Island*, Bishop Mus. Mem.9, 1923.

Mortlock: A. Krämer, *Inseln um Truk*, Erg. Südsee Exped., Hamburg, 1935.

Naga: J. Hutton, ' The Significance of Headhunting in Assam,' *Jour. Roy. Anth. Inst.*, 58, 1928; V. Elwin, *Art of the North-East Frontier of India*, Shillong, India, 1960.

Necker: K. Emory, *The Archaeology of Nihoa and Necker*, Bishop Mus. Bul. 53, 1928.

New Caledonia: J. Guiart, *L'art autochtone de Nouvelle-Calédonie*, Noumea, 1953.

New Hebrides: R. Codrington, *The Melanesians*, New Haven (1891) 1957; F. Speiser, *Ethnographischen Materialen aus den Neuen Hebriden und den Banks Inseln*, Berlin, 1923.

New Ireland: A. Krämer, *Die Malanggane von Tombára*, Munich, 1925; G. Peekel, ' Uli und Ulifeier oder vom Mondkultus auf Neu Meckelenburg,' *Archiv. Anth.*, 23, 1932.

Nias: P. Suzuki, *The Religious System and Culture of Nias, Indonesia*, The Hague, 1959.

Nukuoro: H. Damm, *Inseln um Ponape*, Erg. Südsee Exp., Hamburg, 1935.

Papuan Gulf: F. Williams, *The Drama of Orokolo*, Oxford, 1940; D. Newton, *Art Styles of the Papuan Gulf*, New York, 1961.

Santa Cruz: F. Speiser, ' Völkerkundliches von den Santa-Cruz-Inseln,' *Ethnologica*, 11 1916.

Sepik: O. Reche, *Der Kaiserin-Augusta Fluss*, Erg. Südsee Exp., Hamburg, 1913; R. Gardi, *Sepik*, Bern, 1958.

Solomons: B. Blackwood, *Both Sides of Buka Passage*, Oxford, 1935; W. Ivens, *Melanesians of the southeastern Solomon Islands*, London, 1927.

Southwest Islands: P. Drabbe, *Het Leven van den Tanémbarees*, Int. Archiv. Ethnog. Suppl., 1940.

Sumatra: F. Wagner, *Indonesia*, New York, 1960.

Taiwan: Ling S.-S., ' Human Figures with Protruding Tongues found in the T'aitung Prefecture and their Affinities...', *Bul. Inst. Ethnol. Acad. Sinica*, Taipei, 2, 1956.

Tami: T. Bodrogi, *Art of the Huon-Gulf, N. E.-New Guinea* (in press).

Tonga: P. Buck, ' Material Representatives of Tongan and Samoan Gods,' *Jour. Pol. Soc.*, 44, 46, 1935, 1937.

Torres Straits: A. Haddon, *Arts and Crafts*, Exp. to Torres Straits, 4, Cambridge, 1912; D. Fraser, *Torres Straits Sculpture*, Ann Arbor, Mich., 1961 (microfilm).

America

GENERAL:

W. Bennett. *Art of the Andes*, New York, 1954.
M. Covarrubias, *The Eagle, the Jaguar, and the Serpent*, New York, 1954.
F. Dockstader, *Indian Art in America*, New York, 1961.
F. Feuchtwanger, *Art of Ancient Mexico*, New York, 1954.
R. Heine-Geldern & G. Ekholm in *Civilizations of Ancient America*, Chicago, 1951.
G. Kubler, *Art and Architecture of Pre-Columbian America* (in press).
H. Leicht, *Pre-Inca Art and Culture*, New York (1944) 1960.
T. Proskouriakoff, *Classic Maya Sculpture*, Carnegie Pub. 593, Washington, 1950.

SPECIFIC AREAS

Amazon: J. Steward, ed., *Handbook of South American Indians*, vol. 3, Bur. Amer. Ethnol. Bul. 143, Washington, 1948.
Bella Coola: T. McIlwraith, *The Bella Coola Indians*, 2 vols., Toronto, 1948.
Caribbean: J. Steward, ed., *Handbook of South American Indians*, vol. 4, Bur. Amer. Ethnol. Bul 143, Washington, 1949.
Eskimo: E. Nelson, *The Eskimo about Bering Strait*, Bur. Amer. Ethnol, Ann. Rep. 18, Washington, 1899; S. Ivanov, 'Aleut Hunting Headgear and its Ornamentation,' *Proc. Int. Cong. Americanists*, 23, 1928.
Guianas: P. Dark, *Bush Negro Art*, London, 1954.
Haida: J. Swanton, *Contributions to the Ethnology of the Haida*, Amer. Mus. Nat. Hist. Mem. 8, Pt. 1, 1905.
Kwakiutl: F. Boas, *The Social Organization and Secret Societies of the Kwakiutl Indians*, U. S. Nat. Mus. Ann. Rep. for 1895, Washington, 1897.
Nootka: P. Drucker, *The Northern and Central Nootkan Tribes*, Bur. Amer. Ethnol. Bul., 144, 1951.
Northeast: W. Fenton, *Masked Medicine Societies of the Iroquois*, Smithsonian Inst. Ann. Rep. for 1940, Washington, 1941.
Northwest Coast: R. Inverarity, *Art of the Northwest Coast Indians*, Los Angeles, 1950; P. Drucker, *Indians of the Northwest Coast*, New York, 1955.
Plains: J. Ewers, *Plains Indian Painting*, Stanford, 1939.
Salish: P. Wingert, *American Indian Sculpture*, New York, 1949.
Southeast: E. Fundaburk & M. Foreman, *Sun Circles and Human Hands*, Alabama, 1957.
Southwest: E. Parsons, 'War God Shrines of Laguna and Zuni,' *Amer. Anth.* n. s. 20, 1918; G. Mills, *Navaho Art and Culture*, Colorado Springs, 1959.
Tlingit: A. Krause, *The Tlinkit Indians* (1885), trans. E. Gunther, Seattle, 1956.
Tsimshian: P. Wingert, 'Tsimshian Sculpture,' in *The Tsimshian*, Pub. Amer. Ethnol. Soc. 18, 1951.

316

INDEX

PHOTOGRAPHIC CREDITS

All photographs were supplied by the museums or collectors except as indicated below:

American Museum of Natural History plate 166;
Dr. Block Color Productions 51, 125, 142, 159;
Lee Boltin 171;
Werner Bruggmann 4, 5, 15, 16, 30, 53, 55, 56, 105, 111, 136, 146;
Jean Cussac 27;
Elwin J. Daniel 17, 20, 24, 32, 130, 167, 174, 175, 179, 180, 181, 183;
Ernst Deyhle 93;
Eliot Elisofon 1, 6, 9, 19, 25, 26, 29, 34, 39, 41, 42, 43, 45, 48, 108, 139;
Werner Forman from *Exotic Art*, Spring Books, London 21;
Douglas Fraser 2, 3, 12, 37, 52, 58, 63, 64, 67, 68, 70, 77, 78, 81, 83, 84, 85, 86, 88, 89, 90, 100, 106, 107, 109, 116, 164, 170, 172, 173, 176, 178;
Marianne Goeritz: Rapho Guillumette 141;
Fritz Goro 59;
Whitney Halstead 124;
Friedrich Hewicker 18, 57, 61, 65, 69, 74, 75, 87, 92, 94, 96, 103, 113, 119, 120, 126, 131, 135, 145;
Malcolm Knapp 7, 149, 157;
Larkin Bros; courtesy of Royal Academy of Arts 79;
Paul E. Lefebvre 163;
Photo Meyer 91;
Peter Moeschlin 36, 60, 128, 129, 132;
Al Monner 165;
Nikolas Muray 13;
Frank Newens 23, 35, 38, 127, 182;
Donald Pletsch 102;
Provincial Archives, Victoria, B. C. 177;
Harald Schultz 152, 153;
Edwin Smith 22, 121, 123, 133;
Felix Speiser, Museum für Völkerkunde, Basel 62;
Charles Uht: courtesy of Museum of Primitive Art 72, 117, 156;
John Waggaman, Staff-Sandak 161;
Frank Willett 50;
Paul Wingert 168;
I. Zaffrir 11, 28, 31, 33, 46, 47.

DESIGNED BY ULRICH RUCHTI